Praise for The Nearness of God

Our twenty-first-century world flounders as never before, trying to find a spiritual center of gravity. Here is a contemporary, yet scholarly, text to stabilize, strengthen, and encourage seeking hearts. Burns shoots his arrows straight to the Problem Solver— the ultimate, easily understood answer for inner peace of mind. I highly recommend this excellent tool for pastors, ministry leaders, and anyone in pursuit of ultimate truth.

—**Howard G. Hendricks,** Dallas Theological Seminary

This is an encouraging and helpful book by an insightful and seasoned scholar. In *The Nearness of God*, Lanier Burns sheds much light on a wonderful but neglected biblical theme: God's presence. Readers will find their theology deepened, their hope rekindled, and their joy increased.

—**Christopher W. Morgan,** California Baptist University

God's presence is no minor topic, as *The Nearness of God* shows so beautifully. God with us is about how he draws near. So draw near to this fine book and draw nearer to God."

—**Darrell Bock,** Dallas Theological Seminary

Praise for the Explorations in Biblical Theology series

Neither superficial nor highly technical, this new series of volumes on important Christian doctrines is projected to teach Reformed theology as it is most helpfully taught, with clear grounding in Scripture, mature understanding of theology, gracious interaction with others who disagree, and useful application to life. I expect that these volumes will strengthen the faith and biblical maturity of all who read them, and I am happy to recommend them highly.

—**Wayne Grudem,** Phoenix Seminary

There are many misconceptions today about systematic, biblical, and applicatory theology. One sometimes gets the impression that these are opposed to one another, and that the first two, at least, are so obscure that ordinary people should avoid them like the plague. The series Explorations in Biblical Theology seeks to correct these misunderstandings, to bring these disciplines together in a winsome, clear unity, edifying to non-specialists. The authors are first-rate, and they write to build up our faith by pointing us to Christ. That's what biblical and systematic theology at their best have always done, and the best application of Scripture has always shown us in practical ways how to draw on the rich blessings of Jesus' salvation. I hope that many will read these books and take them to heart.

—**John Frame,** Reformed Theological Seminary

The message of a God who loved us before he formed the earth, called us his own before we could respond to him, died for us while we were dead in our transgressions and sins, made us alive when we were incapable of serving him, unites us to himself so that we can be forever holy, and now loves us more than we love ourselves—sparked a Reformation of hope and joy that transformed the world of faith. Re-declaring that hope and reclaiming that joy is the ambition and delight of this series. Able and godly scholars trace the golden thread of grace that unites all Scripture to make the wonders of our God's redeeming love shine and win hearts anew. The writing is warm, winsome, and respectful of those who differ. The motives are clearly to reveal truth and expose error by glorifying the message and manner of the Savior.

—**Bryan Chapell,** Covenant Theological Seminary

The aim of these volumes is clear: as regards God's Word, rigor; as regards other scholars, respect; as regards current issues, relevance; as regards the Lord himself, reverence. Effective witness and ministry currently require more than extra effort and better methods: the call is heard from churches across the board for renewal in our grasp of Christian truth. Each author in this series contributes admirably to that urgent need.

—**Robert W. Yarbrough,** Trinity Evangelical Divinity School

This is a series that the church needs more than ever, as we forge fresh links between the world of biblical studies and our Reformed theology. The contributors remind us again that the Bible is a book about God and his purposes and encourages us to preach and teach the message of salvation which it contains. It will be an inspiration to many and will give us new insight into the faith once delivered to the saints.

—**Gerald Bray,** Beeson Divinity School

The church of Jesus Christ faces massive cultural challenges today. More and more people in the Western world are ignorant of or hostile to the Christian faith. The moral fabric of our society is unraveling, and as a result of postmodernism many are adopting a relativistic worldview. Some Christians have responded by trying to simplify and dumb down the gospel. Others have tried to catch the cultural mood of the day in order to gain more converts, but they have often been co-opted by the culture instead of transforming it for Christ. What we truly need is to dig down deep into biblical foundations, so that our theology is robustly biblical. Only a worldview that is informed by both biblical and systematic theology can withstand the intellectual challenges that face us today. The series Explorations in Biblical Theology is designed to meet this very need. I commend these volumes enthusiastically, for they explain what the Scriptures teach from the standpoint of biblical theology. What we desperately need to hear and learn today is the whole counsel of God. This series advances that very agenda for the edification of the church and to the glory of God.

—**Thomas R. Schreiner,**
The Southern Baptist Theological Seminary

Explorations in Biblical Theology is a valuable new series of books on doctrinal themes that run through Scripture. The contributors are competent scholars who love to serve the church and have special expertise in the Bible and its theology. Following a thematic approach, each volume explores a distinctive doctrine as it is taught in Scripture, or else introduces the various doctrines taught in a particular book of the Bible. The result is a fresh and unique contribution to our understanding of the Bible's own theology.
—**Philip Ryken,** Tenth Presbyterian Church

Explorations in Biblical Theology is a gift to God's people. Biblical theology was never meant to be reserved for academics. When the verities of the Reformed faith are taken from the "ivy halls" of academia and placed in the hearts and minds of the covenant people of God, reformation and revival are the inevitable result. I believe God will use this series as a mighty tool for the Kingdom.
—**Steve Brown,** Reformed Theological Seminary

The Nearness of God

The Nearness of God

His Presence with His People

Lanier Burns

P&R PUBLISHING

P.O. BOX 817 • PHILLIPSBURG • NEW JERSEY 08865-0817

Scripture quotations are from the HOLY BIBLE, NEW INTERNATIONAL VER-SION®. NIV®. Copyright © 1973, 1978, 1984 by International Bible Society. Used by permission of Zondervan Publishing House. All rights reserved.

Italics within Scripture quotations indicate emphasis added.

Printed in the United States of America

Library of Congress Cataloging-in-Publication Data

Burns, Lanier.
 The nearness of God : His presence with his people / Lanier
Burns.
     p. cm. — (Explorations in biblical theology)
 Includes bibliographical references and indexes.
 ISBN 978-1-59638-056-1 (pbk.)
 1. Incarnation--Biblical teaching. 2. Bible. N.T. John I,
14-18--Criticism, interpretation, etc. I. Title.
 BS2615.6.I53B87 2009
 227'.9406--dc22
                                    2009025398

For Kathy,
who has read my thoughts for over forty years
and has encouraged me to write some of them down
before I forget them

For our wonderful children
and grandchildren, because our heartfelt
prayers for them have been that they experience
a "walk" with the Lord over their lifetimes

Contents

Series Introduction

BELIEVERS TODAY need quality literature that attracts them to good theology and builds them up in their faith. Currently, readers may find several sets of lengthy—and rather technical—books on Reformed theology, as well as some that are helpful and semipopular. Explorations in Biblical Theology takes a more mid-range approach, seeking to offer readers the substantial content of the more lengthy books, on the one hand, while striving for the readability of the semipopular books, on the other.

The series includes two types of books: (1) some treating biblical themes and (2) others treating the theology of specific biblical books. The volumes dealing with biblical themes seek to cover the whole range of Christian theology, from the doctrine of God to last things. Representative early offerings in the series focus on the empowering of the Holy Spirit, justification, the presence of God, preservation and apostasy, and substitutionary atonement. Works dealing with the theology of specific biblical books include volumes on 1 and 2 Samuel, the Psalms, and Isaiah in the Old Testament, and Mark, Romans, and James in the New Testament.

Explorations in Biblical Theology is written for college seniors, seminarians, pastors, and thoughtful lay readers. These volumes are intended to be accessible and not obscured by excessive references to Hebrew, Greek, or theological jargon.

Each book seeks to be solidly Reformed in orientation, because the writers love the Reformed faith. The various theological themes and biblical books are treated from the perspective of biblical theology. Writers either trace doctrines through the Bible or open up the theology of the specific books they treat.

ix

Writers desire not merely to dispense the Bible's good information, but also to apply that information to real needs today.

Explorations in Biblical Theology is committed to being warm and winsome, with a focus on applying God's truth to life. Authors aim to treat those with whom they disagree as they themselves would want to be treated. The motives for the rejection of error are not to fight, hurt, or wound, but to protect, help, and heal. The authors of this series will be godly, capable scholars with a commitment to Reformed theology and a burden to minister that theology clearly to God's people.

Robert A. Peterson
Series Editor

Acknowledgments

ROBERT PETERSON, good friend and editor extraordinaire, whose careful editing of and suggestions for the manuscript have kept it on target.

Chris Morgan, whose careful reading of the manuscript surfaced a number of improvements that have enhanced the copy in your hands.

Friends at Presbyterian and Reformed, who have been kind and gracious to allow me to explore biblical theology for public consumption.

Introduction

I REMEMBER a day in my teens when I wanted to journey across a lake in my single-person sailboat. When I started out, the wind was strong but the weather was not threatening. The sailing was wonderful as I skimmed back and forth across the water. Suddenly, when I was in the middle of the large lake, a storm invaded the area. The wind capsized the boat; lightning crackled overhead; and the waves became so large that I was tossed around like a garment in a washing machine. I desperately needed "presences" to help me. I cried for help, but my voice was drowned in the maelstrom. Where are other people, when I need them! Then I cried to Someone, and somehow I kicked and flailed my way to shore, bloodied and exhausted. Every life is a journey, and every person is formed by presences, for better or worse, the presence of God being the most important of all.

Presences also lurk everywhere beneath the surface of biblical narratives in ways that touch us:

- [To Adam]: "Where are you?" (Gen. 3:9)
- "God called . . . 'Moses! Moses!'" (Ex. 3:4)
- "The LORD is my shepherd, I shall not be in want." (Ps. 23:1)
- "'Who will go for us?' And I said, 'Here am I. Send me!'" (Isa. 6:8)
- "Who do people say the Son of Man is?" (Matt. 16:13)
- "Father, forgive them, for they do not know what they are doing." (Luke 23:34)
- "I have been crucified with Christ . . . but Christ lives in me." (Gal. 2:20)

1

- "And surely I am with you always, to the very end of the age." (Matt. 28:20)

In each instance, God and a biblical character are present—with us. Absence does not seem to be an option in biblical theology.

The dominant theme, "his presence," is a startling notion, when the pervasively secular world around us lives as if God's existence is a diminishing possibility. "Presence" is a biblical term that connotes relationships, human and divine, in all of their facets. Presence means that God is with his creation generally as well as with his people intimately. This book is not about the possibility of God's existence. Instead, it is about the biblical God, who is personally with us in our joys and sorrows, our wants and needs, our successes and failures. If we struggle with the existence of God, are we ready to entertain the belief in a personal relationship with him? What if we are "gods," as proven by our ability to engineer projects, programs, procedures, and people with a profitability that evokes the admiration of our peers? Do I even need God, we ask, if I can be promoted up the chain of command and buy all of the pleasures and happiness that I want? When we ask these sorts of questions or make these kinds of claims, we intuitively suspect that something is missing in our self-based bravado. This is especially true when we reach our goals and are ambushed by emptiness. Robert Roberts tells us why such questions can only terminate with God: "Central to a Christian account of personality is the idea that the human heart needs God. . . . The Christian understanding of the psyche is that it is restless until it rests in God."[1] This Augustinian restlessness is experienced as a sense of alienation, a competitive struggle for survival lest we perish like the millions of people around the world who are embroiled in catastrophes, wars, and pestilences. Colin Gunton laments: "The other becomes the person or thing

1. Robert C. Roberts, *Spiritual Emotions: A Psychology of Christian Virtues* (Grand Rapids: Eerdmans, 2007), 35–36.

from which we must escape or over which one must rule if one is to be human."[2]

The modern human condition, which spawned today's secularity, raises two related issues that concern presence and our need for meaningful relationships on our pilgrimage through life. First is the issue of individuality, secularity's near cousin. The authors of *Habits of the Heart: Individualism and Commitment in American Life* stress the fact that this is the primary roadblock in our attempts to form authentic communities, in which people genuinely care about one another. "Individualism," they state, "lies at the very core of American culture. . . . We believe in the dignity, indeed the sacredness, of the individual."[3] They identified a number of different types of the complex concept of individualism: biblical, civic, philosophical, and personal. They note that as individualism became more dominant in scientifically sophisticated societies, the inadequacies of personal autonomy (or independence) have become more apparent. In other words, many people value their privacy more than their relationships, to their own detriment. Consequently, they forfeit the blessing of others, which the Bible declares to be a basic tenet of meaningful living. One of my students, who came from a more "primitive" country, wrote a paper on loneliness in American society. He stated that this was one of his first observations when he arrived. The problem could be clearly identified, and the evidence was overwhelming. The final project ended up as a ten-page paper with more than seventy-five footnotes!

The second issue is the impersonalness of a technological world, whose primary characteristics have become virtual (as in reality) and artificial (as in intelligence). An incredible century of discovery and innovation has created a difficult environment for thinking about God's presence. He is invisible in our material world of media presences; he is an absentee "clockmaker," who fails to stop the rampant evils that interfere with an empty

2. Colin Gunton, *The One, The Three, and the Many: God, Creation and the Culture of Modernity*, the 1992 Bampton Lectures (Cambridge: Cambridge University Press, 1992), 71.

3. Robert Bellah et al., *Habits of the Heart: Individualism and Commitment in American Life* (New York, San Francisco: Harper and Row, 1985), 142.

optimism that we need as a placebo; and he fails to flaunt his infinite abilities, when we need them most to satisfy insatiable desires. Today, if you have it, you parade it ostentatiously and walk with a swagger. Why does God restrain himself and honor patience, when he could expand his influence so easily with instant gratification?

I needed God and friends in the storm. At other times I have yearned for companionship to share wonderful experiences in life. Sometimes an experience is not at its best when we are alone. Several years ago, I was in Boston for a conference. The Museum of Fine Arts featured a rare display of Egyptian art and artifacts. Having studied "Pharaohs of the Sun" (Akhenaten, Nefertiti, and Tutankhamen) for years, I determined that I had to see the exhibit by that name. I tried to find someone to go with me, but no one shared this passion. So, I stole away from the presentations and committees to see the things that I had read about. The experience was breathtaking! It was neither virtual nor artificial. I stood in front of priceless, irreplaceable displays, wanting to share excitement and insights with someone. Life is formed by presences such as this, and we want to share them with people around us. We are formed by our experiences with God, and believers want other people to know how wonderful he is.

This book is about questions and issues like these. It is about God's revelation of his presence and his desire for relationship with his people. It is about how he providentially works in our world to reproduce his loving character in our communities— and churches. This raises a different set of questions. Why am I unfamiliar with "presence," if the concept is a biblical emphasis? How do I overcome the image of God as an irascible old Judge who drives everyone from his presence? How could anyone have "so loved the world" with its genocidal tendencies that he would come to save those who trust him with their deepest needs and desires? How can my understanding of God's presence enrich my personal relationships, and answer my nagging doubts and persistent problems in areas such as health and finances? Will he guide me to where I am supposed to be, when I do not have any idea where I am going?

The depth of our needs is reflected in our pilgrimage in general. The history of literature has made people aware that the journey is a wonderful metaphor for life. From Homer and Virgil, to the biblical cloud of pilgrims (Heb. 12:1), to Bunyan, among others, we share departure, adventure, and destination in the quest for personal meaning and significance along the way. My study of our journeys indicates that they focus on personal identity, discovering our "selves," a search that begins in our first year of life and continues dynamically to the golden years. John Calvin's magisterial *Institutes of the Christian Religion* centers on the need to know ourselves as the springboard for knowing God as Creator and Redeemer. He understood that a knowledge of God's presence is inextricably connected to a proper view of ourselves as we journey through life.

American individuality involves an unending struggle with issues of diversity and community around us. We start with an awareness of personal and social diversity that makes us crave acceptance from neighborhood playmates, and then peers in kindergarten. We are different from every other person, and we want to be exceptional compared with everyone else. We strive to be king or queen on the royal mountaintop, according to the childhood game, while numerous children imaginatively play in the valleys below for our benefit.

After years of life, we discover that our identity is layered and that we look at life through different lenses according to our stages and seasons: infancy, childhood, adolescence, and early, middle, and late adulthood. Now, I qualify as a "mature adult" and realize with greater clarity who I am: "If they make meaning as young adults by fashioning dreams, now they make meaning by shaping memories."[4] As a child I was formed by the rules and traditions of my family; as a young Christian I was formed by

4. John Kotre and Elizabeth Hall, *Seasons of Life: Our Dramatic Journey from Birth to Death* (Boston, Toronto: Little, Brown and Company, 1990), 377. The list of life's stages is theirs.

5

a very strict regimen of biblical disciplines. As I have aged, the rules and regimen have faded and blended into an adulthood that does not want to go back to my past. However, I would not trade the formative discipline that I received for anything. I walk on a safe path with wise counsel in my heart that warned me about self-destructive pitfalls along the way. For example, I was raised with the Westminster Shorter Catechism principle that "man's chief end is to glorify God and to enjoy him forever." When I came to crossroads in my pilgrimage, this truth guided me in choosing the best paths for a lifetime.

We can add to individuality and personal development the diversity of biblical journeys. One would think that a theme such as presence in personal encounters—with subthemes such as God's Word, prayer, and worship—would mean an uncomplicated synthesis of presence and pilgrimage and a clear-cut procedure on how to walk with the Lord. This expectation ignores the numerous authors under the divine Author, and the distinctiveness of each character's journey in different times and places. Mary the friend of Jesus should not be confused with his mother Mary, and David's pilgrimage should not be understood in precisely the same way as the apostle Paul's. But these distinctions should not interfere with the attempt to show how the presence of the living God, the covenantal principles of grace and faith, and the common goal of the New Jerusalem meld diversities into unities. In fact, the Bible seems to be telling us that looking at the same truths from different angles enriches our understanding. In Bruce Waltke's words, "The disparate melodies of the individual books form a harmony, not a cacophony, because all the books assume the ideas entailed in I AM's covenants with Israel and contribute to themes associated with those covenants."[5]

This harmony is illustrated in the relationship of two famous prophets in 2 Kings 2. Elijah and Elisha apparently had very different personalities, but they were close friends and shared the same calling. The Lord was leading them to the Jordan River,

5. Bruce Waltke with Charles Yu, *An Old Testament Theology: An Exegetical, Canonical, and Thematic Approach* (Grand Rapids: Zondervan, 2007), 50–51.

where he would take Elijah to be with himself and Elisha would assume prophetic leadership in Israel. A company of prophets kept reminding Elisha of Elijah's departure, but Elisha was grieved over his fellow pilgrim's ascension to the Lord, "Do not speak of it" (2 Kings 2:3, 5). The presence of God guided them as they walked along together (2:6, 11). I wonder what these friends said to each other and the Lord on this journey. There were conversations about "the end," because Elijah asked, "Tell me, what can I do for you before I am taken from you?" And Elisha responded, "Let me inherit a double portion of your spirit" (2:9), perhaps because he feared that he could not be the dynamic leader that his mentor had been. When Elijah was taken in the chariot of fire, Elisha cried out "My father! My father!" and tore his clothes (2:12). "Where now is the LORD, the God of Elijah?" he asked (2:14). He lost the presence of his friend, but he gained the enabling presence of God's Spirit, which was evident to his peers (2:15). Life is a journey to our Jericho, and we like Elisha are formed by presence, with the Presence being most necessary.

Finally, different cultures across space and time represent different identities that experience God's presence with diverse priorities and perspectives. A passion of my adult life has been India, which is as remote and different from America as cultures can be. I have been amazed at God's boundless abilities to bless the body of Christ with his presence in radically different circumstances. My Indian friends are among my greatest blessings. They have taught me that in Christ we can transcend differences and walk together to his Holy City. Our countries are growing together. But long before recent trends, we have shared rich fellowship based on our common Source, relationships, values, and destination.

Issues of diversity in personal identity, perspectives about life, biblical journeys, and cultural differences can be disconcerting. With so many options in ways that people live, how do we choose which journey is best for us? Why are so many people choosing paths and affiliations that are different from their backgrounds, a significant trend in America? Were the biblical char-

7

acters content with their choices, and could they change if they became disappointed with God or their peers?

Besides diversity, the second issue in an American pilgrimage is community. I have read a large number of books about spirituality, and they all seem to assume that we need close relationships for spiritual fulfillment. However, they also advise a freedom from distractions, so that we can live with a total focus and commitment. We can walk with God, we claim, if we could escape the impediments that get in our way. We could have community, if we could be free to surround ourselves with people we like. What we fail to consider in our frustrations is that our individuality is inextricably meshed with our communities. We come from families, as dysfunctional as they may be, that involve parental or sibling responsibilities. We are involved with schools, whose curricula have much to do with our futures. We work in companies, where we compete for our livelihood. We may be married with children, whose welfare is dependent on our faithfulness, wisdom, and expertise. We live in cities and countries, which have common standards for citizenship from which we cannot be exempt. If I want to live in my country, I must contribute my taxes and a chunk of time like my fellow citizens. The issue is not whether we experience community or not; the issue is whether we travel with God in the communities in which we participate.

So, how can I mature in my relationship with God when I am forced into overcommitments by authorities over me? As a recent convert to Christianity, if I prioritize my walk with the Lord, then will I jeopardize my family, my job, or my friendships? How do I negotiate the impasses between these rocks and hard places? A very common concern today is compatibility. How can I grow in Christian relationships, if I don't feel welcomed or accepted by Christian communities in my area? What friendships should I cultivate to form my life with God? I would like to marry in Christ, but why don't I feel this kind of attraction in my Christian relationships?

Finally, questions like these have underscored the fact that our Lord is the epicenter of biblical journeys. On the road to Emmaus,

Jesus

"Beginning with Moses and all the Prophets, he explained to them what was said in all the Scriptures concerning himself" (Luke 24:27). Moses regarded "disgrace for the sake of Christ as of greater value than the treasures of Egypt" and "persevered because he saw him who is invisible" (Heb. 11:26–27). Because the Lord Jesus "went before us" into "the inner sanctuary" of God's presence, he is the rightful guide for us through life to the same destination (Heb. 6:20, 19). He is the "author and perfecter of our faith," whose example encourages us through weariness and discouragement (Heb. 12:2–3). As God's supreme revelation, the incarnate Son is "the image of the invisible God," the Creator and Sustainer of all things, the head of the church, the firstfruit of resurrection, and the Savior of the world (Col. 1:15–20). As our Savior, he is also our example in the way of love (John 13:34; 1 Peter 2:21). Yes, our goal is to be like him as we travel through this life. But beyond that, he is the center, who brings perspective and enablement to an otherwise impossible pilgrimage. As we examine parts of the Bible, we must remember that Jesus dwelt among us, so that in the light of his glory we can see the way to his glorious presence in the New Jerusalem. Meanwhile, we remember his assurances, "And surely I am with you always, to the very end of the age" and "I will come back and take you to be with me that you also may be where I am" (Matt. 28:20; John 14:3).

The book begins with the incarnation as God's tabernacle in our midst (John 1:14; 2:19–22; chapter 1). Christ is the perfect mentor for God's people, who are to live wisely in light of the past as they expectantly await the sight of God's city in the future. He is God's immediate presence on earth without parallel. Next, we look at the patriarchs and Moses (chapters 2–3), who walked as prayerful pilgrims before the name, face, Word, and glory of God. They demonstrated the walk of faith that resulted in a special presence of God with believers in addition to his providential presence over his creation. They are witnesses who encourage us to do likewise. A pilgrimage with God necessarily centers in worship (chapter 4). On Mount Sinai, Moses received the pattern for the worship center that mandated a God-centered way of living as exemplified by our Lord. We, like the Israelites, often want to be "like the nations." The chapter on the prophets discusses false worship that accompanies addictive desires (chapter 5). Here we see God's presence among believers in spite of the majority's unbelief and the need for the redeeming presence of the Messiah. The new covenant (Jer. 31) predicted forgiveness in the Messiah's sacrifice on the cross and the indwelling presence of the Spirit to address Israel's needs. We share the benefits of these promises as we follow the Cornerstone of our temple, even Jesus, to the Holy City, whose architect and builder is God.

This book has a couple of distinguishing characteristics. First, it contains an unusually large number of biblical quotations. As far as possible, I have tried to let the Bible tell its own story. I want readers to experience the unforgettable beauty of its language as it aligns God's loyal compassion with his desire for our loving obedience. I hope Christians will use the quotations to reflect on the life-impacting way that the Scriptures deal with *The Nearness of God: His Presence with His People* with our Savior at its center.

Second, the book matches its practical title with application. Each chapter includes some discussion of how the biblical content touches our personal lives, our homes, our churches, or our societies. How do lessons from the ancient world apply to our modern lifestyles? How could Jesus live perfectly without a cell phone, computer, and car? What do the tabernacle and temple teach us about authentic worship? Are we aware that the Spirit indwells us, and are we seen by our neighbors as God's "living epistles"? How does our present life affect our future as the "bride" of the Lamb? What will eternal life be like? I have struggled with these questions and have been blessed by my own encounters with God's presence as I have contemplated them. The book relates a number of extraordinary challenges and extreme illnesses that I have experienced along the way. I share them, because I think that some readers will identify with them and because the Lord has been with me through them. I invite you to join me on this blessed journey.

Incarnation as Presence

Admit that even if Christ were only a character in a great story, the fact that this story could have been imagined and desired by featherless bipeds who only knew that they didn't know, would be as miraculous (miraculously mysterious) as the fact that the son of a real God was really incarnated. This natural and earthly mystery would never stop stirring and softening the hearts of unbelievers.—Umberto Eco[1]

"THE WORD became flesh and dwelt among us." We should be filled with wonder when we think deeply about this truth. A good friend, who has traveled extensively since childhood, recently visited Israel for the first time. She has been a believer for many years and has known the presence of God through the Holy Spirit. She was surprised by her excitement as she visited the holy sites. She saw scenes and sights that the Lord might have experienced before her. This, she reflected, is where God incarnate had actually lived! She now remembers that she felt a special presence of God in that place. Her heart was stirred and

1. Umberto Eco and Cardinal Mara Martini, *Belief or Nonbelief: A Confrontation*, trans. Minna Proctor (New York: Arcade Publishing, 1997), 102.

11

softened by the fact that the Son of the living God had come in love for her and was with her "in his place."

What does "incarnate presence" mean? Interestingly, the Bible expressed the idea of presence with "face" (*panîm* in Hebrew and *prosopon* in Greek). When we see another face, we encounter the immediate presence of the person as opposed to indirect, media-like acquaintances. In experiences of the presence of other people and God, issues of relationship and accountability follow. I remember occasions such as assemblies and classes when the roll was called. I would hear my name and respond with "here." Similarly, from a momentous event in history, God is present in Christ forevermore. He is "here," and all people must respond to his advent. As the apostle John expressed Jesus' presence in 1:9: "The true light that gives light to every man was coming into the world." In the words of Matthew 1:23 (quoting Isa. 7:14): "'The virgin will be with child and will give birth to a son, and they will call him Immanuel'—which means, 'God with us.'"

Even more amazing than the thought of God walking in Palestine as the Messiah is an understanding of the *kind* of person who has lived authentically in our midst. Scholars have advanced theories about what personhood means, without reaching definitive conclusions. We might encounter humanitarians and conclude that we have experienced genuine compassion. Conversely, we might encounter arrogant, cruel, and spiteful people and regret that we have made their acquaintance. Sometimes we wonder whether most of our peers are only using us and others to get whatever will make them happy. In the seemingly endless encounters in life, we might confront the One we most want to meet, the "One and Only" perfection that can meet our needs in this sinful, strife-torn world. In Christ we see priorities for service and salvation, for the poor and the publicans, and for heavenly ideals as well as earthly realities. We will probably be uncomfortable with our imperfections in his presence until we discover that his love graciously dispels our fears. Eco, one of the great writers of the preceding century, reminded us that our Lord has stirred and softened countless numbers of people throughout the world.

This chapter will discuss the subject of presence in the gospel of John's prologue (1:1–18) and attempt to connect the statement of "incarnation as presence" with humanity's timeless needs for an abiding encounter with the Truth. It will challenge us to relate the meaning of God's presence in Christ to our pilgrimage with him until "we shall see him as he is" (1 John 3:2). The chapter will focus on the meaning of John 1:14 in the context of the prologue and, less specifically, the gospel of John as a whole. It will do this in seven parts:

- The Word in Flesh
- The Word and Salvation
- The Word and Perseverance
- The Word as Tabernacle
- The Word as Grace and Truth
- The Word and the Law
- The Word and Our World

"The Word in Flesh," the initial part, is the unifying truth of the incarnation as the full revelation and supreme expression of the presence of God in Jesus Christ. The chapter will advance the elements and aspects of John 1 with a unifying focus on Christ as presence. The concluding part, "The Word and Our World," will present the implications of the incarnation for our lives in today's world.

Christ's incarnation is supremely important because it gives us the perspective and priorities that we need, when we sometimes lose heart because of unbearable circumstances, or when we are so immersed in daily routines that we take his presence for granted. Machines such as computers are attractive because they are subject to our whims and are useful until they break. They are not personal presences and do not require relationships and accountability. People are presences, on the other hand, but very few of them will become the kind of friend who will be there when we need them. Friendships unfortunately break like machines. Neither machines nor people can be substitutes for a saving relationship with our heavenly Father who has loved us in his Son. Christ, in turn, through the Holy Spirit enriches our relationships and ennobles our chores with a meaning and purpose that can transform our days into his service.

The Word in Flesh

The centerpiece for the presence of God in our lives is an emphatic statement of weighty proportions: "the Word became flesh and made his dwelling among us" (John 1:14). As Leon Morris describes it, "In one short, shattering expression John unveils the great idea at the heart of Christianity that the very Word of God took flesh for man's salvation."[2] The expression stands between the deity of the Logos (1:1–3) and the call of John the Baptist: "Look, the Lamb of God, who takes away the sin of the world!" (1:29). John's statement that the Word became incarnate affirms that the unique, divine Son entered the new condition of flesh to fully reveal the Godhead by his glorious signs and explanatory discourses. Because of his authenticated revelation and completed mission, believers have enjoyed extraordinary lives in the presence of God and his people.

The Word from Above

The term *logos* had many shades of meaning in John's world, and most of his readers would have been familiar with them. Philosophers known as Stoics used it for a pervasive, rational principle that ordered life. The rabbis speculated that it was identified with a preexistent *torah* (or word). John's use of *logos* in his prologue is broad enough for a wide range of meanings, because it encompasses creation and varied responses of the world to the advent of the Creator (1:3–5, 10). John presents this breadth of meaning with concrete relationships and events

2. Leon Morris, *Commentary on the Gospel of John*, New International Commentary on the New Testament (Grand Rapids: Eerdmans, 1971), 102.

that he called *signs*: the transformation of water into wine, the need for personal rebirth, the nourishment of truth, the calming of storms, the granting of sight, the security of godly care, and, supremely, the gracious bestowal of life to Lazarus after he died (11:39). Most scholars note, however, that in chapter one *logos* is unmistakably Hebraic and that "in the beginning" points to Genesis 1. Thus, Logos is a name of God that identifies his effective presence in creation, revelation, and salvation. The Word is the unique human person, who, as God in his gracious fullness, brings life to bear on a world that is dissolving itself in its secular acids.

John's teaching about Christ focuses on the statement about incarnation in verse 14. Beasley-Murray has aptly summarized John's use of the title in his prologue:

> The employment of the Logos concept in the prologue to the Fourth Gospel is the supreme example within Christian history of the communication of the gospel in terms understood and appreciated by the nations. As Paul stood on Mars Hill and declared, "That which you worship and do not know, I now proclaim" (Acts 17:23), so the Evangelist set forth to the world his own thoughts familiar to all about the Logos in relation to the world, startlingly modified by the affirmation of the Incarnation, and then went on in the Gospel to tell how the Word acted in the words and deeds of Jesus and brought about the redemption of the nations.[3]

John, in other words, was using a common term with many meanings, so that all of his readers could understand his essential message. The divine Logos made everything and, as the source of all life and light, became flesh and dwelt among us.

3. George R. Beasley-Murray, *John*, Word Biblical Commentary, vol. 36 (Waco: Word Books, 1987), 10. An insightful summary of issues in the prologue can be found in John Painter, "Rereading Genesis in the Prologue of John," in *Neotestamentica et Philonica: Studies in Honor of Peder Borgen*, eds. David Aune, Torrey Seland, and Jarl Henning Ulrichsen (Leiden, Boston: Brill, 2003), 179–201.

The Word as Flesh

"Flesh" (translating *sarx*) refers to people as bodily creatures that are earthly and liable to sin. John could have used more abstract terms for "humanity," but this word was vital for his emphases. The bodily form requires a human birth (1:13), which in Jesus' case also requires deity, for the Logos/Son gave his flesh for the life of his people. In Rudolf Schnackenburg's words, "The Logos becomes *sarx* in order to give this *sarx* over to death; the Incarnation is being taken seriously."[4] Incarnation is the definitive answer to the deadly human condition. The root meaning of the term is simply "humanity" (17:2). However, in John the fleshly world is immersed in unbelief, so its secondary connotations can be very negative.

Insightful

Many interpretations of John 1:14 tend to make deity and humanity antithetical, in part because of the strong connotations of "flesh." They draw contrasts between eternity in 1:1–2 and the historical manifestation in 1:14 as well as in the statement that the Logos was "with the Father" and then "with us" in time. Bultmann, for example, so emphasized humanity that the Revealer is "nothing but" a man.[5] On the other hand, Käsemann underscores deity to the point that the Revealer is "nothing but" God "striding across the earth."[6] John, however, places the natures side by side; the divine Logos became human flesh, because in his uniqueness there is no inconsistency. The "enfleshed" Logos declared, "I and the Father are one" (10:30), and "before Abraham was born, I am" (8:58). His audience "picked up stones to stone him" for blasphemy, but they were forced to wait until his time had come. Present or past, the truths of Jesus as God and man and as God's supreme presence on earth have never been easy to understand.

4. Rudolf Schnackenburg, *The Gospel according to St. John*, 2 vols., trans. Kevin Smyth (New York: Crossroad Publishing, 1982), 2.55.

5. Rudolf Bultmann, *The Gospel of John, A Commentary*, trans. G. R. Beasley-Murray, R. W. N. Hoare, and J. K. Riches (Philadelphia: Westminster, 1971), 62–3.

6. Ernst Käsemann, *New Testament Questions of Today*, trans. by W. J. Montague (London: SCM Press, 1969), 159–61.

A partial explanation of the union of the natures in Jesus lies in the Word's creation of humanity "in the image of God" (Gen. 1:27). As inexhaustible as the incarnation is for discussion, the "image" doctrine affirms that humanity's life was sourced in the breath of God (Gen. 2:7) and that we are godlike as vice-regents (or ambassadors) of the Creator but are not divine. Though we are not gods, we are created to experience the presence of God, and this fellowship is possible because the incarnate One is the precise, perfect Image of the invisible God (Col. 1:15; 2 Cor. 4:4). He is "in very nature God," who was "made in human likeness" to become "obedient to death" at Calvary (Phil. 2:6–8). As both God and man, the Son is "the radiance of God's glory and the exact representation of his being," who "after he had provided purification for sins . . . sat down at the right hand of the Majesty in heaven" (Heb. 1:3). As fully God and fully man united in one person, he could righteously satisfy God's perfection, lovingly forgive our sins that were not his own, and serve as the "one mediator between God and men, the man Christ Jesus, who gave himself as a ransom" for the many who would believe (1 Tim. 2:5–6; Mark 10:45).

The Word as Unique

The councils of Nicea and Chalcedon classically formulated the union of the deity and full humanity of the Son of God as the only kind of person who could save this sinful world. John's prologue similarly emphasizes that the divine Word became human and that Jesus of Nazareth was this unique mediator as validated by his life, death, and resurrection. God created humanity for fellowship with himself, and our sin, rather than our human nature, has tragically separated the world from the Light of Life. By faith in God's mediator alone, believers "become children of God—children born not of natural descent, nor of human decision or a husband's will, but born of God" (John 1:12–13).

A contemporary problem with this understanding of the incarnation is its uniqueness. If Christ is the absolutely perfect

17

answer for human needs, then Christianity is correct and other religions do not address our need for salvation. Many scholars are making every effort to globalize religion; that is, they argue that the world's religions are inclusive ways to the same Deity and that no one can claim to be the only way to truth. We live in an era of resurgent pantheistic movements. Pantheism, which is represented by religions such as Hinduism, believes that everything is god; thus, divine presences are as pervasive as the powers around us that we worship. These kinds of presences are all-inclusive and result in a proliferation of impersonal, natural powers that dissolve in an intoxicating brew of man-centered fantasies. Such impersonal non-presences must deny the exclusiveness of the Light that gives light to every person in the world.

In a century of developing interest in the relationship of religion and science, the trend has been toward "pan-en-theism," pantheism's cousin that hypothesizes that God is evolving with the processes of the world. The presence is the process, but one can hardly be a pilgrim without a definable destination. In our context of "many ways to the same gods," we are confused by an increasing number of spiritual options and the possibility that people are "lost" if they do not know the Lord. However, according to John, there is only a single correct turn in the road of life; pro or con, we choose based on "the Way, the Truth, and the Life."

The combination of unprecedented catastrophes and extraordinary accomplishments in the twentieth and twenty-first centuries has led many scholars to an accommodation of Christianity to the times by redefining Jesus Christ into a less-demanding "Jesus of history" as distinct from a "Christ of faith." We know practically nothing about Jesus' history, they claim, so we can fan our spirituality (our inner sense of innocence or transcendence) into a hope for meaningful living. They hold that an ancient book such as the Bible does not address the magnitude and complexity of modern concerns. We now accept "post-Christian" as a rather common epitaph for cultures around the world. Symptomatic of this trend, at a popular level, are novels that speculate that if Jesus really was "in flesh," then he must have succumbed to his "last temptation" and married with royal offspring. "Codes" that record quests for his grail, accordingly, were suppressed as threats to the power of the church.

Nevertheless, John had commitment to a unique person for all generations in mind, and, strange as it may seem to modern people, contemporary commitment to Christ is included in his call. Though Jesus lived in Palestine long ago, believers have experienced his presence in every generation. His resurrection and God's presence through the indwelling Spirit in the church mean that everyone encounters the same person, who does not change "yesterday, or today, or forever." The Son does not mutate according to the changing trends in different historical periods. He is the Way, and no one comes to the Father except through him. Because he is unique and his saving work is finished, "Salvation is found in no one else, for there is no other name under heaven given to men by which we must be saved" (Acts 4:12).

The Word and Salvation

The issue for the apostle John is salvation, which other religions ignore because they have no meaningful doctrine of sin. One would think that if God so loved the world that he "enfleshed" his One and Only Son to save it, then sinners would see their need and respond in faith. But most of them have not! The rejection of the Logos is sometimes translated in John 1:5 in terms of a darkened world that did not understand him. A preferable meaning of the verse concerns conflict and rejection, so that it would read, "the darkness/world did not overcome him."

"Incarnation as presence" is presented in John as offensive for at least two reasons. First, incarnation offended Jesus' audiences because his claims contradicted their traditions and expectations. That God became flesh, taking on true and full humanity (John 6:52), including known origins (6:42), was a staggering truth. In John 6:52 the Jews argued sharply among themselves: "How can this man give us his flesh to eat?" The idea that "living bread" would give eternal nourishment was more than their manna-oriented minds could digest! The disparity between Fatherly perfection and sinful realities only compounded the offense. In John 6:42 a hostile audience queried, "Is this not Jesus, the son of Joseph, whose father and mother we know?" In the preceding chapter, Jesus explained that "the Father judges no one, but has entrusted all judgment to the Son, that all may honor the Son just as they honor the Father" (5:22–23). The Father and the Son say and do the same things and receive equal worship! Furthermore, the "perfect peasant" claimed superiority to their exalted fathers: "It is not Moses who has given you the bread from heaven, but it is my Father who gives you the true bread from heaven" (6:32). This hostility and conflict seem to crystallize in 8:37: "I know you are Abraham's descendants. Yet you are ready to kill me, because you have no room for my word." Jesus' audiences may have puzzled over these matters, as the church has for centuries, but they clearly understood their charge of blasphemy (19:7): "He must die, because he claimed to be the Son of God."

Second, incarnation as presence is offensive because unbelievers prefer the lusts of the flesh to the love of God: "Men loved darkness instead of light because their deeds were evil" (John 3:19). The hostility is most explicitly expressed in 1 John 2:15: "If anyone loves the world, the love of the Father is not in him." Conflict and rejection were evident when Jesus spoke of his advent in antithetical terms in John 3:10–21: from above (heaven)/from below (earth), life/death, salvation/judgment, light/darkness, and love/hate. The lusts of the flesh are the outgrowth of the negative side of each of these antitheses. Sin has its own risky appeal and illusion of pleasure. In this sin-filled world, sins seem so unnaturally natural, and can be conveniently rationalized.

The world's conflict with its offensive Savior is graphically illustrated at the crucifixion in John 19:1–6 with the various tortures, the false accusations, and the persistent cries for Jesus' death. In this setting we can see the countercultural fact that highlights the grace and love of God. God did not love sinners because they were lovely and worthy. In view of his initiative, God loved even when "his own" were evil. From a human perspective, sinners responded because his grace moved them to a recognition of their need to be changed from seeking illusory pleasures in an evil lifestyle to a relationship with him. In this light, the incarnation as divine presence should be seen as an invasion of love (1 John 4:7–21).

[handwritten margin note: Interesting picture: Jesus a "Invader]

The saving intent of the idea of the Word made flesh in John's Gospel should be understood further in terms of the book's purpose and the prologue's style. The apostle explicitly states his purpose in John 20:31: "These are written that you may believe that Jesus is the Christ, the Son of God, and that by believing you may have life in his name." The book was designed to promote faith in the people whom the Father gave the Son (as described in 6:44): "No one can come to me unless the Father who sent me draws him, and I will raise him up at the last day." The statement introduces issues of sources, background, and authorship that repeatedly surface in John's writings. Many signs that Christ performed were not recorded, and John's selection of signs was designed to engender belief in "Jesus . . . the Christ, the Son of God." Recognizing that Christianity was birthed in the crucible of Israel, he had an evident concern to address the religious and cultural threats against a proper Christology (1 John 4:2–3).[7]

The gospel of John has been an outstanding evangelistic tract for the church, because people read about Jesus' encounters and identify with his audiences. We recognize our resistance to God's love, fearing that he might interfere with a lifestyle that we have enjoyed for years. We realize that we love the world for what it can do for us, instead of loving God in the world to bless people around us. We often feel that we must perform perfectly

---

7. The scholarly consensus is that John the apostle wrote his book around the end of the first century. He addressed, among other things, a "docetic" denial of the humanity of Jesus as well as hostility from the synagogue. The docetic concern is reflected in the emphasis on incarnation as "flesh" and the notion of "fullness" (John 1:16). Gnostics believed that the high god was reflected in emanations of lesser deities. John appears to be arguing that all the blessings of deity reside in the "full" deity of the Word. In this regard, his point is similar to Paul in Colossians 1:19 and 2:9, where "in Christ all the fullness of the Deity lives in bodily form."

to achieve our dreams, yet our evaluations reveal that much of what we do is very imperfect. We can conclude that we are too unworthy to be saved until we discover in John that God graciously saves the least worthy of people. Finally, in the humblest of ways, we acknowledge our sin and trust Christ as our Savior. Why, most of us ask ourselves, did we wait so long to experience the joys of his loving presence?

The Word and Perseverance

In addition to salvation, John was concerned for the well-being of his "children," believers for whom he was pastorally responsible. Hostility toward believers emerges in John 6:60–71, the promise of persecution in 15:18–16:4, and Peter's confrontations and denials just before the crucifixion. John feared that his people would go astray when they were persecuted, so he cautioned them, "so that when the time comes you will remember that I warned you" (16:4). Scholars have concluded that John wrote to churches in Asia Minor. We know that believers in these churches were persecuted as he predicted. He was concerned that they should receive strength from a sense of the presence of their "first love," as "in the days of Antipas, my faithful witness, who was put to death" at Pergamum in Asia Minor (Rev. 2:13). Antipas died for his faith, while most of us experience no worse than occasional discomfort. However, the bottom line is the same; the unique presence of the Logos in flesh should encourage the children of God to abide in their faith (John 1:12) in their hostile world (John 1:10–11).

Furthermore, an understanding of the prologue's "rhythmic prose" can insightfully develop John's pastoral concern.[8] Its distinctive vocabulary (such as *logos*, grace, and fullness) and its thematic integrity are noted in support of the suggestion that it is an early poem or hymn in praise of the Logos. Parallels in

8. The phrase was proposed by C. K. Barrett in *The Gospel According to St. John: An Introduction with Commentary and Notes on the Greek Text* (London: SPCK, 1955), 126.

Paul's writings are frequently cited (e.g., Phil. 2:6–11; Col. 1:15–20; and 1 Tim. 3:16).[9] The core of the hymn in verses 1–5, 10–12, 14, 16 seems to contain a hymn or confession that was familiar to John's readers.

The significance of the poetic style is that John used the Lord's public signs and private teachings as a defense of convictions about Christ with which his readers were already familiar. The presence of God as a comforting truth would have faded in persecution. Like us, they were strengthened by common worship and confessional affirmation. They needed to abide in their commitments rather than leaving the family of believers with whom they had shared fellowship. In this light, the prologue has been compared to an overture of an opera, which is apropos. It introduces the content and sets the tone for the memories that follow, rising in crescendo through dissonance to the completion of salvation. In the face of disorienting opposition, John reminded his readers that the incarnational presence is the Truth that they needed to maintain not only for their salvation but also for the fullness of his grace that they had experienced.

John uses an unusual expression to describe this fullness of grace in verse 16. The New International Version translates the literal "grace instead of grace" with "one blessing after another." The phrase is followed by a comparison with the Mosaic Law. Carson articulates John's point:

> The law, i.e. the law-covenant, was given by grace, and anticipated the incarnate Word, Jesus Christ; now that he has come, that same prophetic law-covenant is necessarily superseded by that which it "prophesied" would come. . . . It is this prophecy/fulfillment motif that explains why the two displays of grace are not precisely identical. The flow of the passage and the burden of the book as a whole magnify the fresh grace that has come in Jesus Christ.[10]

9. For discussion of hymnic parallels, see J. T. Sanders, *New Testament Christological Hymns*, SNTSMS, vol. 15 (Cambridge: Cambridge University Press), 1971.

10. D. A. Carson, *The Gospel According to John* (Grand Rapids: Eerdmans, 1991), 133.

Carson succeeds in establishing the supremacy of Christ's revelation without discounting the grace of God in the giving of the law. He connects the presence of the Word with the grace that sustains the children of God.

Believers in Christ should know that life after salvation is not exempt from ever-present trials in a sin-filled world. We have our own problems in addition to the cares of our families and circles of friends. We huddle in funeral parlors, hospitals, workplaces, and even homes, wondering whether God cares enough to keep us from severe physical and emotional pain. The answers should never be glib, and sometimes we may never receive the answers that we have come to expect as an entitlement. How should we respond?

The story of the man born blind in John 9 captures these tensions. Jesus healed a pitiful outcast, who immediately testified before his neighbors, family, and religious leaders that he had obeyed Jesus and gained his sight. Everyone rejected his testimony; even his parents did not stand with him, because they were afraid they would be cast out of the synagogue if they spoke for him (9:22). The authorities "threw him out" (9:34). His response was "'Lord, I believe,' and he worshiped him" (9:38). Jesus explained that "this happened so that the work of God might be displayed in his life" (9:3). A full explanation of the will of God in the healed man's life was not given, and frequently we lack all that we would like to know about God's ways in our own lives. We do know, however, that the incarnation emphasized the humble way in which the Son of God obediently lived and suffered for the needs of his people: life, nourishment, security, and assurance. We also have a clear presentation of the proper response to incredible suffering—we should persevere in God's presence with faith and worship!

The Word as Tabernacle

John emphasizes two implications of the incarnation. The first one was that the Logos made flesh had "made his dwelling among us." He came as flesh to be the immediate presence of God among his people. "Made his dwelling" (Greek *eskenosen*) can also be rendered "pitched his tent" or "tabernacled." John was referring to the fact that God's presence with Israel was in the midst of the people, whether in the tent of meeting or the Holy of Holies in the worship center. When the tabernacle was completed, "the cloud covered the Tent of Meeting and the glory of the LORD filled the tabernacle" (Ex. 40:34). For rabbinical writers "the divine dwelling" meant the *Shekinah*, the visible presence of God among the Israelites. John seems to have had in mind the visible glory of God, and perhaps even the term *Shekinah*. Thus, he placed the incarnate Word in continuum with Israel's worship center as a culminating expression of God's presence.

The second implication of the incarnation was the fact that John and other eyewitnesses could gaze at divine glory enfleshed.[11] In Thomas's case, the doubter could see *and feel* the risen Lord's scarred hands and side and conclude, "My Lord and my God!" (John 20:28). Inherent in the emphasis is the validation of the Christ who became the cornerstone of the church's confession about the Word of life, "which we have heard, which we have seen with our eyes, which we have looked at and our hands have touched" (1 John 1:1). We are told in John 1:18 that "no one has ever seen God," which recalls Moses' request to "see" the divine glory with God's response that "you cannot see my face, for no one can see me and live" (Ex. 33:18). Moses saw only God's "back" (33:21–23), but even that encounter served as a powerful prelude to the revelation of the law. John, however, tells us, he had "seen" God's glory in the incarnation.

Two aspects of the Son's presence are singled out. First, his dwelling was "the glory of the One and Only, who came from the Father." "One and Only" (*monogenes*) stresses the uniqueness of the Word, unique as God/man who has made known

---

11. Merrill Tenney suggests that this glorious presence alludes to the apostles' experience at the transfiguration, when John was privileged to behold Christ's divine radiance. *The Expositor's Bible Commentary, vol. 9: John–Acts* (Grand Rapids: Zondervan, 1981), 33.

the Trinity (John 1:18).[12] The glory of the Son was manifested in his "signs" (2:11) and in his death (19:35) and resurrection (20:24–30). The miraculous signs were spectacular acts of God that prompted Jesus' observers to inquire about his identity and mission. The connection of miracles and signs suggests that John was using an Old Testament emphasis that focused less on the spectacle of miracle than on the intensification of revelation. The signs, in other words, underscored Jesus' glory as the full revelation of the Father. "No one could perform the miraculous signs you are doing," said Nicodemus, "if God were not with him" (3:2). But the most profound aspect of his glory is the humble way in which the Son of God obediently lived and suffered for the needs of his people. His discourses, like his signs, were "from the Father." Characteristically, John referred to the Father more than twice as often as the other Gospels do. The obvious reason is his concern to place the incarnation in the perspective of Trinitarian presence. Other men may customarily glorify themselves (5:44), Jesus testified, but he sought only God's glory (5:41; cf. 12:43). Thus, when Jesus answered Philip with, "Anyone who has seen me has seen the Father" (14:9), in effect he proclaimed his incarnation as Trinitarian presence.

Therefore, the second person of the Trinity became human to be the saving presence of God on earth. He accomplished salvation for people, whom John describes as gifts from the Father to his Son. His life exemplified an abiding godliness in Trinitarian fellowship. The lives of his children should do the same. We are, in John's terms, born spiritually to dwell in the presence of our Creator.

12. *Monogenes* frequently translates the Hebrew *yahid* in the Septuagint, the Greek translation of the Old Testament. The term is derived from *ginomai* rather than *gennao*; thus it is connected etymologically with being rather then begetting. We should avoid any notion that suggests the Son is not eternal. An alternative rendering is "beloved" (*agapetos*). In Genesis 22 *agapetos* renders *yahid* with reference to Abraham's "uniquely beloved" Isaac (cf. Heb. 11:17). The theme surfaces indirectly with John's emphasis on the love of God that should characterize his beloved community (John 13:34–35; 1 John 4:7–21).

The Word as Grace and Truth

The second aspect of the Son's glory concerns his being "full of grace and truth" (1:14–16). The combination of terms occurs only here in the New Testament, and John's single use of the term "grace" is here, even though the concept pervades his writings. "Grace and truth," however, occurs frequently in the Septuagint, the Greek translation of the Old Testament, reflecting the Hebrew terms *hesedh* and *'emeth*. We can note Exodus 34:6, where the Lord manifested his glory to Moses and identified himself as "the compassionate and gracious God, slow to anger, abounding in *love and faithfulness*." In Psalm 85:9–10, the psalmist celebrates the nearness of salvation to those who fear the Lord, "that his glory may dwell in our land" where *"love and faithfulness* meet." Grace and truth together emphasize the covenantal faithfulness of God, which received its complete expression in the advent of the Messiah.

John's point is that God's proclamation of grace and truth to Moses has now been incarnated in the Word. Unlike "grace," "truth" is one of his most distinctive terms. His use of the concept, in a variety of forms, far surpasses the other Gospels. Like the Old Testament, John defines truth as characteristic of God. And he affirms that Jesus is God's reality and Truth. "I am the way and the truth and the life," Jesus claimed in 14:6, the source of all grace and truth in the world (1:17). Hence, truth is not teaching about God so much as God's very reality—occurring!—in Jesus. The difference is between personal encounter, "Do you know him?" and impersonal assent, "Do you believe it?" In him is life as "the only true God" (17:3). Consequently, in him the believer is freed from guilt and slavery to the world (8:31–32). God's steadfast love and trustworthiness in the prologue are in view in spite of unbelief. In short, Jesus is the Truth regardless of how many votes he gets; truth, according to John, is not a matter of popular choice. Yancey captures the implication well: "It would be easier, I sometimes think, if God had given us a set of ideas to mull over and kick around and decide whether to accept or reject.

He did not. He gave us himself in the form of a person."[13] Thus, Christianity is not only adherence to beliefs but also relationship with a Person, a commitment that assumes the presence of God in the believer's life. A Christian is a follower of Christ, and this identification has been validated by the faith of believers, who have been his abiding body and family for millennia.

God has been gracious to the world as well. In Buechner's words, "The poor, the brokenhearted, the disinherited, the riffraff—from the beginning of his ministry these were the ones that Jesus particularly addressed himself to rather than to the ones who would have given him a more powerful following."[14] The issue was faith without regard for worldly status and circumstances. Nicodemus and Joseph of Arimathea exemplify the "leaders [who] believed in him" (12:42), but the preponderance of "the needy" substantiates Buechner's point. John could have called these people "pilgrims" who were passing through the wilderness of the world and were questing for "a spring of water welling up to eternal life" (4:14).

No episode demonstrates God's grace and truth in Christ more clearly than Jesus' encounter with the Samaritan woman in chapter 4. While the disciples had gone for food, Jesus was resting by Jacob's well. He requested a drink from a woman, who was surprised because "Jews do not associate with Samaritans" (4:9). Jesus answered her with his ability to provide "living water" that would satisfy her thirst forever. His invitation to her "husband" revealed his knowledge that she had loose relationships with several men rather than a marriage. Interestingly, his knowledge and her response led Jesus to invite her to worship God "in spirit and truth" (4:23). Realizing that he was the Messiah, she went to her town, where many believed that he really was "the Savior of the world" (4:39–42). Meanwhile, he explained to the disciples that his "food" was to reap the harvest of the Father (4:34–38). Thus, the glorious presence of God was manifested in his incarnate Truth to the Samaritan woman and her town.

13. Philip Yancey, *The Jesus I Never Knew* (Grand Rapids: Zondervan, 1995), 261.

14. Frederick Buechner, *The Faces of Jesus, A Life Story* (Brewster, MA: Paraclete Press, 2005), 38.

The Word and the Law

The prologue's uncharacteristic "grace upon grace" ("one blessing after another" in NIV) in John 1:16 is further explained with the revelation of the Lord through Moses (John 1:17). The rabbis identified Moses as "the first deliverer." He was remembered for his extraordinary intimacy with God: "My servant Moses . . . is faithful in all my house. With him I speak face to face, clearly and not in riddles; he sees the form of the LORD. . . . Since then, no prophet has risen in Israel like Moses, whom the LORD knew face to face" (Num. 12:7–8; Deut. 34:10). The law, reflecting this intimacy, expressed the "enduring love" and truth of the Lord's will for his people (Deut. 32:10–12, 46–47). Moses authored the law that pointed to the full expression of truth in "Jesus Christ," the first time that this title is used in the book (John 1:17). Its use here serves as a literary bridge to messianic speculations that were abroad (1:19–28). In 1:44–45, Philip alludes to the coming "prophet like [Moses]" (Deut.18:18) in saying, "We have found the one Moses wrote about in the Law, and about whom the prophets also wrote." If Moses was to an extraordinary degree a revered mediator for Israel, then Christ is the Mediator *par excellence* for all people.

This comparison raises the issue of Jesus' relationship to the Jews and the patriarchs in John's gospel. The matter is of utmost importance because questions have been raised about possible anti-Semitism in the book. There are seventy-one references to "the Jews" in sixty-seven verses; thirty have a neutral meaning or refer to Jewish believers, and forty-one depict the Jewish people or their leaders as hostile toward Jesus. The tendency in the book is for references to hostility to be implied in earlier chapters, while they become increasingly explicit as the crucifixion approaches. We should note that Jesus insisted that "salvation is from the Jews" (4:22). Therefore, since anti-Semitism must mean general hostility toward Jews and since John was a Jew writing for Christian Jews, he obviously desired to commend Christ for his comment on their allegiance.[15]

The issue in the comparison was between faith in Mosaic tradition or the incarnate Son of God, who is Truth. John wrote at a time when exclusion from the synagogue threatened many Hebrew Christians, a persecution that had been directed first at Jesus (John 15:18–25).[16] In 6:30–34 the Jews asked for a sign like the manna that had been given by Moses. Jesus responded that his Father, rather than Moses, had given the manna and had now given "the bread of God . . . who comes down from heaven and gives light to the world" (6:33). Similarly, in 8:31–59, the children of Abraham debated with Jesus about the Fatherhood and family of God. The Jewish leaders suffered from blinding "cataracts," because their faith was in their identity as descendants of Abraham and disciples of Moses (9:28). In summary, one can conclude that the Gospel reflected intra-Jewish issues and conflicts in which believers were being distanced from nonbelievers.

In John 1:18, John advanced a similar point in saying: "No one has ever seen God, but God the One and Only, who is at the Father's side, has made him known." Moses, as noted earlier, did not see God's full presence (Ex. 33:23). Now, however, God the Son fully reveals the Trinity. He is God's self-communication issuing from his own position of intimacy in the Father's presence. Even though "Father" often means "God" in John, we do well to remember Raymond Brown's caveat on John 1:1: "By emphasizing the relationship between the Word and God the Father, 1:1b

15. Sigfred Pederson has a very helpful discussion of the problem in his "Anti-Judaism in John's Gospel: John 8," in *New Readings in John: Literary and Theological Perspectives. Essays from the Scandinavian Conference on the Fourth Gospel, in Århus, 1997*, Journal for the Study of the New Testament Supplement Series, vol. 182, eds. Johannes Nissen and Sigfred Pederson (Sheffield, England: Sheffield Academic Press, 1999), 172–93. He concludes that the evangelist does not condemn Jewish people as such, 193. Andreas Köstenberger similarly concludes, "It must be said that any such charge against a document whose writer (the apostle John) is a Jew, and whose major 'hero' (Jesus) is a Jew (cf. 4:9), seems at the outset rather implausible," *Encountering John: The Gospel in Historical, Literary, and Theological Perspective* (Grand Rapids: Baker, 1999), 248.

16. The Jewish opposition seems to be related to the *Birkath ha-minim*, a "Twelfth Benediction" issued at Jamnia by Samuel the Small that expelled Christians from the synagogue as heretics (ca. AD 85).

at the same time implicitly distinguishes them."[17] Thus, the issue is revelation of Trinitarian relationships rather than a confusion of the persons of the Godhead.

The intimacy of the Father and the Son extends to believers who share their familial relationship in grace: "All that the Father gives me will come to me," Jesus reveals in 6:37–40: "For my Father's will is that everyone who looks to the Son and believes in him shall have eternal life." Again, in 10:29, "My Father, who has given them to me, is greater than all; no one can snatch them out of my Father's hand. I and the Father are one." Barclay captures the desired effect in God's family when he concludes: "God can never be a stranger to us again."[18] When we consider John's teaching that the children of faith are the family of God, then perhaps we can soften the emphasis by saying, "God *should* never be a stranger again," because, in honesty, we can feel like strangers in the presence of passages like these.

The Word and Our World

The apostle invites his readers to participate in the blessings of life with the present tense. In John 1:5 he writes that the Life and Light of men "shines" in the darkness. "I am the light of the world," Jesus emphasizes. "Whoever follows me will never walk in darkness, but will have the light of life" (8:12; cf. Ps. 36:9). The function of light is to dispel darkness, but the implied advent of the Logos in the initial verses means that he never ceases to shine. Like the invisible, infrared rays that are revealed by a spectroscope, so God's presence is made visible in the incarnation and in the lives of believers. Then, another shift to the present tense occurs in verse 15, where John the Baptist testifies concerning the One and Only Word. The author's intent is evidently that John the Baptist's sermons are still "audible" and that recipients of

17. Raymond Brown, *The Gospel According to John*, 2 vols., Anchor Bible Commentaries (Garden City, NY: Doubleday, 1966), 1.5.

18. William Barclay, *The Gospel of John*, 2 vols., The Daily Study Bible Series (Philadelphia: Westminster, 1955), 1.56.

God's grace "must become less," so the Son can be increasingly glorified (3:30). He challenges us to ask ourselves whether Jesus counts for us as he counted for him.

In Eco's words, the incarnation stirs and softens hearts. This chapter on the incarnation has affirmed his observation, because Jesus was the immediate presence of the living God, "God with us." Presence means being there with someone. The advent of the Son brought a timeless accountability, a confrontation of the Trinity with creation. In light of the incarnation, God's people must encounter their need for faith in heavenly ideals to follow the Savior's life of loving service. It should affect the way we live and the priorities that characterize us. "The Truth and the Life" is the unique way to experience God in salvation and perseverance, the man who "tabernacled" in our midst. In other words, that presence of the incarnate and resurrected Christ means that the Someone with us is God and man. He has confronted pilgrims with his fullness of grace and truth, the revelational presence of the otherwise invisible God. John's distinctive doctrine of rebirth points to the fact that people have been made to dwell with their Creator.

How do we project the absolute terms of John into today's relativism? How do we sense the personal presence of God as enfleshed Logos in our technique-oriented, mechanized world? How do we gaze at the glory of our God in a secularized culture, where God has become strange and the notion of pilgrimage has become a complicated and confusing process of self-discovery?

The State of the World

The riveting focus of the prologue's Christology may seem very distant to some readers who are torn between hope for the "good life" and threats of social catastrophes. We are too familiar with the fact that the public seeks escapes from reality with addictions that seemingly ease the pain of empty lives. John points us to the better way of a commitment to the Word that brings perspective and priorities to our walk in his ways. We need perspective in darkness, so that we can honor the Light in our midst.

We learn over time that his light and life in human flesh will lead us to his home, which our fleshly desires tend to obscure.

Concerning perspective, we must understand that the chaos of our times, as interesting and energetic as it might seem to be, is not worth a detour from the "grace upon grace" of a pilgrimage with the Lord. Change toward globalization in the last century is everywhere evident. Scientific progress has captured our collective imagination with revolutionary advances in fields such as transportation, information, communication, entertainment, engineering, and health care: from cars to space stations, from the telephone to wireless miniatures, from over-the-counter remedies to exotic surgeries, and from radio to virtual realities. The world and its corporations have become globalized machines with insatiable appetites for competitive growth, in an intense quest to be the biggest, brightest, and best.

Natural catastrophes and wars in recent decades have reminded us that our pride in human progress is inappropriate, since it has detracted from our sense of God's presence. At times we have become more comfortable with some things rather than some One. We have advanced technologically, even as we have declined morally. I have also read repeatedly in recent days that people are weary of the vague race for a success that has no substance in the end. We "succeed" and then wonder at what cost, or ask, "Is this what I have lived for?" We are taught that the way to succeed is to be faster, stronger, and more creative and visionary. But the years of a workaholic's pace wear thin, and we begin to wonder about Jesus' question, "How can you believe if you accept praise from one another, yet make no effort to obtain the praise that comes from the only God?" (John 5:44). As Christian pilgrims, how do we break through our prideful ambitions that reject the grace and love of the Word who came to assure us of God's presence with us?

The Path of the Pilgrim

Christians in developed nations cannot easily escape the perspectives and priorities that are based in our common histories and societies. We can ill afford to throw darts at a world that we enjoy so much. We appreciate the excitement of scientific discoveries, from genetic possibilities to stellar exploration. We enjoy modern conveniences and would hardly trade them for the Spartan simplicity that served Jesus so well. We survived the century and entered the new millennium without a technological meltdown. Yet, our world too often has trapped us in its vise-like grip. We, like others around us, have become addicted to the adrenaline rushes of successful performances and new things. We too are driven by a quest for the mythical best. We cannot ignore the trends of the world, the critical comments of our neighbors, the frenzied pace of everyday living, and the ever-present competitions that threaten to entangle us. Yes, honestly, we have often "loved praise from men more than praise from God" (John 12:43), perhaps not realizing that praiseworthy lives before God result in respect and mutual appreciation in the church.

The darkness of the world in John, I have discovered, is so unrelenting that God has had to use personal crises to remind me that my deepest hunger is for assurance of his loving presence. Reynolds Price is insightful in his writing on John as "The Strangest Story": "Bizarre as it is in so many parts, he says in the clearest voice we have the sentence that mankind craves from stories—*The Maker of all things loves and wants me.*"[19] The issue for us is whether the crisis is worth the assurance of his love.

In 1980 I traveled to teach in a seminary in India that I was privileged to start in partnership with an Indian believer. I remember my excitement as I taught eager students in a vastly different culture. Midway through the experience, however, my joy waned as I began to feel very sick. A steady diet of aspirin kept fever at bay for a time, but one morning I could not get up from my cot. I felt as though I was on fire. I remember a doctor and my students discussing my malaria and dysentery. I learned that the students had been praying over me constantly. In these kinds of experiences, alone and so far from home, one can gravitate toward

---

19. Alfred Corn, ed., *Incarnation: Contemporary Writers on the New Testament* (New York: Penguin Books, 1990), 72.

either anger or peace. Why would God allow sacrificial service to end with a life-threatening illness? For me, the answer was a peace "that passes all understanding." Without all the trappings of modern comforts, I saw the glory of the Lord in a distinctively purifying way and experienced a memorable fullness of his grace. Despite the fifty pounds that I lost in those weeks, I have been to India many times since that initial visit. Each time I see faces that remind me of God's work in my heart many years ago. The seminary has grown, and a secondary school has been added to reach Hindu and Muslim children. A hospital now ministers to village people who cannot afford medical care without charity. And the House of Joy is a home for abandoned children, where they can grow in an atmosphere of the loving presence of the Lord.

Of course, we do not have to have crises to understand our need for God's loving presence in the Spirit. We can recite the disciplines that have helped many believers in their development: prayer, Bible study, worship, and regular fellowship. What I received, on the other hand, was a wake-up call to determine whether my Christianity was personally authentic! Paul Tournier, after careful reflection on superficial relationships, concluded, "Outside close intimacy and the miracle of the presence of God, real honesty seems to be utopian."[20] Without the crutches of customary conveniences and comforts to lean on, I had to ask myself whether my beliefs were real. Is our "One and Only Hope" alive? Is Easter true? If so, what difference does the Truth really make in the way I live?

The change in my perspective after my life-threatening illness may be compared to driving on a familiar road. At night (amid the pressures of the world) we can see the road and, if careful, perhaps drive without an accident. However, an unexpected obstacle in the road can surprise us and lead to tragic circumstances. But, in the daytime, we see everything with clarity and depth of field. Suffering and difficulties can be the blessings that lead us to a closer walk with the Lord. They shed light on the most important things in this life. We enjoy the blessings of the road because we

20. Paul Tournier, *The Meaning of Persons*, trans. Edwin Hudson (New York, Evanston: Harper and Row, 1957), 30.

can see the dangers as well as the beautiful sights that the darkness formerly hid. My illness gave me urgency about the reality of John's appeal. It was as if God asked: "Do you love me? Then love me like your students loved you, when they prayed for you in my presence." I have learned that it is better to prioritize covenantal faithfulness with the Savior than to expend myself in the caprices of worldly demands. On that basis, in spite of our fears, failures, and hesitancy, we should invite him to "dwell" in our real, fleshly lives that he shared. By God's grace, we can live with godly priorities. We look forward now to the patriarchs in general and Moses in particular, who experienced God's presence in an unparalleled way before the incarnation.

"For the law was given through Moses; grace and truth came through Jesus Christ" (John 1:17).

> 'Twas grace that taught my heart to fear,
> And grace my fears relieved;
> How precious did that grace appear
> The hour I first believed!
>
> Through many dangers, toils and snares,
> I have already come;
> 'Tis grace hath brought me safe thus far,
> And grace will lead me home.
> —John Newton, 1779

The Presence with the Patriarchs

It was, I remember thinking, the most difficult walk that anyone ever had to make. In every way, a walk to remember. . . . In front of God and everyone else I'd promised my love and devotion, in sickness and in health, and I'd never felt so good about anything. —Nicholas Sparks[1]

Religion as a word points to that area of human experience where in one way or another man comes upon mystery as a summons to pilgrimage; where he senses meanings no less overwhelming because they can only be hinted at in myth and ritual; where he glimpses a destination that he can never know fully until he reaches it. —Frederick Buechner[2]

WE HAVE SEEN that "presence" connotes relationship, whether human or divine, as exemplified by the Son who was with his Father in the beginning (John 1:1). Relationship with God involves

1. Nicholas Sparks, *A Walk to Remember* (New York: Warner Books, 1999), 237–39.
2. Frederick Buechner, *A Room Called Remember: Uncollected Pieces* (San Francisco: Harper and Row, 1984), 152.

a commitment, usually a lifetime, of faithfulness and loyalty. It requires a process of growth toward maturity rather than an instant vaccination against spiritual disease. When we consider the patriarchs, we cannot help but notice the ongoing processes of their relationships: communication (Word), commitment (walk), personal encounter (face), and faithfulness (covenant). A meaningful experience of God's presence mandates more than instant gratification.

I think about this when I garden, which is one of my favorite hobbies. I wonder whether creation in a garden was an intentional model of God's ways with humanity. Gardening requires a growing knowledge of plants, just as a biblical walk involves a developing wisdom about God and his people. This experiential knowledge means that we will appreciate the diversity of plants and people. You cannot plant acid-loving shrubs in alkaline soil, or they will wither and die. Changing soils involves considerable labor and expense. You don't plant sun-loving flowers in the shade, or they fade and die. When you learn where plants flourish, they grow and bloom with a beauty that attracts "pilgrims" from near and far. Arboretums in our cities testify to this attraction. Everyone loves beautiful plants and people that adorn the world. All relationships with God, people, and plants have to be nurtured on a daily basis. Fertilizer and water must nourish the ground with appropriate applications. The wrong diet or fluids can kill plants—and people.

A neighbor of mine grows roses professionally and advises me regularly on the health of my garden. The other day I asked her about her roses. "They're in lousy shape," she said. "I am tired of caring for my plants day after day and year after year. I am going to cut them down and start over." I know dozens of people who are tired of God and their friends after years of nurture and maintenance. They want to start over, but they cannot do it, because relationships, once broken, are very difficult to replant. You can put new flowers in the ground, but you cannot simply create a new God or try to restore disillusioned friends. Plants and people have to be pruned, cared for, and encouraged to maintain their health. They have to be protected from a myriad of fungi and pests that are more than happy to reduce them to barren stems. So, as we think about patriarchs and presence, we should think in terms of habits and routines that mature godly people.

In the next three chapters, we will trace God's presence with his people in the initial five books of the Bible. This chapter will develop the theme from Adam to Moses. We come to the chapter with an initial understanding of God's presence in mind. It means that he is with his people, a covenantal and revelational companion on their journeys. His intent is to show them that he made them to dwell with him. The chapter will also note the effect of sin on God's presence: "Though the world was made through him, the world did not receive him" (John 1:10). The importance of the presence from the beginning of the Word and its urgency after sin's intrusion into creation will be developed in four sections:[3]

- The Presence from Adam to Abraham
- The Presence and the Fall
- The Presence from Abraham to Moses
- The Presence on the Way

We will note the role of mediators of God's presence, but we will emphasize the terms and concepts that characterized his relationships with his people: Word, walk, face, and covenant. The issue of sin will be discussed in connection with the fall and the flood. Finally, the application of his presence for our pilgrimages will use the images and emphases of the chapter to show that the walk of the patriarchs is ours as well.

3. The reader will note the use of capital letters in unusual places such as the Presence, the Glory, the Name, and the Word. In Old Testament studies, equivalents of God are sometimes capitalized as names when situationally appropriate. This practice works well with the theme of this chapter and the book. Thus, the Presence and the Glory are designations for the LORD with his people, the Name focuses the way that he wishes to be known, and the Word is God as revealer and communicator.

The Presence from Adam to Abraham

Genesis is the revelation of beginnings that center on covenantal relationships between God and people. Only at the culmination of ordered life in creation is humanity introduced. Trinitarian relationships in the Godhead ("us") were reflected in the creaturely dust and breath in Adam, a "living being" who was made to serve the living God (2:7).[4] To establish humanity's place under God, Adam was commanded to obey by not eating "from the tree of the knowledge of good and evil . . . in the middle of the garden" (2:17, 9).[5] The order of creation, accordingly, revolved around the axis of obedience as expressed by love. Loving God with all one's heart became the central standard of Israel's faith (Deut. 6:5). It represented obedience with love that was exemplified and underscored by Christ (John 13; 15:9; Matt. 22:37). This covenantal order undergirded relationship with God and was normally symbolized in the midst of life, from the tree to the altar and Holy of Holies. God did not intend for his highest creation to "know evil" by yielding to temptations to be like himself (Gen.

4. The plural "us" is much debated. Normally, Old Testament scholars prefer "either a plural of majesty or a potential plural, expressing the wealth of potentials in the divine being," Allen Ross, *Creation and Blessing: A Guide to the Study and Exposition of Genesis* (Grand Rapids: Baker, 1988). Ross's further comment is apropos, "These plurals do not explicitly refer to the triunity of the Godhead but do allow for that doctrine's development through the process of progressive revelation." With Barth, we have opted for a Trinitarian meaning, because Trinity is an incommunicable attribute of God and we have imported clear texts on this matter from the New Testament (John 1; Col. 1): Karl Barth, *Church Dogmatics*, vol. 3, pt. 1: *The Doctrine of Creation*, trans. J. W. Edwards, O. Bussey, and Harold Knight (Edinburgh: T. & T. Clark, 1958), 183–207. Thinking by analogy is the basis of our understanding of God and his ways, but it must not compromise the absolute distinction between creature and Creator. In other words, humanity can be creative in ruling creation, but we can never be Creator.

5. The word for "knowledge" refers to experiential knowledge (Prov. 2:6, 10; 3:19–20). The contrasting extremes should be understood as a merism, opposites that suggest knowledge of all things, which is an exclusively divine prerogative. Knowledge of God, according to Vriezen, concerns all of one's life without sacred and secular distinctions. It is a "communion with God, and it is also faith; it is a knowledge of the heart demanding man's love (Deut. vi); its vital demand is that man should act in accordance with God's will and walk humbly in the ways of the Lord (Micah vi. 8)." Th. Vriezen, *An Outline of Old Testament Theology*, 2nd ed. (Newton, MA: Charles Bradford Co., 1970), 154.

3:5, 22). His intent was to dwell in the midst of his people with fullness of grace and truth (cf. John 1:17).

Adam's labor in the garden and his naming lower creatures taught him God's principle that "it is not good for the man to be alone" (Gen. 2:18) and that only woman who is "bone" and "flesh" from him could be a suitable partner. Reflecting the plural oneness of the Trinity, Adam and his wife were "one flesh" in marriage, unashamed until the fall (cf. Eph. 5:22–33). From the beginning, people were made to experience presence with another person, human relationships being analogous to fellowship with God. The ideal was expressed by the Lord Jesus with his Father in John 17:11 that his people might be one as the Father and Son are one, a unity of persons on a common mission under God. According to Genesis 1:26–28, this mission is to rule and reproduce; that is, in a metaphorical sense, to be lights to the nations by "birthing" lovers of God to the ends of the earth (Isa. 49:6).

God's Presence as Word

The Bible begins with God's creation of the heavens and the earth. His presence was expressed as his creative Word that ordered life on earth, "And God said . . . and there was." The world was formed in two sets of three days, culminating in the creation of humanity in his image to rule as his vice-regents over lower orders. The image of God, among other nuances, established humanity's role on the earth, personal affinity with God, and the possibility of receiving revelation and communicating in prayer. In a word, it bonded people and the rest of creation to the relational presence of the Creator forever, for blessing or curse. The psalmist summarized this initial form of divine presence eloquently:

> For the word of the LORD is right and true. . . .
> For he spoke, and it came to be;
>   he commanded, and it stood firm.
> The LORD foils the plans of the nations;
>   he thwarts the purposes of the peoples.

41

> But the plans of the LORD stand firm forever,
>> the purposes of his heart through all generations. (Ps. 33:4a,
>> 9–11)

From creation, the Word was an authoritative presence that set the stage for the Creator's plan for the earth. The psalm testifies that God is not silent, and we can experience "the purposes of his heart through all generations."

God's words in the Bible have preserved his presence as "very near," so that we may "walk in [the] ways" of our Creator and Savior (Deut. 30:14–16). The emphasis on the Word as a trustworthy standard for godly living continues in Paul's foundational statement: "All Scripture is God-breathed and is useful for teaching, rebuking, correcting, and training in righteousness, so that the man of God may be thoroughly equipped for every good work" (2 Tim. 3:16–17). It is a "living" presence, "dividing soul and spirit" (Heb. 4:12), as well as a dynamic force that communicates with nations and natural forces in spite of themselves. More than a petrified ancient epic, God's Word penetrates to the innermost issues of life and self. On the other end of creation's history, God himself instructed John to "write this down, for these words are trustworthy and true" (Rev. 21:5; see chapter 7 later in this book).

The Word is God's revelation about himself, about our relationship with and under him, and about his will for the earth. However, the patriarchs did not have the written Word as we do. How did they experience his Word as his presence in their midst? Two themes will help us to understand his Word for them.

First, the biblical pattern places Word before event. The Word revealed an event and explained or cautioned the audience about its meaning or consequences, respectively. This is illustrated by direct communication in divine appearances (to the patriarchs), in event (as in the Assyrian defeat in Isaiah 36–37), or in worship (see chapter 4 later in this book). God warned Cain that "sin is crouching at your door," and Abel's murder was carried out with catastrophic consequences for the murderer. God told Noah: "I am going to put an end to all people, for the earth is filled with violence," and the flood followed. He called Moses to deliver his oppressed people, and the exodus came as predicted. And the Lord promised "a new covenant" to Jeremiah, and the messianic fullness of all things has blessed his people. We must remind ourselves that the Word given to the fathers is our presence as well, because the same God who spoke to them is working with us to bring his unchanging will to pass. The Sovereign of history does not have to repeat himself, for we have been gifted with a retrospective awareness that his Word is a trustworthy guide for our pilgrimage on the same earth where all people have walked.

Second, Word is presence, because biblical knowledge involves relationships. Friendships are not based on a list of principles, and we should not think of fellowship with God in this way either. In both cases, a growing, mutual knowledge with guidelines forms the long-term, stable friendships that people desire. Knowledge for us usually pertains to information about life that we process as memory, understanding, insight, and related cognitive needs. However, we moderns tend to forget the biblical emphasis on knowledge as experiential familiarity. William Dyrness is correct: "Revelation in the Old Testament always leads to a personal relationship between God and his people."[6] For example, sexual intimacy in the Bible is described as "knowing" one's mate. Modern people, who seek to explain knowledge apart from their Creator, walk down a path that ultimately denies the possibility of a meaningful relationship with God. The patriarchs, on the other hand and in another time, received God's Word by faith and walked in his guidance. They comprehended issues in their world, because they honored their "personal affinity" with the Creator.[7] Thus, the Bible repeatedly affirms that God acts, so that "you [or they, including the nations] will know that I am the Lord."[8]

6. William Dyrness, *Themes in Old Testament Theology* (Downers Grove, IL: InterVarsity Press, 1979), 26.

7. The apt phrase is used in connection with the doctrine of the image of God by Elmer Martens, *God's Design: A Focus on Old Testament Theology* (Grand Rapids: Baker, 1981), 83.

8. Variations of this phrase occur about seventy-eight times in Ezekiel alone. Of

God's Presence as Face

God's presence in his creation is characteristically expressed by "face" in addition to his Word. The usual term for presence was *panîm* (Greek, *prosopon*), and the biblical understanding of relationships was based on an understanding of the phrase "face to face" in human or divine encounters. When God graciously turned toward Israel, his people received blessing: "The LORD make his face shine upon you and be gracious to you; the LORD turn his face toward you and give you peace" (Num. 6:25–26). On the other hand, when God hides or turns away his face, judgment follows: "When you hide your face, they are terrified; when you take away their breath, they die and return to the dust" (Ps. 104:29). Thus, in Genesis 1:2, the Word describes the Spirit's creative presence over the "face" (or surface) of the waters. After the fall, however, the anthropology of presence comes to the fore as "the man and his wife heard the sound of the LORD God as he was walking in the garden in the cool of the day, and they hid from the 'face' [presence] of the LORD God among the trees of the garden" (3:8). When personal beings are face to face, they encounter one another with the presence (or absence) of appropriate communication that determines the quality of the relationship to follow. Wolff summarizes the point:

> In the face as the *panîm*, man turning towards another, his organs of communication are gathered together; and among these the eyes, the mouth and the ears are the most important. . . . For the ear and the mouth provide not only the specifically human exchange between men, but also that between Yahweh and Israel, between mankind and its God.[9]

We have seen that people were not created to be alone; we were created to encounter, in love, both God and people. David

---

course, it carries the weight of God's covenantal name, which will be discussed in chapter 3.

9. Hans Walter Wolff, *Anthropology of the Old Testament*, trans. Margaret Kohl (Philadelphia: Fortress Press, 1974), 74–75.

earnestly prayed, "My heart says of you, 'Seek his face!' Your face, LORD, I will seek" (Ps. 27:8). He addressed God not as an impersonal idea but rather as a living personality, who was vital in his daily relationships (27:10–12). Thus, self-knowledge necessarily comes through such encounters in which commands and conversation set the tone for relationships. The expressions of the face indicate various attitudes and emotions such as joy, anger, candor, or shame. Thus, the couple's "eyes" of knowledge were opened; they were aware of their nakedness, which indicated alienation, fear, and insecurity; so, they hid from the "face" of God (3:8–10). "The trust of innocence," Wenham observes, "is replaced by the fear of guilt."[10]

God's Presence as Walk

After Word and face, "walk" is introduced as a metaphor of God's presence. "Enoch walked with God" and was taken from the corrupt world at the time of the flood (Gen. 5:24). And Noah "was a righteous man, blameless among the people of his time, and he walked with God," which brought comfort to his family in their toilsome labor on cursed ground (Gen. 5:28–29; 6:9). We are given no details except for the fact that they lived righteously.

"Walk" as a way of life and personal character has been used in literature around the world for generations with similar meaning and emphases. Therefore, a summary of its figurative use, particularly in the Bible, will help us to understand the pithy references in Genesis. To this end, we will describe three characteristics of the concept.[11]

10. Gordon J. Wenham, *Word Bible Commentary: Genesis*, 2 vols. (Nashville: Nelson Reference and Electronic, 1987), 1.76.

11. In Hebrew, *halak* (to walk), *sub* (to return, walk the other way), *derek* (a way, path), and *rus* (to run, achieve) are used. In Greek, *(peri)pateo* (to walk), *(su)stoicheo* (to walk in rank or series, harmony, or agreement), *hodos* (way, journey), *poreuomai* (to walk in obedience), *trecho* (to run, achieve), and *dromos* (to run) are used. *Peripateo* is the preferred term in the New Testament, while *poreuomai* with *hodos* is used most frequently in the Greek translation of the Old Testament (LXX). The Old Testament emphasizes obedience to the Torah, while the New Testament underscores the believer's position in Christ with a Christlike "walk" in the Spirit (see chapter 7).

45

First, the notion of "walking before God" is developed with an extraordinary variety of terms. Its richness of vocabulary indicates its importance for godly living. The terms refer to a way or path of life that characterizes a person's conduct and character. Believers were to obediently "walk in God's ways" (Deut. 10:12) with a sense of his presence, so that they reflected his righteousness in responsibilities such as work, daily chores, and healthy relationships. Leupold described it as "a very expressive description of how a believer realizes the very real presence of God."[12] To describe such a relationship the word "intimacy" would not be inappropriate.

Second, the concept of a "life walk" assumes choices or decisions that lead to antithetical ways (or paths) in life. Extrabiblical literature allowed for a comparatively broad range of options, but the Old Testament reduced the Israelites' walk to obedience or disobedience to God's Word. Covenantal stipulations meant that their choices determined blessings or curses: "See, I am setting before you today a blessing and a curse—the blessing if you obey the commands of the LORD your God . . . the curse if you disobey the commands of the LORD your God" (Deut. 11:26–28; cf. 30:15–18). Psalm 119:1 states, "Blessed are they whose ways are blameless, who walk according to the law of the LORD." Contrary to this blessing, the arrogant are cursed in verse 21, "You rebuke the arrogant, who are cursed, and who stray from your commands." Proverbs 2:13 defines the wicked as those "who leave the straight paths to walk in dark ways." This is in contrast with verse 20, "You will walk in the ways of good men and keep to the paths of the righteous."

Evil was always observed and judged, as demonstrated in God's interventions at the flood and Babel: "The LORD saw how great man's wickedness on the earth had become, and that every inclination of the thoughts of his heart was only evil all the time" (Gen. 6:5). Thus, the absence of a walk with God, biblically speaking, was presented as an extremely serious condition. Cain's face

12. H. C. Leupold, *Exposition of Genesis*, 2 vols. (Grand Rapids: Baker, 1942), 1.514.

was downcast with anger before he killed Abel (4:6). As a consequence, the Lord cursed him as a "restless wanderer" in search of a fruitful land. "I will be hidden from your presence," Cain grieved, "and whoever finds me will kill me" (4:14). So, with a protective mark from God, he "went out from the LORD's presence and lived . . . east of Eden" (4:16).

The New Testament continues the emphasis on opposing ways. Paul, in Romans 8:4, declared that believers should "not live according to the sinful nature but according to the Spirit." In Galatians 5:16–25 he declared that we should "live by the Spirit," a lifestyle that is in conflict with the flesh. Living in this way means that "we should keep in step [or walk] with the Spirit" (Gal. 5:25). Detailed descriptions of the godly walk can be found in 1 and 2 Timothy, in which Paul applies godliness for his beloved disciple who had known the holy Scriptures from infancy (cf. 2 Tim. 2:15).

John extends the antitheses: faith vs. unbelief, light vs. darkness, love vs. hate, and life vs. death (cf. John 3:10–21). In 12:35–36 Jesus addressed a crowd in terms of walk as presence: "Walk while you have the light, before darkness overtakes you. The man who walks in the dark does not know where he is going." Of course, he was referring to himself and his impending glorification: "Whoever follows me will never walk in darkness, but will have the light of life" (8:12).

Third, the emphasis on the godly journey was presented as obedience to God's Word as the content of the righteous walk or the boundary of the blessed path. This presence could be experienced as divine interventions or in anthropomorphic ways. In Isaiah 43:16 and 19 the Lord "made a way through the sea, a path through the mighty waters," and he was "making a way in the desert and streams in the wasteland" for his people. The reference is to God's direct deliverance of his people from imperial captivity. Anthropomorphically, in Genesis 3:8 the Lord God was audibly "walking in the garden in the cool of the day." And "I will walk among you and be your God, and you will be my people" (Lev. 26:12; cf. 2 Cor. 6:16). But the weight of the Old Testament

47

rested on walking before the Lord according to his Word as David charged Solomon: "I am about to go the way of all the earth . . . observe what the LORD your God requires: Walk in his ways, and keep his decrees and commands, his laws and requirements, as written in the Law of Moses" (1 Kings 2:2–3; cf. 3:14).

Presence as "walk" in the New Testament could be viewed as obedience to the Word. In the New Testament, the concept focused on Christ and his abiding presence with believers, who are "in him" through the Spirit. He is the incarnate Word, the full revelation of the Father "in these last days" (Heb. 1:1–2). With Day of Atonement imagery in the background, the Holy Spirit showed that "the way into the Most Holy Place had not yet been disclosed as long as the first tabernacle was still standing" (Heb. 9:8). But "by the blood of Jesus, by a new and living way opened for us through the curtain," the Savior is the Way to the very presence of God, and "no one comes to the Father except through [Jesus]" (Heb. 10:19; John 14:6). He is our example of the "most excellent way" of *agapic* love (1 Cor. 12:31; cf. John 13), and Christians exemplify "the Way" as they walk as Jesus walked (Acts 9:2; 24:14; 1 John 2:6; 3:16–20).

The union of walk, Word, and God's presence is summarized in Psalm 119. This magisterial psalm served as prayerful instruction about biblical living in the realities of life. The psalmist identified himself as God's servant who was persecuted without cause by arrogant rulers and their henchmen, "who stray from your commands" (119:21, 86, 121). Before his affliction by these enemies, he confessed, "Before I was afflicted I went astray, but now I obey your Word" (119:67, 176). Now his ways are blameless in "the way of truth," and he has "kept [his] feet from every evil path," because his relentless obedience has "run in the path of your commands" (119:30–32).[13] He says, "I seek the LORD with

13. The psalmist uses eight Hebrew terms for the Word: *torah* (law), *'edot* (statutes), *piqqudim* (precepts), *miswot* (command[ment]s), *mishpatim* (laws), *huqqim* (decrees), *dabar* (word, law, promise), and *'imrah* (word, promise). These terms are repeated throughout the psalm, but all of them are used in the *He, Waw, Heth, Yodt, Kaph,* and *Pe* sections. Again, the richness of vocabulary points to the seriousness with which the psalmist took the Lord's communication about our personal walk in his presence.

all my heart" and desires faithfulness to God's commands as a "stranger on earth" (119:10–19). "Your Word," he testifies, "is a lamp to my feet and a light for my path" (119:105). He prays that his obedience will bring comfort in affliction and deliverance from his enemies (119:52, 76, 93–94, 123). "I have sought your face with all my heart; be gracious to me according to your promise. . . . Make your face shine upon your servant" (119:58, 135). Thus, the psalm exemplifies a prayerful walk on a straight path in the presence of God's "face" according to his Word.

In summary, the brief yet suggestive statements about God's presence with the patriarchs become a wealth of detail, when word, face, and walk are traced through the Scriptures. Moreover, the details form a clear pattern around the single image of life as a journey. In the last chapter, we noted that "God with us" reflects his desire for us to walk with him, a theme that resonates from creation. Life, by his design, is a journey on a personally distinctive path with unity among believers. We are to travel with him in obedience to his Word. The Word is God's "face-to-face" teaching through stages of life and diverse circumstances about life-affirming, righteous character. It is a walk of love and devotion, in which we learn to trust him for his purposes for us. As we seek the light of his presence to keep us on the path, he shows us the Way of the living Word, the Son of God, under the guidance of the Holy Spirit.

For every aspect of the path of light, the dark ways have their equivalent. Most people (Enoch, Noah, and Abraham are rare examples to the contrary) prefer to walk in darkness, rebelling against the Word to gain knowledge on how they can form their own ways to be "gods." God hides his face from them, and they wander restlessly like Cain in the ways of death. Their journeys, says the Preacher of Ecclesiastes, are exercises in vanity. They reject the Son of God, and stride in the steps of the flesh rather than the Spirit. Without the presence, they seek a renown in which "the thoughts of their hearts are only evil all the time" (Gen. 6:5). This is the setting for the flood.

49

The Presence and the Fall

The brevity of the biblical account of the fall should not conceal the shattering consequences of mankind's *hubris*, the sin of self-centeredness. The gracious source of people's love, security, well-being, and life itself had now become their primary threat in aloneness and death. Their attempt to be independent had cursed them, and now their dependence was shadowed by the menacing presence of sin (Gen. 4:7), the knowledge of evil's consequences (3:22), and the need for the shedding of blood (3:21; cf. Lev. 17:11).

One can hardly overemphasize the relational emphasis of the account, which helps us to understand the importance of God's healing presence in our lives. It means that God's living presence in the resurrected Christ through the indwelling Spirit is a gift that allows us to live with confidence and love instead of alienation and fear (cf. 2 Tim. 1:7; 1 John 4:8). Presence means that God is with his people, and its blessings are companionship, guidance, and enablement for the needs of the day. It helps us to appreciate the supreme love of God in Christ and his answers for our basic needs (note Heb. 9:22). The forgiveness of sins is a reality that turns the effects of sinfulness into effective service for the Savior.

The biblical emphasis on God's presence has his actions as its corollary. The focus, accordingly, is not so much on the abstract notion of immanence—God's providential involvement in history—though that is true, as it is on his encounters and his consequent actions in blessings and curses. Thus, "The Lord God [mercifully] made garments [or tunics] of skin for Adam and his wife and clothed them" (Gen. 3:21). In doing so, he redemptively reminded them of their sinfulness and covered their shame. He promised them that the son of the woman, the Messiah, would mortally crush the satanic serpent (3:15) and deliver his people from their wayward paths.

We should note that after Genesis 3 the "face" of mankind has been depraved, affecting our sight and hearing. John Calvin

50

expressed this in an unforgettable way: "The miserable ruin, into which the rebellion of the first man cast us, especially compels us to look upward."[14] God's presence was veiled, and people have wandered from his path in a sinful world, blindly groping for truth. God's Word proceeds with grace, but we hear inarticulate speech and see an offensive Savior until the Spirit leads us to his loving presence.

We should note two aspects of the presence of God at the time of the flood that are normative for Scripture. First, God did not abandon the world because of the pervasiveness of evil. The world is always accountable to its Creator, even though its thinking is often futile and its heart darkened (Rom. 1:21). We have seen that the Bible expresses the effect of sin as a judgmental "hidden-ness" from God's presence. The Psalms are replete with prayers that God not hide his face from the believer (69:17; cf. 30:7), or the reverse, "hide your face from my sins" (51:9). Though he "sees all mankind" on an earth "that is full of his unfailing love" (Ps. 33:5, 13–14), his "face . . . is against those who do evil" (34:16), who "strut about when what is vile is honored among men" (12:8), "the wicked who [in his pride] does not seek him" (10:4).

Second, based on the relational analogy, "the eyes of the LORD are on those who fear him, on those whose hope is in his unfailing love, to deliver them from death" (Ps. 33:18–19; cf. 27:7–9). In Enoch's and Noah's terms, those who "walk" obedi-ently with him live in his favor. Thus, in God's providence, the wicked in heart are judged, while the seekers for relationship in his presence are blessed.

The Presence from Abraham to Moses

The same themes continue with mediators, who advanced God's unchanging will for the earth until Israel's formation under

14. John Calvin, *Institutes of the Christian Religion*, 2 vols., ed. John T. McNeill, trans. Ford Lewis Battles, The Library of Christian Classics, vol. XX (Philadelphia: Westminster, 1960), 36.

its fathers and Moses. Noah inherited God's decree to Adam with notable transition, since his covenant factored in sin and judgment (Gen. 9:1–17). Abraham (then called "Abram") was called from Ur of the Chaldees as mediator of blessing to the families of the earth (12:1–3). His call was the election of a few people, who were chosen to be the light and leaven of the world. The Lord said, "I am God Almighty; walk before me and be blameless. I will confirm my covenant between me and you. . . ." (17:1). "Walking before," in the Old Testament, meant to live openly without shame, so that God's favor could be evident to others and enjoyed by the obedient believer. In Israel's memory, Abraham's walk resulted in his reputation as a friend of God (Isa. 41:8), for he was willing to sacrifice his only son to experience the sufficiency of God's bounteous provision (Gen. 22).[15] Eliezer, Abraham's servant, communicated his master's words to Laban: "The LORD, before whom I have walked, will send his angel with you and make your journey a success. . . . " (24:40). To Isaac, God promised, "I will be with you and will bless you . . . and will confirm the oath I swore to your father Abraham" (26:3). God's promise that he would be "with Isaac" underscores the reality of his protective presence.

Abraham's Covenant under God

God's oath to Abraham was given in Genesis 15, a noteworthy "presence" text. Abraham had left his ancestral home in Ur (15:7) to travel several hundred miles in search of God's Promised Land (12:1; 13:15–17). The pilgrimage was anything but easy and pleasant, involving a severe famine (chapter 12), a generous gift of the best land to his nephew Lot (chapter 13), a regional war to rescue Lot (chapter 14), and God's apparent lapse in memory regarding land and offspring. So, after the conflict, the "word of the LORD

---

15. Angels were an indirect form of God's presence as well, messengers of their Master's sovereign will: "But the angel of the LORD called out to Abraham from heaven, 'Abraham! Abraham!'" (Gen. 22:11).

came to Abram in a vision" (15:1). In a promise dialogue, God grants Abraham a promissory oath to guarantee his calling.

The chapter contains two parallel sections (15:1–5 and 7–21) that include God's Word of promise (15:1 and 7) and Abraham's request for assurance (15:2–3 and 8). In the concluding assurance, God graciously swears that Abraham's descendants will inherit the Promised Land. The two sections are bridged by the governing principle of Abraham's faith in the Word of promise, which God "credited . . . to him as righteousness" (15:6). Abraham's faith meant that he accepted God's gracious initiative as his Sovereign in life (15:2, 8). He accepted God's Word as the only hope for his future.

Abraham was understandably fearful about the passing of time and his persistent childlessness, so the two sections concern offspring and land respectively. The Lord answered that his presence would reward Abraham and that a son, not the servant Eliezer of Damascus, would inherit the patriarch's household. "The word of the LORD came to him . . . [and] he took him outside" to compare Abraham's offspring to the stars, as innumerable as the dust of the earth (15:4–5).[16]

The second section of Genesis 15 relates to the pilgrimage from Ur to the land of the Amorites. The patriarch again sought assurance: "How can I know that I will gain possession of it?" (15:8). God then instructed Abraham to prepare a sacrificial ritual that would guarantee his royal grant of the land (note 1 Chron. 16:14–18; Ps. 105:8–11). The sacrifice was accompanied by Abraham's driving away birds of prey from the carcasses before he fell into "a deep sleep, and a thick and dreadful darkness came over him" (15:12). Abraham, no doubt, sought certainty of the land in the near future rather than a distant time. God declared that his descendants must be "strangers in a country not their own [Egypt]" for about four hundred years before they would be morally prepared for peace in the land (see Gen. 38 for the depravity of the Hebrews before exile). God then promised their

16. A glance at the Middle East today demonstrates that the offspring of Ishmael and Isaac are engaged in the largest family conflict in world history.

deliverance from slavery with great possessions. Abraham, however, was told that he would "go to your fathers in peace and be buried at a good old age" (15:15).

A second reason for darkness before deliverance, besides the discipline of God's people, was that "the sin of the Amorites had not yet reached its full measure" (15:16). The mutual discipline of Israel in Egypt, accordingly, related to judgment of the Promised Land's inhabitants. What does fullness of sin mean? Just as the earth had become hopelessly evil at the time of the flood (Gen. 6), so the Amorites' polytheistic idolatry with its attendant corruptions would become hopelessly evil. Divine justice is deeply embedded in the passage. People fail to consider the long-suffering of God before he ordered the ban in the land, thus they look at the conquest as intolerably cruel. But until they acknowledge the malignancy and destructiveness of evil, they will never comprehend the need for its extraction so that history can move forward. Would God have forgiven the Amorites had they turned to him in repentance? Yes. But they would not have turned after going beyond a point that only God can discern. Sinners' guilt in time becomes inoperable, so their only recourse is to blame God for their self-imposed condition.

In the darkness an oven with torch appeared and passed between the split animals.[17] At this point the promises of God became a covenantal guarantee by divine oath: "To your descendants I give this land from the river of Egypt to the great river" (Gen. 15:18). Thus, as Allen Ross states insightfully: "The expositor must see the promise in light of the doubts and the dangers and, conversely, must see the doubts and dangers in light of the promise."[18]

The presence of God is presented as his Word and, symbolically, as the oven with torch that would have signified his holy light in the darkened world. The presence gave the patriarch a

---

17. Abraham, as a former Mesopotamian, would have recognized the ritual. Cf. E. A. Speiser, *Genesis: Introduction, Translation, and Notes*, Anchor Bible, ed. W. R. Albright and D. N. Freedman (Garden City, NY: Doubleday, 1964), 113–14.

18. Allen Ross, *Creation and Blessing*, 364.

wonderful gift and a sobering caution. The gift was assurance in fearful circumstances. Twice Abraham sought certainty about God's promises, and twice God personally guaranteed the trustworthiness of his Word. People crave some degree of assurance in a perpetually changing world, and God's Word blesses those who have the faith to accept his promises. The caution is that God answers prayers in light of his sovereign perspective, which we can rarely see. God guaranteed his Word, and without aging or changing over hundreds of years, guided Abraham's descendants to their land. The hard part for Abraham's descendants, and for us too, is patience. The principle of faith in the Word for the credit of righteousness is the same for any generation (Rom. 4:3, 20–24; Gal. 3:6; James 2:23). If we die without receiving the promises (Heb. 11:13, 39–40), we can know that we will receive them when God's Word comes to fruition.

Jacob's Encounters with God

Between the Abraham and Moses narratives, Jacob's encounters with God contain the most vivid descriptions of patriarchal experiences of the presence. Jacob, in flight from Esau, stopped at Luz and, in a dream, encountered "the God of your father Abraham and the God of Isaac." From the top of the "stairway . . . reaching to heaven," the Lord reconfirmed the promises of the fathers to Jacob as chosen mediator: "I will give you and your descendants the land on which you are lying. Your descendants will be like the dust of the earth" (Gen. 28:12–14). He continued, "I am with you and will watch over you wherever you go. . . . I will not leave you until I have done what I promised you" (Gen. 28:15). Fearful because of the awesomeness of the experience, Jacob renamed the city Bethel (meaning "house of God"): "Surely the LORD is in this place. . . . This is none other than the house of God; this is the gate of heaven" (28:16–17). Later, at Peniel (meaning "face of God"), he wrestled with God's messenger who changed Jacob's name to Israel (meaning "one who has prevailed with God"): "It is because I saw God face to face, and yet my life was spared" (32:30; cf. Hosea 12:3–4). The lasting impact of Jacob's encounters was memorialized in his new name in addition to his lifelong limp: "Therefore to this day the Israelites do not eat the tendon attached to the socket of the hip, because the socket of Jacob's hip was touched near the tendon" (Gen. 32:32). Israel by custom remembered "Israel," their forefather, who persistently struggled with God until brokenness made blessing possible. "The law [prohibition against eating the tendon] reminds them, negatively, that Father Jacob was injured in the process of grappling with God, positively, that God was close enough to be encountered and grappled with, yet without destroying him."[19] Jacob later blessed Joseph with memories of God's sustaining presence: "May the God before whom my fathers Abraham and Isaac walked, the God who has been my shepherd all my life to this day . . . bless these boys" (48:15). Joseph, in turn, told his brothers, who were terrified "in his presence," that God had sent him to Egypt to deliver a remnant of the Israelites (45:7; 50:20). Finally, we come to Moses, whose pilgrimage gave the primary forms of God's presence their highest expression before Christ—his Name and Glory.

The Presence on the Way

We began the discussion of the patriarchs with quotations from Sparks and Buechner about our lives as memorable pilgrimages. Like plants in a garden, they require knowledge and nurture to maintain their health. We have discussed how a few heroes of biblical faith were summoned to walk in the light of the Word, and how they lived, very imperfectly at times, in God's presence on the path of life. Most of the memorable texts are snapshots instead of movies, so the chapter provokes as many questions as answers. What would a daily schedule in the lives of Enoch and Noah look like? What were the habits and routines of these

19. Leon Kass, *The Beginning of Wisdom: Reading Genesis* (New York: Free Press, 2003), 465.

righteous men in their extraordinarily wicked generation? What gave Noah the daily strength to hammer away on his barge in condemnation of the world around him (see Heb. 11:7)? What went through Abraham's mind when his Promised Land turned out to be a place of famine? How did their wives cope with their seemingly vaporous promises? Sarah (then called Sarai), we know, entered Pharaoh's palace as Abraham's "sister," and she became an emissary of diseases in the ploy (note Gen. 12:17). Did the couple learn their lesson? What were they thinking when Sarah offered her maidservant to her childless husband? There were times when the patriarchs' "walk" slowed to barely more than a crawl. We learn about the pilgrims' walk through individuals, so what did their households think when all males had to be circumcised, when Hagar and Ishmael were expelled, and when Abraham left to sacrifice his only son? We can identify with the patriarchs' imperfections and halting steps, but how do we read between the lines of their faith?

There are many questions, but a clear answer radiates from crucial verses in the Bible. Genesis 5:24; 6:9; 17:1 are brief trail markers for Enoch, Noah, and Abraham respectively. Their message points the way to a godly pilgrimage: "Obedience is the way to righteousness." The patriarchs walked with God with an "open face" toward his Word. They reflected God's light, when the world around them was dreadfully dark. Their lives collectively testify that the Creator honored people who dwelt in his presence. The message may be simple, but it is a lifesaver in a sinful world.

The lengthy prayer in Psalm 119 is a helpful commentary. However, I have gained additional insight from a Christian classic and a concrete illustration of what a pilgrimage with God's presence entails. The classic is Jonathan Edwards's discourse on "The Christian Pilgrim, Or, The True Christian's Life a Journey toward Heaven," which he wrote in September of 1733.[20] The illustration is the Appalachian Trail (hereafter referred to as AT), "The People's Path," which is more than 2,100 miles of walk-

20. Jonathan Edwards, *Works*, 2 vols., rev. Edward Hickman (Edinburgh: Banner of Truth Trust, 1974), 2.243–46.

ing trail that connects two mountains, Springer in Georgia and Katahdin in Maine. It is a 250,000-acre greenway along the ridge of the Appalachian Mountains, a swath of land that traverses 75 federal and state forests.

Edwards's thesis is that all believers should view this life as a journey toward heaven. His supporting text is Hebrews 11:13: "All these people were still living by faith when they died. They did not receive the things promised. . . . And they admitted that they were aliens and strangers on earth." For Edwards this meant that life always should be lived with the destination in mind, involving planning, priorities, perspective, and partnerships.

He believed that a preoccupation with the goal of heaven is paramount:

> We ought not to rest in the world and its enjoyments, but should desire heaven . . . the journey's end is on the pilgrim's mind.

He argues that this is mandatory, because believers are made to enjoy God's presence:

> God made us for himself. . . . Therefore, then do we attain our highest end, when we are brought to God; but that is by being brought to heaven; for that is God's throne, the place of his special presence. . . . But when we get to heaven . . . we shall be brought to a perfect union with God, and have more clear views of him. There we shall be fully conformed to God, without any remaining sin; for "we shall see him as he is."

Again,

> we may attain that glorious region which is the habitation of angels; yea, the dwelling place of the Son of God; and where is the glorious presence of the great Jehouvah.

For Edwards, this is the purpose and goal of life, which makes a difficult journey eternally significant.

The second section of "Christian Pilgrim" deals with why life is a pilgrimage. First, this world is clearly not the Christian's home. It is a short and transitory existence, in which "death will blow up all our hopes, and will put an end to its enjoyments." Second, all are on the journey, and they must choose one of two paths. The "broad way" of the unconverted "spends lives in traveling toward hell." Believers, on the contrary, "press forward in the straight and narrow way of life, and laboriously travel up the hill toward Zion."

One does not plan to hike the AT without a focused desire to reach its defining mountains. Four million people annually dabble with some part of the AT, but only a few hundred "thru-hike" the entire length in a single season. The complete hike takes about six months, involving careful planning, incredible strength of body and mind, and considerable expense. It requires specific goals along the way for nourishment, evaluation, and rest. There are way stations within the larger destination, where a hiker can review the progress of past days, the position of today, and the anticipated needs of days to come.

This focused planning, in my opinion, is the most important part of the challenge. Edwards spoke of the pilgrimage as a life-long journey that is filled with "the work of every day." For years I have kept a daily schedule that prioritizes necessary responsibilities, relationships, and chores for the following day. I have never accomplished everything on the schedule. But I go to bed at night, having done what I had to do at work, having fellowship with friends and family, and having turned my thoughts to the Lord in various ways. The day will include time in his Word and with his people. Today Brian, Josh, David, and I spent two hours together, in which we laughed, prayed, and encouraged one another in our walks with the Lord. We can do this because we have developed a vested interest in each other's lives over a couple of years. Things that I did not do today will make their way to a proper priority on tomorrow's schedule. Edwards defined the content of the Christian journey as "obedience to God's commands" (the Word), which leads to "following Christ, the paths he traveled was the right way to heaven." He was correct, and disciplined days lead to restful sleep at night without regrets.

After proper planning, Edwards counseled a strong sense of priorities in life. Pilgrims should not be distracted by beauty or pleasures on the way: "A traveler is not wont to rest in what he meets with, however comfortable and pleasing, on the road. If he passes through pleasant places, flowery meadows, or shady groves; he does not take up his content in these things." Certainly, we can take time to "smell the roses," but we do not need weeks to do it. We mut be mindful "to surmount the land we have to travel through . . . there are many mountains, rocks, and rough places that we must go over." Again, the reason for the priority of the narrow path is that "all the steps we shall take are subordinated to the aim of getting to our journey's end."

The AT has magnificent vistas. Places in the Smoky Mountains or at Annapolis Rock can mesmerize hikers and cause them to veer from the path and face life-threatening dangers in darkness or storms. We have the Word, and the AT has about 165,000 signposts that guide travelers through turns and junctions, so that they can stay on target. One can lose the destination simply by wandering from the path. Edwards warned Christian pilgrims about the need for patience, but I wonder how Abraham and the Israelites felt about a four-hundred-year detour in their walk to the Promised Land!

To planning and priorities, Edwards added the need for proper perspective. Life and the AT are marathons, not sprints. We know from fellow travelers that the AT is difficult and demanding, just as we know from God's Word that life is not easy. If we expect difficulties, we are not surprised and profoundly disappointed by them. If we realize that some good things will happen to us, we can keep our perspective and not be spoiled by them. Often hard times are not as demanding as we expected, and we can negotiate the hurdles with ease because of the wisdom of former pilgrims who have walked the same path. I remember a section of the AT that involved traversing a cliff. We were told about the proper way to accomplish this to avoid a fall that would have killed or paralyzed us. The traverse was not easy, but we did it and gained confidence in our ability to handle other obstacles on the way.

Edwards's third section is "instruction," and he informs us that maturity, or closeness to our destination, gives us wisdom about death. When we lose loved ones, we can realize that believers are traveling to a better place: "We are following after them, and hope to be with them again, in better circumstances." So, the longer we walk on the AT, the more we long to reach our destination. Sometimes the most difficult parts of the trail are the long, flat portions across meadows and through woods. "Couldn't we just hurry along, so that we can find some excitement or beautiful views?" Life is like that. Everyone who undertakes the journey of life can testify that it is a walk to remember. Experiences like this spawn a wealth of stories that pilgrims share for years to come. The patriarchs used to do that with their households around the fire, something that scholars refer to as "oral tradition."

Finally, Edwards's concluding advice is that we must not walk alone: "Let Christians help one another in going on this journey. There are many ways whereby Christians might greatly forward one another on their way to heaven, as by religious conference, etc. Therefore let them be exhorted to go this journey as it were in company, conversing together, and assisting one another." Edwards is one of a long line of wise believers, who know that companionship is essential for the godly walk in spite of the occasional messiness of relationships. Peterson wrote of his fictitious disciple Gunnar Thorkildsson, "You could be a solitary wanderer; you can't be a solitary Christian."[21] Yancey similarly concludes, "As God's children we become who we are through relationship with God and God's people."[22] People who hike the AT almost always testify that the highlight of their journey was the people that they walked with on the way. When we share the walk, we enrich the experience.

21. Eugene Peterson, *The Wisdom of Each Other: A Conversation Between Spiritual Friends* (Grand Rapids: Zondervan, 1998), 25.
22. Philip Yancey, *Reaching for the Invisible God: What Can We Expect to Find?* (Grand Rapids: Zondervan, 2000), 107.

So, I suspect that Edwards's discourse, as illustrated by the AT, tells us a great deal about the content of the patriarchs' journeys from Mesopotamia (Abraham) and back (Jacob). They probably could not plan as we can. Hebrews tells us that "Abraham . . . did not know where he was going" (11:8). They took a number of detours, because their distractions were famines and life-threatening conflicts. On occasion, the patriarchs lost perspective and passed out naked in their drunkenness, passed off their wives as sisters, and twisted reality with their deceptions. However, they had the Word as we do, and they are remembered as having walked in God's presence. We are told that Jacob/Israel, the old deceiver, "worshiped as he leaned on the top of his staff" (Heb. 11:21). If he could, we can too. So, the patriarchs encourage us across the ages with the fact that God multiplies imperfect faith as we journey to our common destination in his presence.

> When we walk with the Lord
> In the light of His Word
> What a glory He sheds on our way!
> While we do His good will
> He abides with us still,
> And with all who will trust and obey.
>
> Trust and obey,
> For there's no other way
> To be happy in Jesus,
> But to trust and obey.
> —Daniel Towner, 1886

3

The Presence with Moses

Many of us will honestly say, "I would like to believe in God. If only I could see something, anything, that proves that God exists, I would gladly accept and believe." Unfortunately, what most people can see of God would be irrelevant or nonsensical, and what is relevant and sensible cannot be seen. . . . This is not an issue of high theology. It is a very close, concrete matter that affects people in every station of life, whether they are intellectual and sophisticated, or simple, emotional types.—Adin Steinsaltz[1]

WE CAN recall John's comparison as the keynote of this chapter: "For the law was given through Moses; grace and truth came through Jesus Christ" (John 1:17). God's presence was revealed supremely in the Son, and we noted in chapter 2 that Jews remembered Moses for his unique relationship with God: "No prophet has risen in Israel like Moses, whom the LORD knew face to face" (Deut. 34:10). Philip referred to the coming prophet "like Moses" in John 1:45, "We have found the one Moses wrote about in the Law, and about whom the prophets also wrote." Moses had

1. Adin Steinsaltz, *Simple Words: Thinking About What Really Matters in Life*, ed. Elana Schachter and Ditsa Shabtai (New York: Simon and Schuster, 1999), 201–2.

received the law that contained instructions for proper worship in Israel's tabernacle and temple, and John noted in language reminiscent of the tabernacle (John 1:14) that the incarnation was to be understood as the Word becoming flesh and dwelling among us.

Presence is a weighty concept that should not be taken lightly. It is so central to human experience that some people pay fortunes for a chance to see or be with celebrities. When I was in military service, one of my duties was to protect the president of the United States when he and the first lady came to our base for medical checkups. The helicopter formations, the cadres of armed personnel, the elaborate procedures, and the weight (*gravitas* is the technical word) of the moment were breathtaking. We knew that these were mere people, but the aura that surrounded them seemed to be something more. Many people think of the presence of God in this way. "You wouldn't act like that in front of the president," we hear them say. There were times like Isaiah's call (Isa. 6) when the divine presence was overwhelming. However, when the president is present, military personnel stand at rigid attention with absolutely no speech or movement. We cannot know people like this unless we share their circles of power. The Lord, though infinitely more powerful, is not like this. He made himself knowable for his people. In this chapter we shall see that Moses lived in God's presence in surprising ways.

The chapter on the patriarchs concerned "God with us" in terms of his desire for his people to walk with him from creation. This means that believers are to travel through life on a trail with markers such as obedience to the Word and righteousness. His light on the path points to the Way of the living Word under the guidance of the Holy Spirit. Those who walk in rebellion away from the face of their Creator wander aimlessly in the steps of the flesh rather than the Spirit, toward death rather than life.

This chapter will advance our survey of the presence of God in the initial five books of the Bible. The preceding chapter forms the background of Moses' narratives, and this one will treat five aspects of Israel's pilgrimage:

- The Presence in His Call
- The Presence and His Intercession
- The Presence in His Confrontations
- The Presence as Glory
- God's Presence in Our Prayers

Moses' extraordinary relationship with God is especially evident in Exodus 32–34, where the Israelites' idolatry at Sinai provoked a crisis that threatened their status as God's people. We will consider Moses' transformation, which was based on his experience with God's presence as Name. We will see his strength as mediator, when he confronted and disciplined Israel. He challenged God as well to lead Israel personally to the Promised Land. "Presence as Glory" comes to the fore in the covenant renewal, as Moses radiates the glorious presence before the people. Finally, we will apply Moses' unparalleled example in prayer to our pilgrimage.

The Presence in His Call

The crowning experiences of God's presence in the Torah came to Moses in God's revelation of his Name in Exodus 3:1–15 and in the subsequent crisis at Sinai after the exodus. As the narrative begins, Moses was tending the flock of Jethro, his father-in-law, in the vicinity of Mount Horeb. The first verse emphasizes his daily routine as a prelude to Moses' detour to investigate a bush that was flaming but was not being consumed. Moses turned aside, and his extraordinary encounter with God transformed him from shepherd to deliverer. The gracious initiative of the divine presence dominates the narrative. Moses was instructed to remove his sandals to honor "the God of your father, the God of Abraham, the God of Isaac and the God of Jacob" (3:6). Moses complied and "hid his face, because he was afraid to look at God." The Lord explained that he had seen the misery of his people and "heard them crying" (3:7), so he determined to send Moses as his prophet and their deliverer. "So now, go. I am sending you to Pharaoh to bring my people the Israelites out of Egypt" (3:10). Moses remembered the momentous event as follows: "Because he loved your forefathers and chose their descendants after them, he brought you out of Egypt by his presence and his great strength" (Deut. 4:37). The deliverer would continue to lead them "into a good and spacious land, a land flowing with milk and honey" (Ex. 3:8).

In characteristic presence language, clusters of verbs are used from the same Hebrew root to capture the drama of the encounter: "see" (seven times in Ex. 3:2–7), "send" (five times in 3:10–15), "believe" (four times in 4:1–9), and "speak" (seven times in 4:10–17). The traditional title "the God of Abraham, the God of Isaac, and the God of Jacob" occurs in 3:6, 15, 16, and 4:5. The phrase "I will be with you" is stated or implied in 3:12 and 4:12, 15. The speeches of God dominate the narrative, while Moses' responses are rather brusque in comparison. Moses was not irreverent or rude. Instead, he was overwhelmed by the sudden shift in his role from command of the sheep to submission to the Shepherd. What can one say, when one can hardly believe what he sees and the destination of the calling? Each of Moses' objections was answered with assurances, "I know" and "I will be with you." Presence, as we have noted before, is encounter and communication, usually with a call to a common mission that mandates obedience. The eyes, the mouth, and the ears established a relationship that would last for the rest of Moses' life. The literary effect established an atmosphere of confidence and expectation that overcame the resistance of the mediator.

The Objections of Moses

Moses' objections arose from his knowledge of past experiences, while God's answers pointed forward to new realities of faith (Ex. 3:12, 14; 4:5, 11–17). We can infer that Moses had mixed memories and a split identity from his initial forty years in Egypt. There was a vast gap between his position as an Egyptian prince and his heritage in a persecuted people (2:11–13). The call, in retrospect, had disorienting implications. Moses was commanded to uproot his ingrained routine as a shepherd with its measure of social stability, and to adopt a humanly absurd campaign against Egypt in the sole security of God's Word. He was allowed to express his inability and fear of rejection, but God, effective and gracious, did not allow personal hesitations from the past to thwart his redemptive work for the future. God's redemptive purpose for his people, including the irresistible call of his deliverer, permeates the commissioning narrative. The human agent dragged his feet, but ultimately he would ally with God in spite of himself (4:18).

Moses' first objection was, "Who am I, that I should go to Pharoah?" (3:11). God's prophets usually felt inadequate for the task. Later Jeremiah would plead that he was only a child who did not know how to speak (Jer. 1:6). God called the least-qualified person and the smallest nation for this reason, so that the power of his presence would be evident for everyone to see. God assured Moses of the sufficiency of divine enablement through the graphic demonstration of the unconsumed bush. The theophany demonstrated a power that trumped human hesitation with divine promise. "You cannot do it by yourself," God seemed to say, "but I will be with you, so that you can." Then he linked his deliverer with his chosen people by announcing the sign that Moses and Israel would worship him together at this holy mountain after the exodus. The point is that Moses and others were called to do things for which they felt inadequate—just as we are! We think of them as great heroes, but they did not think of themselves that way. They would tell us that the living presence of God was the explanation for their success.

Presence as Name

The second objection, "Who are you?" or "What is [your] name?" is a rhetorical response to the Israelites' expected question (Ex. 3:13). The question is intriguing, because God had identified himself already as "the God of your father." The Bible does not articulate Moses' motive in voicing the objection, but his memories and the Israelites' experience as slaves would seem to suggest a probable explanation. The question appears to couch the classical concern about God and evil. The Israelites' thinking would be, "If God really is the covenantal God of our fathers, then why would he allow us to be ruthlessly oppressed as slaves for hundreds of years?" We could infer that Moses heard such things before he murdered the Egyptian. We are still occupied with these kinds of questions, when we suffer adversity as the Israelites did.

Most people would be deeply offended by the objection, but God is personal and wise. He receives Moses' question with utmost seriousness and dignifies it with the revelation of his covenantal name. Names, in ancient Near Eastern thought, were a presence that communicated identity and character.[2] God said, "I AM WHO I AM [Eheyeh 'asher 'eheyeh]. This is what you are to say to the Israelites: 'I AM ['Eheyeh] has sent me to you'" (3:14). The Name conveys information as well as an implied explanation of its significance. His answer is a wordplay that, though positive, neither condoned Moses' doubt nor satisfied his curiosity. It was a mysterious revelation that begged for faithful obedience since God's plan would be further revealed in his future redemptive acts rather than abstract explanations. Unpronounceable (YHWH, which is traditionally rendered Jehovah), the name signifies God as the trustworthy, covenantal God of the fathers. In view of the preceding "I will be with you," Buber captures the emphasis:

2. Since naming meant so much more then than now, we note Walther Eichrodt's statement as reinforcement of its significance: "Hence knowledge of the name is more than an external means of distinguishing one person from another; it is a relation with that person's being. . . . He at the same time threatens dire punishment for any misuse of the Name, thus educating men in a truly personal relationship with their God," *Theology of the Old Testament*, Old Testament Library, 2 vols., trans. J. A. Baker (Philadelphia: Westminster, 1961), 1.207. This Name has been problematic, because its sanctity was carefully guarded from irreverence. Some scholars use Yahweh or its English equivalent Jehovah. We follow the NIV's LORD. Bruce Waltke and Charles Yu use "I AM" in their *An Old Testament Theology: An Exegetical, Canonical, and Thematic Approach* (Grand Rapids: Zondervan, 2007), 11–13.

I am and remain present. Behind it stands the implied reply to those influenced by the magical practices of Egypt. . . . YHVH is 'He who will be present' or 'He who is here,' he who is present here; not merely some time and some where but in every now and in every here. Now the name expresses his character and assures the faithful of the richly protective presence of their Lord.[3]

He is the Living God, who will not only deliver his people but also will be fully revealed in the incarnation of the Logos/Son (cf. John 8:58).

God continued, "This is my name forever, the name by which I am to be remembered from generation to generation" (Ex. 3:15). God's response has moved beyond Moses' original objection. The Name was meant to provoke abiding worship. Thus, Israel was to avoid idolatry by seeking "the place the LORD your God will choose from among all your tribes to put his Name there for his dwelling" (Deut. 12:5). Jerusalem, accordingly, became the city "where I chose to put my Name" (1 Kings 11:36), and its temple was the "dwelling" of his earthly presence (1 Kings 8:12–19; 9:3; 2 Chron. 20:8; cf. Ps. 74:7). That is, without compromising his transcendence, God ordained the temple in Jerusalem as the "dwelling" place where the Israelites could worship in his presence (1 Kings 8:27–30). The dwelling was the assurance of God's favor, a "house of prayer" for those who loved his name (Isa. 56:6–7).

God further expanded his response (Ex. 3:16–22) to include the obstacles that Moses would face. The elders of Israel will believe; the Pharaoh will resist; the exodus will be accomplished; and the Egyptians will be despoiled. God knew that the immediate future, with its trials, would fit together in his plan. We need to remind ourselves that the same God who was faithful to his

---

3. Martin Buber, *Moses: The Revelation and the Covenant* (New York, Evanston: Harper Torchbooks, 1958), 52–3. Edmond Jacob similarly stated: "God is he who is *with* someone . . . his effective presence near the individual or amongst his people. To make the people aware of the presence of Yahweh in their midst was exactly the task committed to Moses," *Theology of the Old Testament*, trans. A. W. Heathcote and P. J. Allcock (New York, Evanston: Harper and Row, 1958), 52.

Israelites is the One we should trust in the midst of our objections and questions.

Moses' third objection reflects his fear that the leadership of Israel would not listen and would deny that the Lord had appeared to him (4:1). Doubt about the audience always accompanies self-doubt and questions about the sending authority. Moses was in a position where he could be profoundly embarrassed, and he knew it! In the Old Testament this chain of doubt characteristically accompanied a prophetic call. To Jeremiah, for example, God said, "From the time your forefathers left Egypt until now, day after day, again and again I sent you my servants the prophets" (7:25), but the people of Judah had made "this house, which bears my Name . . . a den of robbers" (7:11). Jesus applied the indictment to a later generation when he "cleansed" the temple (Matt. 21:12–17 and parallels), showing Israel's "stiff-neckedness" through history.

God's response moves seamlessly through the signs of the staff and serpent to Moses' leprous hand (Ex. 4:2–8) to confirm his mediatorial office, "that they may believe that the LORD, the God of their fathers—the God of Abraham, the God of Isaac, and the God of Jacob—has appeared to you" (4:5). The signs are the validations of the mediator that could not be used indiscriminately. The audience of the signs shifts from the Israelite elders to the Pharaoh and the Egyptians (4:9), and the signs shift as well to the first plague. The point can hardly be misunderstood; God paves the way for his servants regardless of the size of the obstacles.

The projected hesitancy of the people was actually an echo of Moses' own reluctance, so his fourth objection is a plea for "someone else" based on his lack of eloquence (Ex. 4:10–13). Public speaking has always been a fearsome qualification for leadership. Forceful words in historical crises are quite different from the pleasantries of daily conversation. We sometimes wonder, "What if I motivate as well I can, and the people don't move?" After all, Moses had once heard, "Who made you ruler and judge over us?" (2:14).

70

The Lord's answer was: "I will help you speak and will teach you what to say" (Ex 4:12). God conceded Aaron as Moses' "mouthpiece," but his will was unchanged and effectual for bringing "my people the Israelites out of Egypt" (3:10). He had the power to govern history and the universe, and he loyally loved his people, so he saved them as the apple of his eye. This prompts us to remember that God, not us, is the Savior and that he can use our stammers and stutters to accomplish his will.

Moses' call is about God's Name as his presence, a Name that bridged his faithfulness to the fathers and his mighty acts that would deliver his people. God had seen and heard Israel's laments in captivity. He was present even when he seemed to be absent. He encountered Moses by name (Ex. 3:4), and Moses responded, "Here I am." Yet, even though God was stunningly present in shocking ways from an unconsumed bush to a leprous hand, Moses' objections and inadequacies were repeatedly voiced in spite of his initial assent. God's presence demanded an obedient heart that could see his sufficiency in the walk of life. Our problem is that we have learned in human relationships that people often are not what they claim to be. It takes time, therefore, in our relationship with the Lord before we can appreciate the perfection of his integrity. In short, Moses had to walk with God through Egypt and back to the wilderness to see the wonders of the Savior. Similarly, the apostle John gazed on the wonders of the Word's miracles as signs, so that he could testify for the ages that life is in "Jesus the Christ, the Son of God." And so we must apply truths such as these as we sing Meyer Leoni's eighteenth-century arrangement of the Hebrew "Yigdal":

> The God of Abraham praise,
> Who reigns enthroned above;
> Ancient of everlasting days,
> And God of love.
> Jehovah, great I AM,
> By earth and heaven confessed;

71

I bow and bless the sacred Name,
Forever blest.

The Presence and His Intercession

We rejoin Moses after the exodus and discover that his former hesitancy has been transformed into an extraordinary boldness as mediator between God and Israel. Chapters 32–34 form
a literary unit that is structured around common themes such
as sin and forgiveness. God and Moses confront the Israelites
and one another as the broken covenant (Ex. 32) is restored
in chapter 34. Chapter 33 centers on Moses' intercession that
healed the breach and brings the theme of presence to the fore.
Moses' encounters with God dominate the narrative. However,
Aaron and the Israelites, the Tent of Meeting, the tablets of the
law, the Sabbath and the feasts, and the prospective pilgrimage
to the land are interwoven with the effect of placing the theme
of divine presence in bold relief.

The Consecration of Israel

With the exodus as the backdrop and Sinai as the stage,
God summoned Moses to consecrate Israel as a "kingdom of
priests and a holy nation" (Ex. 19:6). Mount Sinai was crowned
in smoke and fire and trembled violently as the Lord validated
Moses' leadership and began to reveal the law. For their part, the
Israelites responded, "We will do everything the LORD has said"
(19:8), an ironic refrain in view of their rebellion to come. In
a remarkable passage (24:9–11), Moses, Aaron, Nadab, Abihu,
and the seventy elders of Israel shared a mountaintop meal
in fellowship with the Lord. Moses then "entered the cloud"
(24:18) alone for a forty-day session with the presence, which
culminated in the sign of the Sabbath for the creation of the
nation (31:16–17). God gave Moses "the two tablets of the Testimony . . . inscribed by the finger of God" as a prelude to Moses'
descent from Sinai.

The Idolatry of Israel

Meanwhile, in the interval, the people reasoned that Moses had inexplicably disappeared: "We don't know what has happened to him" (Ex. 32:1). They asked Aaron to make "gods who will go before us," a request that indicated their desire for a visible presence for guidance and protection. A vanished leader and an unseen God meant that they had to take matters into their own hands. Their request reflected their perceived need for divine assistance for their journey. Aaron, without resistance, collected their jewelry and carefully "made it into an idol cast in the shape of a calf, fashioning it with a tool" (32:4). Egyptian plunder (3:22) was now transformed into Israelite idolatry. He announced a festival for worship and celebration, and the Israelites "got up to indulge in revelry" (32:6). The idolatry had a surprising hint of self-justification, for the festival was to be "to the LORD" (32:5). Hence, Yahweh was not being replaced in Aaron's proclamation. Rather, he was being misrepresented in a deception that allowed the Israelites to express their disobedience in the Lord's name.

Brevard Childs summarized the impact of the sin as follows: "Indeed, one can say that the whole subsequent history of Israel's unfaithfulness (note especially Jeroboam I) has been reflected in the request. In the words of Ps. 106:20, 'They exchanged their Glory for an image of a bull, which eats grass.'"[4] One can extend the summary even further by observing the characteristic behavior of all sinners in Romans 1:20–25, which indicates the same exchange of Creator for creation as an indicator of timeless human rebellion. Thus, the chapter demonstrates clearly that the presence of God, even recently experienced, is no guarantee of righteous behavior.

The tragic turn of events at the foot of the mountain keynotes several contrasts in the narrative. On the summit above, God and Moses fellowship in covenantal intimacy, while in the valley below restlessness erupts in boisterous folly. The lamentable scene pro-

---

4. Brevard Childs, *The Book of Exodus, A Critical, Theological Commentary*, The Old Testament Library (Philadelphia: Westminster, 1974), 564.

voked God's angry response to Moses: "Go down, because your people . . . have become corrupt. . . . Now leave me alone so that my anger may burn against them" (Ex. 32:7, 10). The personal pronoun communicates the speakers' contrastive tone in the passage: your gods (Israel, 32:4) . . . your people (the Lord, 32:7) . . . your people (Moses, 32:11). Moses as mediator proceeded to confront the people, Aaron, and the Levites, and then returned to intercede with God. He binds the parts of the episode into one of the Old Testament's most extraordinary narratives.

God, the reader should observe, was not only present with his people, but also was fully aware of their idolatrous activity. Exodus 32:8; and Deuteronomy 9:12, 16 emphasize the quickness of Israel's departure, a catastrophic self-corruption that the nation should "never forget" (Deut. 9:7). The utter seriousness of the offense is highlighted by its proximity to God's immediate presence and the mighty act of the exodus. Indeed, Israel sought to replace worship of their living God with pagan idols that had been fashioned from their earrings!

We often think that we can behave as if no one is aware of our actions or thoughts. The passage teaches us that God is aware of what we think and do, so we should strive to live in ways that honor him, even when he seems far removed from our valleys.

But Moses "sought the favor of the LORD" with unparalleled boldness, and in his intercession he exemplified the characteristic role of his office, bridging God's will and the well-being of his people. Literally, the verse reads, "Moses attempted to soften the face of the Lord." "Softening the face" is used in the Old Testament for the repentance of sinners that turned God away from his intended judgment. Here, since Israel had not repented, Moses advanced three arguments that were based on God's covenant with Israel and his promises to the patriarchs. First, Moses turned God's wrath in verse 7 into a covenantal reminder: "Why should your anger burn against your people . . .? do not bring disaster on your people" (Ex. 32:11–12). In effect, he asked: "Are you going to contradict the exodus?"

Second, Moses prayed that God would not be blameworthy in the eyes of the Egyptians (Ex. 32:12; Deut. 9:28). Would the Lord be like the capricious Egyptian gods? Did he save the Israelites only to destroy them? He pleads with the Lord to turn from his anger: "Relent and do not bring disaster on your people" (32:12).

Third, Moses reminded God of his promise to the patriarchs "to whom you swore by your own self" (Ex. 32:13). Specifically, he noted the promises of numerous descendants and the land. In short, God's integrity depended on his sovereign accomplishment of his oath, so that destruction of his people was unthinkable.

The effect of Moses' intercession was a satisfaction (or, propitiation) of God's righteousness through the chosen mediator's use of his Word. "Atonement" is the biblical word for God's work to reconcile sinners to himself. In Exodus 32:30 Moses was willing to personally atone (or serve as a substitute) for Israel's sin. "Propitiation" is the aspect of atonement that indicates God's satisfaction with the offering; that is, the appeal of Moses was based on God's promises and the exodus. Since Israel's sin was flagrant, the nation was dependent on God's sovereign discretion for its existence. The brevity of the narrative should not obscure the intensity of Moses' prayer. Deuteronomy 9:25 recalled his prostration for forty days and nights to plead Israel's case. In one of the most remarkable verses in the Bible, "the LORD relented and did not bring on his people the disaster he had threatened" (Ex. 32:14).

God had ordered the world so that a covenantal spokesman could intercede for his glory. The tension between God's justice and compassion radiates from the passage. The Israelites' sin justly demanded their destruction. But the reminder of his Word by the people's priestly intercessor satisfied and freed him to discipline the guilty ones, even as he compassionately preserved his unchanging will for the earth through the seed of the patriarchs. Psalm 106:45 poetically recalled, "For their sake he remembered his covenant and out of his great love he relented." We are reminded of the Lord Jesus, the supreme Mediator, who is "greater than Moses" and "is able to save completely those who come to God through him, because he always lives to intercede for them" (Heb. 7:25). In the balance of his attributes, God could be compassionate and gracious in response to Moses' intercession.

The Presence in His Confrontations

Moses descended with the tablets of the Testimony, engraved by God himself, and rejoined Joshua who drew his attention to the raucous camp below. Moses' "anger burned," and he shattered the tablets and the golden calf. As part of their judgment, he forced the Israelites to drink water that he had mixed with the pulverized gold. Every detail dramatizes the breach of the covenant and the people's own participation in the judgment of their golden image (Ex. 32:19–20).

In another sharp contrast, Moses initiated a dispute with Aaron. Moses' identification with the Israelites (Ex. 32:11–13, 31–32) is strikingly different from Aaron's accusatory disclaimers (32:22–24). He blamed the people and minimized his own role to the extent that he claimed that the calf was magically formed. Moses, on the other hand, offered himself for Israel's forgiveness (32:30).

Moses then turned from Aaron to complete the disciplinary process for the nation's sin. In response to his call for allegiance to the Lord, the Levites rallied and were commanded to execute three thousand of their brothers, friends, and neighbors. Clearly, Aaron and the Israelites teach us that sin is destructive and cannot be dismissed or euphemized. In sharp contrast with Aaron's confusion of idolatry and worship, Moses assumes the role of prophet and draws an uncompromising distinction: "This is what the LORD, the God of Israel, says. . . ." (32:27). In other words, Moses, as deliverer of the Word, became the presence of God in the midst of the nation. The chapter closes with God's justice on display, first in the plague and then in a promise to send an angel before the people rather than his personal presence.

Dialogue between Moses and the Lord continues in chapter 33, centered in the issue of an angelic escort to the land (33:1–3). The chapter's dominant theme, in Moses' view, is the necessity of God's personal, enabling presence among and in front of the nation. Moses' intercession had spared the Israelites from annihilation, but God now declared: "I will not go with you, because . . . I might destroy you on the way" (33:3).

The first reaction came from the people, who began to mourn and remove their ornaments as a sign of repentance. They seemed to have realized the necessity of God's personal presence for their lives as his people. Perhaps they also understood the profundity of the consequences of their recent willfulness for their relationship with the Lord. Their regret sparked Moses' renewed intercession for God's abiding presence for their journey to the land. Thus, Moses' confrontations with the people transition to his confrontation with the Lord.

The reconciliation of Israel with the Lord was initiated at the Tent of Meeting "outside the camp some distance away" (33:7). In the law, "outside the camp" connoted a sinfulness that prevented God from dwelling in their midst (Ex. 29:14; Lev. 4:11–12; 13:46; Num. 15:35). It was a reminder that their sin had alienated them from God. The tent was not the tabernacle to come, but was a place of consultation where Moses spoke face to face with God, whose presence was evidenced by the pillar of cloud. Though God's presence was still questionable for the nation's pilgrimage, the pillar at the tent affirmed his pleasure with their repentance.

A clue to the significance of presence as relationship is indicated by the phrase "as a man speaks with his friend" (Ex. 33:11). Prayerful dialogue with God is like conversation between good friends, candid and respectful. Moses' prayers would not have been casual but would have expressed his awareness of the need for the Israelites' constant dependence on the Lord for their daily needs: for guidance, protection, and provision. At the deepest level, we learn from this passage that God's presence is absolutely essential in the formation of his people. Israel could not be God's kingdom of priests without his distinguishing presence (33:16). Durham's observation concerning the passage is profound: "Its theological insight is universal, equally applicable to divine-human relationship and ministry in any age. No people, no matter how religious they are and for whatever reasons, can be a people of God without the presence of God."[5] In today's terms, a church cannot be God's people without his distinctive dwelling in its midst. Success in any form must be quantified by an earnest desire by the believers to seek the Lord for their guidance, protection, and provision. His presence gives meaning and significance to goals, plans, and projects.

The Israelites observed Moses' intercession with the Lord, worshiping at the entrances of their tents. One should note the sharp change in their attitude toward Moses as well, from disrespect (Ex. 32:1) to respect (33:8). Our attitude toward God is reflected in our treatment of his servants. We may infer that this camping sojourn was a training session over an extended period of time to impress the Israelites with the radical difference between worshipful behavior and lawless idolatry.

The training was the setting for Moses' confrontation in Exodus 33:12–18. His initial request (33:12–13) was marked by intensity, beginning and ending with exclamations, "Look!" He reminded God that he had called him by saying, "Lead these people" and had shown him favor when God said to him, "I know you by name and you have found favor with me" (33:12). Moses objected that God now declined to go with him. So, with the issue of presence in view, he asked God: "Teach me your ways so I may know you and continue to find favor with you" (33:13). The several parts of the prayer formed a single request that God

5. John Durham, *Word Bible Commentary: Exodus* (Nashville: Nelson Reference and Electronic, 1987), 448. Similarly, Samuel Terrian states, "Presence is that which creates a people. . . . Initiated by presence, it leads to presence. Out of all peoples, the new people will become Yahweh's 'special treasure' (*segullah*)," *The Elusive Presence: Toward a New Biblical Theology*, Religious Perspectives (San Francisco: Harper and Row, 1978), 124.

himself would accompany Israel in the future. Moses requested an affirmation of God's personal commitment, notably his compassion and favor in light of his recent wrath.

The divine response was positive, "My presence will go with you, and I will give you rest" (Ex. 33:14). His "face" will not be "turned" from the Israelites, a promise that comforted Moses with the assurance that he would know God by name and continue in his favor. Instead of anxiety about God's absence (vv. 12–13, 15–16), Moses could rest in the assurance that God would honor his promises, so that the people need not fear restless wandering like Cain. They would have a home where God would dwell with them, in his time and in his way.

Moses' answer underscored the seriousness of God's presence for their departure. In essence, he asserted, "If you don't go, then we can't go" (Ex. 33:15). His two reasons were presented as questions. First, without the divine presence, how would observers recognize God's covenantal pleasure with Moses and the nation? Second, without him, why should an indistinguishable people even try to drive hostile tribes from their land? God's presence, Moses argued, was necessary to validate his promises to himself and Israel. For Moses' sake ("because I am pleased with you and I know you by name"), the Lord committed to "do the very thing you have asked" (33:17). Thus, the way was prepared for the formal renewal of the covenant.

Moses' second request advanced his desire to know God's ways, "Now show me your glory" (33:18). His request was deflected by God, "You cannot see my face [panîm], for no one may see me and live" (33:20). God was saying that a direct encounter with his glory was "too heavy" (kabod means "weightiness") for a sinful person to bear. Glory is the overwhelming power of God's personal Being that was characteristically manifested as radiant light, which Moses somehow reflected in chapter 34. It is closely associated with his holiness and perfection, which distinguish him from all creatures, especially in their sinful condition.

However, the Lord offered an expansive reply with mercy and compassion for his chosen friend. He paraded his "goodness" in front of Moses with personal proclamations of his name (Ex. 33:19; 34:5–7). There are limits for God's presence, even for a face-to-face friend. Thus, in this setting, the Glory was seen through the lens of his goodness, with his attributes of mercy and compassion expressed in terms of his sovereign freedom as in 3:14. The Glory was also manifested in its mysterious passing and the protection of God's hand in the cleft of the rock (33:21–23). Moses' confrontation was now complete.

The Presence as Glory

The restoration of the covenant in Exodus 34 serves as an excellent summary of Israel's experience at Sinai. In a theophany, Moses received laws that were focused on the threat of idolatry both in light of Israel's recent unfaithfulness and in the impending conquest of Canaan. The chapter unfolds with the Lord's gracious answer to Moses' intense intercessory prayers and ends with a pattern for the living will of God, "The LORD made this covenant . . . with us, with all of us who are alive here today" (Deut. 5:3).

Moses obediently chiseled two tablets like the first ones, so that he could write the same words on them in God's presence (Ex. 34:1, 27–28). Moses was to climb Sinai alone, while the people and flocks were to remain at a distance (34:2–3). He ascended "as the LORD had commanded," and the Lord descended "in the cloud." He "stood there with" Moses, proclaiming his name and attributes as a further response to Moses' request to see his glory. The confession of his character reflected the justice and forgiveness that were evidenced in the preceding chapters, a "credo of adjectives" that was remembered by later generations (Ps. 86:15; Neh. 9:17).[6] In dialogue for forty days and nights, Moses worshiped (34:8) and asked God to "take us as your inheritance" (Ex. 34:9). "It comes naturally to men to bow in fear and trem-

6. The apt phrase is from Walter Brueggemann, *The Theology of the Old Testament: Testimony, Dispute, Advocacy* (Minneapolis: Fortress Press, 1997), 215.

bling before this gracious Being," Eichrodt noted.[7] The Lord, in turn, promised to "do wonders never before done in any nation in all the world" (34:10). Israel's tradition, thus formulated, was not one of proud faithfulness but rather of dependence on God's sustaining mercy and judgment for the sake of his unchanging will. In this way, Israel was to be distinguished from other people on earth (33:16).

The nation was to resist the idolatries of the nations in honor of "the Lord, whose name is Jealous" (Ex. 34:14). And "three times a year all your men are to appear before the Sovereign Lord, the God of Israel" to worshipfully celebrate the feasts of Unleavened Bread, Weeks, and Ingathering (34:23). The Sabbath, in all circumstances, was to be observed to remember the goodness of the Creator and Sovereign of history in behalf of his people (34:21). Accordingly, the feasts expressed their thankfulness for the fruitfulness of the land.

When Moses descended from the mountain, "he was not aware that his face was radiant because he had spoken with the Lord" (34:29). Aaron and the Israelites saw the radiance, and "they were afraid to come near him" (34:30). However, because of his glowing face, they knew that God was pleased with him. Moses would summon them and give them all the commands that the Lord had given him (34:32). Customarily, Moses would speak unveiled with the Lord in the Tent of Meeting, and then "put the veil back over his face" in his reports to the Israelites (34:33–35). The point of the narrative is that Moses was to be a reflection of God as he communicated the Word to the people. In chapter 6, we will see that Paul uses the radiance and veil to demonstrate the superiority of the new covenant for us in the Spirit.

We have traced the theme of God's presence from Eden through the patriarchal narratives in Genesis. The theme of presence was underscored from creation as a walk of obedience to God's Word on the way to the son of Eve, who would crush Satan's opposition to God and his people. The patriarchs' encounters

7. Eichrodt, *Theology of the Old Testament*, 1.44.

with God intensified as Israel's history progressed from Jacob to Moses. Moses experienced God's presence "face to face as with a friend" with intensity and transparency. When God as I AM called him, Moses expressed his objections and inadequacies. The God of Abraham, Isaac, and Jacob promised him guidance and protection as he experienced mighty acts of deliverance from the Egyptian empire. God's relationship with his prophetic mediator grew to the point that Moses witnessed the Glory to the extent that God could allow for his beloved servant leader. In this way Moses pointed forward to the Prophet like himself (Deut. 18:15, 18) who would mediate salvation for the world. Moses' intense and transparent experience of the presence can be summarized as prayer. From his call, through the exodus, to the giving of the law, God and Moses shared a unique "duologue" in behalf of a wayward nation. How do we pray toward a personal relationship with the Holy Spirit and the Word today?

God's Presence in Our Prayers

This chapter began with Steinsaltz's quotation concerning a willingness to believe, if only we could see anything that proves God's existence. This is a common excuse for unbelief. It is, as he stated, a concrete appeal that affects people in every station of life. As a plea for God's presence, the statement seems self-evident. Honestly, do we not sometimes wonder about God, who at times seems to be invisible, silent, and remote?

The problem is that Israel's Sinai experience proves that the statement is incorrect. The Israelites witnessed the plagues, crossed the sea, and were represented by Aaron and others at the covenant ceremony. "They responded with one voice, 'Everything the LORD has said we will do'" (Ex. 24:3). Sometimes the idolatry in chapter 32 is disclaimed as the behavior of riffraff who somehow connected with the Israelites in the exodus. The Old Testament does not treat the episode in this way, although we would like to think that it is true. The nation saw God's mighty acts and rebelled anyway.

A Pilgrimage in Prayer

On the other hand, Moses saw the same things and became one of God's closest confidants, in spite of his earlier reservations. We are reminded of the apostles, who cringed at the cross before they became transforming agents in their world through the special presence of the Spirit. What caused Moses' remarkable change from a stammering shepherd to an eloquent advocate with God for his people?

The Sinai narrative teaches us that prayer is the pivot of the change, and it challenges us to compare our prayer lives with Moses' communication with God. Significantly, he reminded the Israelites in Deuteronomy 4:7 that prayer keys their distinctive relationship with their personal, living God: "What other nation is so great as to have their gods near them the way the LORD our God is near us whenever we pray to him?" Granted, we are not special mediators like the patriarchs nor have we been called into the presence of a flaming bush. Our incarnate Lord, who is now in session at the right hand of his Father, is a much greater Mediator than Moses! However, we yearn to know that God "will do the very thing" that we ask because he is pleased with us (Ex. 33:17). Is this possible?

My pilgrimage has led me to the possibility of knowing God in a greater way through prayer. I grew up in an atmosphere of formal prayers. There were liturgical prayers, blessings at meals, family prayers at gatherings, and prayers at bedtime. The liturgies were as beautiful as the Scriptures that formed them. The family prayers have endured as a significant part of my early memories. Several of the familiar refrains were preserved in framed handiwork that adorns our walls. These kinds of prayers still bless my life. But Moses seems to tell us that a walk with the Lord involves more. We underestimate the power of intercessory prayer in the will and work of the Lord. God looked for a person in Israel just before the exile "who would build up the wall and stand before me in the gap on behalf of the land so I would not have to destroy it, but I found none" (Ezek. 22:30).

I have taught theology for decades, and, in the process, my understanding of prayer and its priority in life has changed. I trace this change to three new perspectives—from theology, from relationships, and from this passage. First, my view of God and my prayers were disjointed. I taught that God is omniscient, that he knows all things actual and possible. Yet I prayed as if he shouldn't know about the shameful or negative parts of my life. I hid my face from him out of a fear that he would hide his face from me if he knew what I was really like. An unstated reason for prayer, for me, was for success in *my* endeavors, prosperity in *my* circumstances, and relief from *my* hardships. My prayers lacked details and honesty. I sometimes doubted that a lofty, exalted God really cared about the messy stuff that consumed my days. Eventually, I reasoned that a lofty God who is confined to a sanctuary is not great after all. However, the biblical God is so great that he can enter the lives of his people and sustain them through their circumstances, successful or otherwise. I discovered that prayer should be conversation with God as we practice his presence every day. Besides, if the Holy Spirit indwells me, who am I trying to fool!

Second, I began to see the relational analogies in Scripture with greater clarity. God made Adam and Eve in his Trinitarian image, and mutual communication (or prayer) has been central to all relationships ever since. The fall did not change this; it simply caused us to hide from his face, so that our shame would be unseen. I have frequently contemplated the fact that if I communicated with my family and friends like I often pray to God, then I would lose my friends. Does Exodus not say, "The LORD would speak to Moses face to face, as a man speaks with his friend?" (33:11). No human being wants formal, formulaic relationships, and neither does God. One cannot help but note that our conversations are saturated with "Can you . . . ," "Will you . . . ," "I want . . . ," and similar requests. The problem is that our prayers tend to follow the pattern of our conversations. God is personal, and he loves to be loved! Verses such as Proverbs 8:17 come to mind: "I love those who love me, and those who seek me find me." When I am with friends these days, we find ourselves praying for others' needs with gratitude for his bountiful provision for us. This is a wonderful way to shift attention away from ourselves. During times of intense suffering, I have confessed to God that, on a number of occasions, I had only pretended to have a personal relationship with him.

Third, I have enjoyed Moses' prayers in Exodus for a number of years. I may not be a mediator, but I can learn from him. I can identify with all of his objections to God's call—namely, his fears of embarrassment, inadequacy, and rejection. My primary lesson has been Moses' bold honesty in dialogue with God. He confronted the Lord with "Remember!" about his promises to the fathers. He pleaded for God to "Look!" at reasonable arguments for divine leadership of his people. He dared to tell God that "if you won't go, then we won't go." I am still amazed that God relented, and that he would do the very things that Moses asked. Yes, I want that kind of relationship with the Lord.

The Possibilities of Prayer

"So what?" you ask. First, my prayer life has shifted to conversational prayer, where I share with the Lord life as I experience it. I try to pray about everything, including the words of this chapter! I pray about family members, friends, finances, and daily concerns such as broken appliances and bad cars. Yes, I praise him for graciously giving me so much to be thankful for, such as intangible blessings that I often take for granted. Of course, I try to pray constantly, not just in times of illnesses and emergencies. The more I pray, the more I realize my need to ask God to enable me to live in a way that reflects his presence in my life. This kind of prayer has helped me to understand portions of the Bible that seemed unreal before. I understand Job's demand for an audience with God, Jacob's all-night wrestling match, and our Lord's need for regular prayer with his Father. Why does God the Son need to talk to God the Father, since God has no needs? There is a depth of prayerful communication beyond requests. There is presence! Yes, my prayer life has enhanced my sense of God's presence in my life.

One of the great classics of the Christian faith, Brother Lawrence of the Resurrection's *The Practice of the Presence of God*, relates our walk with the Lord to a life of conversational prayer. We may suppose the life of Nicholas Herman (his given name) as a Carmelite monk on Rue Vaugirard in Paris in the seventeenth century was so simple that he could pray continually. What chance do we have in our stress- and pressure-filled, modern lives for even occasional prayers? But his story evidences struggles common with ours, such as his work in the kitchen that was very stressful. He was "lord of all pots and pans," because he was slow and unskilled. He lived in the seventeenth century, which was a turbulent time of change in Europe. While fighting in the Thirty Years' War, he was wounded and walked with a noticeable limp.

The cornerstone of his advice on the spiritual life was conversation with God: "Above all else, the main ingredient of a genuine spiritual life is practicing God's presence—living for God's closeness, day by day; getting used to spending time with Him; and praying to Him humbly (remember who you are!) and with love (remember who He is!)."[8] Brother Lawrence described this kind of prayer in many ways: daily closeness with the Lord; the joy of divine companionship; spontaneous prayer; unbroken conversation with God; regular, quiet, loving, private conversation; prayer bursting with life; simple, all-day worship; chats with God; a fond regard for God; and "that holy habit." His assumption is that God is real and personal. How do we learn to pray this way? We "practice" through the initially difficult stages and discover the power of prayer for ourselves.

Second, my appreciation of God has been enriched. God wants for me to be honest with him. He knows my weaknesses

8. Robert Elmer, ed., *Practicing God's Presence: Brother Lawrence for Today's Reader* (Colorado Springs: NavPress, 2005), 85.

and failures. He wants me to move beyond issues of theoretical thinking to asking him to help me with my everyday challenges. I realize that I have not because I had not asked (James 4:2). I also realize that he, who knows me best, loves me most. Steinsaltz suggests that "issues of high theology," theologians' use of abstract syllogisms to develop their thinking, sometimes can dishonor God and his Word. I can understand the correctness of his point. The Sinai experience, like much of the Bible, engages life with a disarmingly realistic perspective. I realize that, as a younger person, I would have said that conversational prayer is irreverent. Now I know that God honored the honesty of Moses, because he took God seriously in the difficulties of this life. I have also learned that God is offended by attempts to ignore him or to treat him as if he is not living and present.

Third, in spite of my prayers, this world has not changed for the better, at least in moral and spiritual terms. I have given up my desires for instant gratification and eye-catching miracles—desires that were constant companions in former years. I am content in the silent answers to my prayers that God is present, even when he seems to be absent. Somehow, I now believe that I do not have, because I have not asked God for what would please him, and that we cannot walk well in life without his presence. I have also learned that sometimes when I have asked, I did not receive because I asked with the wrong motives, for my own pleasures (James 4:2–3). In an ironic sort of way, I can feel God's presence in a more vivid manner as I go through trials, because these are the times that his sufficiency is most evident. John Bunyan's *The Pilgrim's Progress* is a classic on the Christian life. His "Christian" is in constant danger of death, yields to temptation, and almost abandons his quest for the Celestial City. Mr. Hopeful encourages him with the "solid ground" of God's promises. In the end, true to the promise, he finds God's rest. Untold numbers of fellow believers have discovered that life at its best is built upon a prayerful practice of the presence of God in the footsteps of "Christian."

A wonderful Savior is Jesus my Lord,
He taketh my burden away;
He holdeth me up, and I shall not be moved,
He giveth me strength as my day.

He hideth my soul in the cleft of the rock
That shadows a dry, thirsty land;
He hideth my life in the depths of His love,
And covers me there with His hand,
And covers me there with His hand.
                              —Fanny Crosby, 1890

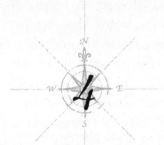

The Presence
and the Sanctuary

The church exists primarily not to provide entertainment or to encourage vulnerability or to build self-esteem or to facilitate friendships but to worship God. . . . Taken as a whole, the Bible clearly puts the emphasis on what pleases God—the point of worship, after all. To worship, says Walter Wink, is to remember Who owns the house.—Philip Yancey[1]

The Word became flesh and made his dwelling among us.—John 1:14

WE HAVE SEEN that Jesus Christ is the supreme revelation of God's presence (John 1:1–18; Heb. 1:1–2). In John's prologue, Jesus as Creator is with the Father, a Trinitarian presence that surfaces from creation in the mutual fellowship of God with his people. As the Logos, the Son of God was compared with Moses, who received the law that contained precise instructions for worship in Israel's tabernacle and temple. We have seen the

1. Philip Yancey, *Church: Why Bother? My Personal Pilgrimage* (Grand Rapids: Zondervan, 1998), 25–26.

importance of divine presence from the creation as manifested in concepts such as the Word, face, walk, Name, and Glory. We focused on Moses' face-to-face friendship with the Lord as he led the Israelites from Egypt to the reception of their covenant at Sinai. The first three chapters have associated the presence with incarnation, obedience, and prayer, respectively.

The presence of God is often associated with worship. Yancey reminds us that the church exists to worship God. What does worship mean? What did it mean for Israel in comparison with contemporary congregations? A member of our church recently stimulated my thinking about questions such as these. He had achieved the American dream by middle age: a devoted wife, a wonderful family, and entrepreneurial success. About five years ago, apparently without warning, he was struck by Lou Gehrig's disease. We since have watched his body decline even as the Lord has given him a measure of spiritual maturity that few attain. His paralysis has advanced to the point that he can no longer care for himself in ways that healthy people take for granted. For example, he cannot get into bed and pull up the covers at night. He has told us that evenings at home are worship times, when he meditates and discusses his physical disabilities with the Lord. God has faithfully answered his prayers, including "his wife's pulling up the covers every evening—twice!" before she realized that she was serving God by doing so. They worship in their home throughout the week and then bless the church by attending its Sunday services. Surely, stories like this teach us that believers must take worship beyond the walls of their sanctuaries. The Old Testament affirms the fact that true worship takes place in the sanctuary, in the home, and in the fields. For every Israelite, however, the trail of obedience intersected with worship in the sanctuary.

This chapter is about "The Presence and the Sanctuary," focusing on the part of the law that describes the nation's tabernacle and temple as God's "dwelling" and, accordingly, the center of its corporate worship. The preceding chapters have had an individual focus. Here we will examine the presence of God with emphasis on Israel's corporate fellowship with God in its midst. It will be developed in four ways:

- The Presence according to the Covenant
- The Presence on the Pilgrimage
- The Presence in the City
- The Presence in Our Worship

"The Presence according to the Covenant" will cover themes such as holiness, pattern, and dwelling that were consistently associated with the tabernacle and temple. "The Presence on the Pilgrimage" will compare the Tent of Meeting with the tabernacle and their implications for covenantal relationship between God and his people. "The Presence in the City" will compare the tabernacle and the temple, showing that the Israelites' desire to be "like the nations" led to compromise in their worship. The lessons for our churches that come from the Israelites' decline will conclude the chapter in "The Presence in Our Worship."

A foundational principle for our purposes is that worship in Israel was very serious business. A casual attitude that accepts the possibility of faith and worship, if they are comfortable and convenient, is biblically unacceptable. In Numbers 16, Korah, a descendant of Levi through Kohath, "became insolent and rose up against Moses" (vv. 1–2). He rallied Dathan, Abiram, and 250 community leaders to try to usurp Moses' authority. Korah, interestingly, had important duties at the tabernacle, but he wanted more power! Moses summoned the rebels to appear "at the entrance to the Tent of Meeting," where a significant part of Israel's worship was conducted, to receive the Lord's validation of his leadership. "The glory of the LORD appeared to the entire assembly" (16:19), and "the earth opened its mouth and swallowed [the rebels] . . . all the Israelites around them fled, shouting, 'The earth is going to swallow us too!'" (16:32, 34). This reminds us that we should enter all discussions of sanctuary and holiness with sobriety and reverence for the Lord.

The Presence according to the Covenant

The biblical presentation of Israel's sanctuary is governed by God's precise plan in the Sinaitic Covenant. Moses had read the book of the covenant, and the people had pledged obedience under the blood of the covenant. He had returned to the mountaintop alone to receive the tablets of the law, and "the glory of the LORD settled on Mount Sinai" (Ex. 24:16), which looked like "a consuming fire" to the Israelites below. On the seventh day, the Lord invited his mediator into the cloud covering, where Moses stayed for forty days and nights. The Lord requested offerings from the Israelites to construct the tabernacle and said: "Then have them make a sanctuary for me, and I will dwell among them. Make this tabernacle and all its furnishings exactly like the pattern I will show you" (25:8–9). In a similar passage the Lord affirmed: "Then I will dwell among the Israelites and be their God. They will know that I am the LORD their God, who brought them out of Egypt so that I might dwell among them. I am the LORD their God" (29:45–46). The passage teaches the purpose of God's dwelling among the Israelites with a view to his consecration of the nation with their sanctuary and priesthood. In his presence they will learn his ways and the holiness that will distinguish them from other peoples on the earth.

We should pause to note that, although Israel's sanctuary was featured, the nation's worshipful activity was not confined to the tabernacle or temple. The Bible views worship as a necessity in all of life, which extended beyond places of sacrifice and corporate prayer to daily responsibilities and relationships. The Israelites' life before their living God was to be characterized by worshipful work and rest in the breadth of God's covenant, as indicated by the plethora of laws that defined holy living. The laws deal with godly behavior in a framework of familial relationships, personal health, celebration of harvests, and maintenance of harmony between citizens. The absence of sacred-secular distinctions in their society probably seems strange to most of us, but, as we shall discuss later, it could help us with our need for more nourishment from the Holy Spirit than a weekly service can provide. So, all of life was meant to be worshipful, but the center of corporate worship was the sanctuary.

Sanctuary and Holiness

Sanctuary (*miqdas*) is derived from the root meaning "holy" and refers to the "holy or sacred space" where the divine presence was corporately experienced. Israel's concept of sanctuary was revealed in Exodus in a nexus of themes such as covenant and dwelling, which have the holiness of God as their unifying center. The emphasis is on the God who sanctifies rather than the sanctity of the place or the people. The holiness theme had surfaced with Moses, who was told: "Do not come any closer . . . for the place where you are standing is holy ground" (Ex. 3:5). Holiness was the overarching condition of the covenant that separated the perfection of God from the uncleanness of his people. When Moses went alone to Sinai's peak to receive the law, he was separated not only by the cloud but also by his seven days of preparation before he was summoned by God (24:15–16). And in Leviticus 21:23, we read, "I am the LORD, who makes them [the priests] holy." Separation, we must emphasize, was for protection, not exclusion, and did not contradict the Lord's desire for proximity with his people.

The Lord's dwelling in the midst of his people required special safeguards to protect them from his annihilating perfection. The priestly washings and sacrifices were God-given measures to ensure a reverential entry into his presence. The Lord sanctified his sanctuary *from* profane conditions such as drunkenness (Lev. 10:8–9) and *for* sacrificial worship. Unequivocally, he commanded, "Observe my Sabbaths and have reverence for my sanctuary. I am the LORD" (Lev. 19:30). The laws governing sacrifices emphasized that they were to be carried out "before the LORD." Conversely, gross disobedience by individuals or the nation was punished by death or separation from his covenantal community (Ex. 19:21;

Lev.17:10; 20:1–6; 26:17); in other words, God would set his face against them.

The priests were instructed to "distinguish between the holy and the common, between the unclean and the clean" (Lev.10:10). These terms must be carefully distinguished. "Holiness" reflected the character of God, a God-initiated condition without blemish or sin. "Common" things had not been made holy and, if polluted, could be made "unclean." "Cleanliness" was a "normal" state of things. "Uncleanness," the crucial distinction and the opposite of holiness, was contagious and was to be strictly separated from all things holy, notably the tabernacle. Thus, "your camp must be holy, so that he [the LORD your God] will not see anything indecent among you and turn away from you" (Deut. 23:14).

A brief description of uncleanness is necessary because of its implications for the holiness of the nation. The conditions are described in Leviticus 11–15 as a prelude to the Day of Atonement in chapter 16. Uncleanness was based on regulations regarding dietary limitations, reproductive issues, disease, bodily discharges, and death. The rules were designed to teach the Israelites about integrity in worship as well as to protect them from unhealthy practices. These rules were the expression of God's concern for the wholeness of his people at their time in history. While the regulations do not directly apply to us, nevertheless, God cares about us as his people in the same way. Accordingly, we are to honor God with our bodies and spirituality (cf. Rom. 12:1–2). On the Day of Atonement, the high priest performed blood rituals to cleanse the sanctuary, carried a smoking censer into the Holy of Holies to screen the holy presence, and sprinkled blood on the mercy seat. The day was most holy in the life of the Israelites.

There is a remarkable contrast drawn between the holiness of true worship and the profaneness (or uncleanness) of Israel's idolatry in Exodus 32. The Israelites had requested a visible representation of God, had contributed gold for the image's construction, and had offered corrupt sacrifices. These elements of "worship," which were a terrifying twist away from God's truth, threatened their existence—and were a virtual charade of God's later instructions for worship. When God's people fulfilled the God-centeredness of true worship to the letter, they were assured of his forgiveness and presence in spite of their sinfulness. The difference in worship was the chasm between prideful rebellion in the image of a fallen creature and humble obedience to the glory of the Creator.

Sanctuary according to Pattern

The sanctuary's importance was keynoted by its detailed, God-given specifications in Exodus 25–31, the exact pattern that God revealed to Moses on Sinai. Its prominent location, architectural details, and visual impact focused on the presence of God in the holiest room in the midst of his people. Its design, in Piper's words, promoted "true worship that reflected back to God the radiance of his worth."[2] The Bible emphasizes that God's "dwelling," with all of its furnishings, visually portrayed his explicit directions to Moses rather than being a product of human ingenuity (Ex. 25:8, 40; 26:30; 27:8; 31:11; 39:32, 42–43; Num. 8:4). Its dimensions exhibited a harmonious design that focused the observer's eyes on the holiest place with his presence. The numbers three, four, and ten as well as gradations of metals, colors, and cloth supported the visual focus. All Israelites would have lived and celebrated formal gatherings with a visual awareness of the presence. The author of the Epistle to the Hebrews added the fact that the sanctuary was "a copy and shadow of what is in heaven" (Heb. 8:5).[3] In other words, the tent/temple was,

2. John Piper, *Desiring God: Meditations of a Christian Hedonist* (Portland: Multnomah Press, 1986), 70.

3. The notion of an earthly sanctuary as an imperfect copy of heavenly realities has led some scholars to see "temple" as a comprehensive theme in the Bible. Thus, noting parallels, they interpret Eden as the initial form of space where deity and humanity enjoyed covenantal fellowship. Specifically, God's presence as walking in the garden is resumed in Lev. 26:12 and Deut. 23:14 as walking among his people. The theme is then discussed prospectively to the eschatological Holy City in Rev. 21. See Desmond Alexander, *From Paradise to the Promised Land: An Introduction to the Main Themes of the Pentateuch* (Grand Rapids: Baker, 1995); and for lengthy discussion, G. K. Beale, *The Temple and the Church's Mission*, New Studies in Biblical Theology, vol. 17 (Downers

among other things, a visual statement of covenantal relationship that taught the Israelites about life with the one and only living God. In the words of Elmer Martens, "In very concrete ways, such as in a building, the tabernacle, or through instructions, or in the social gatherings of a festival, Israel participated in life with Yahweh. From these settings she knew him as present with her, manifesting himself, but always the Other, holy."[4] As it was in heaven, so it would be on earth; the people's attention would be drawn to him.

Sanctuary as "Dwelling"

While sanctuary designated the worship center with its fenced courtyard, "dwelling" (*miskan*) was the tent (or building) with its holy and holiest rooms, the latter being the residence of the cloud of the presence.[5] The holy place contained the bread of the presence, an altar for incense, and a lampstand. A table with the "arranged bread" was displayed with twelve loaves in two rows (Lev. 24:5–9) to symbolize the Israelites' covenantal presence before the Lord and their dependence on him for their needs. The table was separated from God's immediate presence by a curtain.

Similarly, the high priest's ephod and breastpiece had engraved stones with tribal names, signifying priestly mediation for the nation. A golden plate on his turban with the words "HOLY TO THE LORD" (Ex. 28:36) complemented the identification of the tribes on his official garments.

The holiest place (or Holy of Holies) was half the size of the holy place, a cube with dimensions of fifteen feet. It featured the ark, a wooden chest that contained the ark of the covenant

---

Grove, IL: InterVarsity Press, 2004). Our concern, however, is merely with the issue of divine presence in the Mosaic context.

4. Elmer Martens, *God's Design: A Focus on Old Testament Theology* (Grand Rapids: Baker, 1981), 96.

5. Horst Dietrich Preuss is helpful when he describes the emphasis of the metaphor: "The temple became therefore the 'house of YHWH,' not because he dwelt there, but rather because he may be encountered there." *Old Testament Theology*, 32 vols., Old Testament Library (Louisville: Westminster John Knox, 1996), 2.43.

(designated as such forty-two times) or the ark of the testimony (thirteen times). The tablets of the law were the featured contents of the chest. Over the ark was placed an atonement cover (*kapporet*), appropriately translated "mercy seat" or "propitiary." The ark was overlaid with gold, but the atonement cover was pure gold (45 by 27 inches). The large quantities of gold in the holiest place indicated royalty. The ark was viewed as the Lord's "footstool" in his throne room (1 Chron. 28:2), while the sanctuary was his palace, which was suitably adorned with royal colors. Two cherubim of hammered gold, facing one another at the ends of the cover, enhanced the throne imagery of the heavenly pattern. On this "throne," God, as holy Sovereign, met with Moses and gave him commands for the Israelites (Ex. 25:22). In the same vein, "the LORD your God moves about in your camp to protect you and to deliver your enemies to you" (Deut. 23:14). The ark represented the presence of God among his people as well as the union of the families with each other. As such, it commemorated his mighty act of forming Israel, since any sort of visible image was strictly forbidden by the second commandment. Later, on the Day of Atonement, the high priest sprinkled sacrificial blood on the cover "to make atonement for the Most Holy Place because of the uncleanness and rebellion of the Israelites, whatever their sins have been" (Lev. 16:16).

The connection of presence with unity points to an important emphasis in the Bible. When the Israelites worshiped the Lord at their center, they experienced joy in the sense of their common mission. When they wandered from a sense of his presence, they would begin to break apart in their self-centered interests. In Numbers, the jealousy and rebellion of Moses' siblings (Num. 12) and Korah (Num. 16) illustrate this. We would do well to remember that God is the unifying presence for families and the nation.

Repeatedly, the Old Testament identified the tabernacle as "the place the LORD your God will chose as a dwelling for his Name" (Deut. 12:4–12; cf. Neh. 1:9; Ps. 74:7). The presence of God is, as Moses prayed, the distinguishing mark of his favorable relationship with them (Ex. 33:16). "Dwelling" could be rendered as "abode" or "home," which points to a crucial point of continuity between Sinai and Eden. From the beginning, God used marriage and the household as models for covenantal relationships. Adam and Eve were fruitful and multiplied, and the genealogies reaffirm this familial pattern of human life. Through Abraham and Sarah's family, God would bless all the families of the earth. Exodus began with "names of the sons of Israel," who multiplied and filled the land of Egypt (Ex. 1:1–7). So, God's "tent" in the midst of the Israelites' tents was a royal household, in which God was jealous for the affections of his family (Ex. 20:5; 34:14). However, we must always remember that God's dwelling was among his people rather than rooted in one place.

A second thematic connection with creation is the Sabbath, "a sign between me and you for generations to come, so that you may know that I am the Lord, who makes you holy" (Ex. 31:13). It was a "tithe of time" to celebrate the God of creation and covenant.[6] The fourth commandment mandates the creational pattern of labor for six days with a Sabbath for rest. Every household was to remember the goodness and faithfulness of the living God, who was their Liberator from Egyptian bondage (Lev. 26:13; Deut. 5:15). Durham summarizes the significance of the day well: "The intention of this sign and the reason it must be kept so regularly and conscientiously is that Israel might know Yahweh's presence by experience, in every generation, and be reminded constantly that only by that presence are they a people set apart."[7] The Sabbath was a perpetual reminder of Israel's holiness under the living Creator, and the tabernacle was the place of corporate renewal to sustain the mission of his people to the ends of the earth. Israel could rest, knowing that her loyally loving Lord would provide for his people's needs in the wilderness and the land. Thus, the

---

6. The insightful phrase is from Roland de Vaux, *Ancient Israel*, 2 vols. (New York, Toronto: McGraw-Hill, 1965), 2.480.

7. John Durham, *Word Biblical Commentary: Exodus*, vol. 3 (Nashville: Nelson Reference and Electronic, 1987), 412–13.

creation of the world and the new creation of Israel as a "royal family" were linked for the generations.

A concluding implication of "dwelling" looks forward to Jerusalem and its temple. The unique, living God of creation in the midst of his people made Zion the center of the earth from which the gift of life was extended to the ends of the earth. The psalmist expressed this truth in Psalm 48:1–2 in praise of Zion: "The city of our God, his holy mountain . . . is beautiful in its loftiness, the joy of the whole earth . . . the city of the Great King." In his judgment of Jerusalem in Ezekiel 5, the Sovereign Lord stated: "This is Jerusalem, which I have set in the center of the nations, with countries all around her" (Ezek. 5:5). This meant that all nations were accountable to God for their treatment of his "dwelling" and people. Israel was to be severely disciplined for her idolatries and injustices, but the nations received their oracles of judgment as well. In a positive sense, though God is omnipresent, he was present on the earth particularly in Israel.

To this point, we have seen God's covenantal presence with his nation focused in his sanctuary, a corporate worship center that was known as his dwelling in the center of the Israelites. The unifying stipulation of worship was holiness, from the meaning of sanctuary as holy space to the Holy of Holies—which was designed to rivet the people's attention on God's presence as the essential condition of their existence. The God-given pattern with its enshrined law distinguished them as the people of the living God, protected them from uncleanness within and hostility without, and unified them before their Lord. As with the patriarchs, their paths as families intersected corporately at the sanctuary with an attitude of humble obedience to God's Word. The Sabbath was their perpetual tithe of time to remember that the sovereign Creator of the earth was the Lord of the royal "household" whose will was for them to take life to the ends of the dying world.

The Presence on the Pilgrimage

How could God be uncompromisingly transcendent yet imma-
nent with his people? By his design, the tabernacle with the ark
was the answer. Exodus concludes with the completion of the
tabernacle exactly "as the LORD commanded" (Ex. 40:29). Then,
"the cloud covered the Tent of Meeting, and the glory of the LORD
filled the tabernacle" (Ex. 40:34). Whether mobile or stationary,
Israel's sanctuary consistently functioned as an ordering center
of national life, a place of revelation (or guidance), sacrifice, and
divine presence. This continuity was based on the tabernacle as a
shelter for the ark of the covenant. The tabernacle's completion is
a turning point in the narrative and introduces the transition from
the Israelites' encampment to their march to the land.

The Tent and the Tabernacle

Although the significance of the sanctuary was consistent,
the transition introduced several changes from tent to tabernacle
in view of Israel's wilderness sojourn. The Tent of Meeting was
a place to rendezvous that was some distance outside the camp
while the tabernacle was under construction. The tabernacle, on
the other hand, was a portable shrine that was carried in front of
the Israelites while on the march and then assembled in the midst
of their encampments. God's design was for every Israelite to see
his presence in the cloud and fire as they moved to the Promised
Land. However, one should not infer coziness between Israel and
her Lord. The separation of holiness and sin was always a paramount consideration, so the veil that protected the holiest place
served as a suitable barrier to uncleanness, even as Mount Sinai
had done earlier.[8] The pillar of cloud was at the entrance of the Tent

8. In the words of Walther Eichrodt, "For the light or fire phenomena in which the
divine majesty shows itself is a formless brightness fully in keeping with the strong sense
of God's intangibility. And even this pledge of the actual presence of God does nothing to lessen the emphasis on his unapproachableness," *Theology of the Old Testament*,
2 vols., The Old Testament Library, trans. J. A. Baker (Philadelphia: Westminster, 1961),
1.408–9.

of Meeting, where the Israelites could consult the Lord or receive revelation (Ex. 33:7; 34:34). But the "dwelling glory," the *Shekinah*, moved to the holiest place above the cherubim in the tabernacle. The altar was at the entrance of the Tent of Meeting, but in the tabernacle and temple it was in the courtyard. Moses mediated for the Israelites until the Lord's glory filled the tabernacle, and then he could no longer enter the tent (40:35). In his prophetic role he received and recorded the law. The book of Leviticus, for example, apparently was given to Moses at the door of the Tent of Meeting (1:1). However, the functions of national assembly and revelation transitioned to priestly ministry after the ordination of Aaron and his sons (Lev. 9:23–24). "Meeting," in a formal sense, was transferred to the annual appearance of Aaron before the altar on the Day of Atonement (Lev. 16). Joshua had maintained the tent (Ex. 33:11), but the care of the tabernacle was entrusted to the Levites. Yet, in spite of these changes, the presence of the Lord in the midst of his people remained the dominant truth.

The Covenant Relationship

On the journey, the presence of God in the holiest place defined the covenantal relationship. God demonstrated his loyal love by revealing a code of behavior in Leviticus 17–26. The Israelite was to "be holy, for I, the LORD your God, am holy" (Lev. 19:2). The refrain characterized the code. The reason for the instructions was a similar refrain: "I am the LORD your God" (Lev. 18:4). The issue was obedience to the wise Protector of the people rather than a full understanding of their way of life.

The Israelites, in turn, were to love the Lord their God with all their hearts as expressed by obedience to his commands (Deut. 6:1–5). In Numbers 9:15–23 we are given a magnified view of the importance of abiding obediently in the presence of God. The passage affirms:

> Whenever the cloud lifted from above the Tent, the Israelites
> set out; whenever the cloud settled, the Israelites encamped. At

the LORD's command the Israelites set out, and at his command they encamped. As long as the cloud stayed over the tabernacle, they remained in camp. (Num. 9:17–18)

We wonder how such behavior could be expected when the Israelites, like all of us, were prone to wander. They, like us, must have wondered from time to time whether their flaws disqualified them from relationship with God.

Nevertheless, we are rather surprised that punishments for disobedience were severe, because God intended for his presence to bring joy and blessing (Lev. 23:40; 1 Kings 8:65–66). The believers' understanding of sin and its effect on their life and nation reconciles the tension between severe punishments and joyful worship. The root of sin is self-centeredness that generates an insatiable desire for personal pleasures. Sins seem so inviting in the present until they diminish godly values, foster rebellious behavior, and destroy relationships. The joy of the Lord is based on a love for him that expands into a love for his people. This kind of life seems so contrary to the "freedoms" of sin that we so cherish. Buechner observes that obedience has become a bad word, incompatible with "independence" and "freedom." He continues, "When Jesus asks people to obey above everything the Law of Love . . . it is above everything for their own sakes that he is asking them to obey it."[9] We are surprised to discover that our deepest needs and desires are found in the One who made us (Ps. 139) and cares most for our well-being. We would be wise to realize that godly obedience helps us to avoid pitfalls and enriches fellowship with the Lord and his people on the path of life.

We only have glimpses of "presence and sanctuary" as the Israelites journeyed across the wilderness. Joshua 18:1 records that the nation gathered at Shiloh, after conquering much of the land, and set up the Tent of Meeting. There, Joshua apportioned the land "in the presence of the LORD" (18:8–10). Joshua 22:29 adds that the whole assembly of the Lord said, "Far be it from

9. Frederick Buechner, *Whistling in the Dark: An ABC Theologized* (San Francisco: Harper and Row, 1988), 90.

us to rebel against the LORD and turn away from him today by building an altar for . . . sacrifices, other than the altar of the LORD our God that stands before his tabernacle." The verses indicate that the nation was to have a single sanctuary for sacrifices to maintain their unity under the covenant.

The primary text, preparatory to temple worship, is Deuteronomy 12, which is Moses' valedictory on unifying worship. His instruction was bracketed by commands to destroy Canaanite altars and idols— "wipe out their names from those places" (12:1–4; cf. 12:29–31). Instead, the people were "to seek the place the LORD your God will choose from among all your tribes to put his Name there for his dwelling" (12:5; cf. 12:11). "There, in the presence of the LORD your God, you and your families . . . shall rejoice . . . because the LORD your God has blessed you" (12:7; cf. 12:12, 18). The passage emphasizes God's choice of a dwelling for his Name and a spirit of rejoicing as the Israelites celebrated his blessing.

The Presence in the City

The ark briefly appears in 2 Samuel when David brought it to Jerusalem by way of the homes of Abinadab and Obed-edom. The divine presence was associated with the ark by description and action. It was "called by the Name, the name of the LORD Almighty, who is enthroned between the cherubim that are on the ark" (2 Sam. 6:2; 1 Chron. 13:6).[10] And "the LORD's anger burned against Uzzah," when he irreverently grabbed the ark after the cart's oxen stumbled (2 Sam. 7). They proceeded to Jerusalem and "set it in its place inside the tent that David had pitched for it" (2 Sam. 6:17; 1 Chron. 15:1; 16:1).[11] We learn from 2 Chronicles

10. The parallel passages in 2 Samuel, 1 Kings, and 1 and 2 Chronicles, and parallel psalms can be distracting at best and confusing at worst. For clarification, the reader may consult James D. Newsome Jr., ed., *A Synoptic Harmony of Samuel, Kings, and Chronicles with Related Passages from Psalms, Isaiah, Jeremiah, and Ezra* (Grand Rapids: Baker, 1986).

11. Samuel Terrien, *The Elusive Presence: Toward a New Biblical Theology*, Religious Perspectives, vol. 26 (New York, San Francisco: Harper and Row, 1978), 168. "The pres-

1 that the Tent of Meeting, the tabernacle that "Moses the LORD's servant had made in the desert" (2 Chron. 1:3), was in Gibeon at the time. So, the ark had been separated from the tabernacle until it was restored to its central position in the temple. Solomon had gone to Gibeon to sacrifice in front of the tabernacle. His purpose was to seek wisdom and knowledge for governance and for the temple's construction (2 Chron. 1:1–13; cf. 1 Kings 2:46–3:15).

After David had settled in his palace, he told the prophet Nathan, "Here I am, living in a palace of cedar, while the ark of God remains in a tent" (2 Sam. 7:2; 1 Chron. 17:1). Consequently, the Lord counseled Nathan in 2 Samuel 7:5–7:

> Go and tell my servant David, "This is what the LORD says: Are you the one to build me a house to dwell in? I have not dwelt in a house from the day I brought the Israelites up out of Egypt to this day. I have been moving from place to place with a tent as my dwelling. Wherever I have moved with all the Israelites, did I ever say to any of their rulers whom I commanded to shepherd my people Israel, 'Why have you not built me a house of cedar?'"

God did not allow David to build the temple, but he honored his request by naming Solomon as the builder (2 Sam. 7:12–13; 1 Chron. 17:11–12). The point of the "tent" is that the issue of structure was less important than the Lord's presence with his people. The stated reason that God had not initiated construction of the temple was that David was a warrior king, whose role was to conquer the land (1 Chron. 22:6–8), a point that David gratefully acknowledged (1 Chron. 28:2–3). Solomon, on the other hand, would have "rest from all . . . enemies" (2 Sam. 7:11), and with his abundance of wisdom, he could devote himself to the project (1 Kings 5:1–5; 2 Chron. 2:1–4).[12] God told David: "'Because it

---

ence of the ark near a stronghold which had been until then a center of Canaanite worship could be viewed not only as a symbol of Yahweh's triumph over the deities of the land but also as a link with the faith of the fathers in the wilderness."

12. 1 Kings 5:3–4; 1 Chron. 22:8–9; 28:3 contrast David and Solomon as men of war and rest respectively. These characterizations suited their roles in God's providential

was in your heart to build a temple for my Name, you did well to have this in your heart," but Solomon, "your own flesh and blood," will have the time and means to accomplish the task (2 Chron. 6:7–9; 1 Kings 8:17–20).

Similarities of the Tabernacle and the Temple

A comparison of the tabernacle and temple is instructive, as the foundational truths of the presence of God were parallel. First, as the tabernacle was built according to God's precise plan, so he gave David "the plans of all that the Spirit had put in his mind" (1 Chron. 28:12). "All this," David said (to Solomon), "I have in writing from the hand of the LORD upon me, and he gave me understanding in all the details of the plan" (1 Chron. 28:19). Craig Koester underscores the connection: "Israel's sanctuary was central to its life as a people, and its character—first as a tent and later as a permanent house—was determined by the will of God, not human presumption."[13]

Second, the design of the structures was similar. Like the tabernacle, the temple had two courts separated by a veil with adornments of gold, royal colors, and fine linens. The Holy of Holies contained the ark and the mercy seat with cherubim, so that the royal motif of the throne, footstool, and palace continued (1 Chron. 28:2). In Psalm 132:7–8 we read, "Let us go to his dwelling place; let us worship at his footstool—arise, O LORD, and come to your resting place, you and the ark of your might." Of course, the temple was larger, and the cubical Holy of Holies had dimensions of thirty feet (1 Kings 6:19; 2 Chron. 3:8). The worshipers' attention, as before, was directed to the holiest place and the divine presence. According to the pattern, the tabernacle can be seen as a prototype of the temple.

---

will for the nation. The name "Solomon" (*Shalomoh*) in verse 9 is a wordplay for "peace" (*shalom*) and represented God's sabbatical ideal for Israel during his reign.

13. Craig Koester, *The Dwelling of God: The Tabernacle in the Old Testament, Intertestamental Jewish Literature, and the New Testament*, The Catholic Biblical Quarterly Monograph Series, vol. 22 (Washington: The Catholic Biblical Association of America, 1989), 15.

Third, as the glory of the Lord filled the completed tabernacle, so the temple, when finished, was filled with a cloud of glory so dense that "the priests could not perform their service because of the cloud, for the glory of the LORD filled the temple" (1 Kings 8:10–11; 2 Chron. 5:13–14). After Solomon's dedicatory prayer, "fire came down from heaven and consumed the burnt offering and the sacrifices," confirming that the temple was the divinely appointed successor to the tabernacle (2 Chron. 7:1). Furthermore, all the Israelites worshiped by saying, "He is good; his love endures forever," echoing David's hymn of thanks and confirming the continuity of their covenant (1 Chron. 16:34; 2 Chron. 5:13; 7:3; cf. Ezra 3:11; Ps. 136:1).[14]

Differences between the Tabernacle and the Temple

Important differences between the structures should be noted as well. Changes in motive in the construction of God's dwelling reflected a decline in the values of the nation and its allegiance to the Lord. First, the building of the temple was characterized by the grandeur of royal ambition that was different from the comparative spontaneity of its Mosaic precedent. The dominant concern of the tabernacle's generation had been the necessity of the presence of God and the consequent need for holiness. This reflected theocratic leadership and a relatively simple arrangement of the tribes around the mobile cloud of the presence. The temple generation, on the other hand, reflected a concern for a monumental structure that fostered a more complex and less personal relationship with God in his holiest place. David initiated preparations for the temple with a concern that "the house to be built for the LORD should be of great magnificence and fame and splendor in the sight of all the nations" (1 Chron. 22:5). Solomon continued the emphasis in his message to Hiram of Tyre in 2 Chron. 2:5: "The temple I am going to build will be great ["large and magnificent," 2:9], because our God is greater than

14. Earlier, "fire from heaven" on the sacrificial altar had confirmed Jerusalem as the center of Israel's worship for David (1 Chron. 21:24–22:1).

all other gods." And, at the installation of the ark, Solomon testified to God, "I have built a magnificent temple for you, a place for you to dwell forever" (2 Chron. 6:2; 1 Kings 8:13). The temple grandeur was a powerful memory for Israelites who returned from their Babylonian exile and wept when they saw the modest appearance of the post-exilic temple (Ezra 3:12).

The Bible gives us a conflicted assessment of Solomon's reign. We know that God was with Solomon in his developing reputation and temple building. We also realize that he sanctioned the temple with fire and his glory. God was pleased that the king requested wisdom as his greatest wish, so he promised wealth, riches, and honor as secondary blessings. He was pleased with Solomon's dedicatory prayer in which the king praised his incomparable God for his faithfulness and emphasized the need for the Israelites "to walk before" God "according to [his] law" (2 Chron. 6:16; cf. 1 Kings 8:25). His prayer in God's presence for forgiveness, protection, and provision for the future was exemplary. Solomon correctly declared: "The heavens, even the highest heavens, cannot contain you. How much less this temple I have built!" (2 Chron. 6:18; 1 Kings 8:27; cf. 2 Chron. 2:6). His statement affirmed God's exaltedness, balancing his nearness in his "dwelling."

However, the issue was the presence of God in covenant relationship with Israel rather than the brilliance of the temple. Circumstances have multiple ways of affecting our attitudes and behavior. The prophets constantly warned about a perfunctory formality in religious services, in which impressive appearances concealed deceitful hearts and hypocritical lives. Soon after the dedication of the temple, the Lord appeared to Solomon and cautioned him about perverting good things into evil practices: "If you turn away and forsake the decrees and commands I have given you and go off to serve other gods and worship them, then I will uproot Israel from my land, which I have given them, and will reject this temple I have consecrated for my Name" (2 Chron. 7:19–20; 1 Kings 9:6–7). The words must have sounded strange to Solomon at that crowning moment of his life, even as God's cautionary words to us sound strange when we are in moments of seemingly untainted success.

Later, when the Israelites had filled the temple with "idols of jealousy," Ezekiel saw the glory of the Lord depart from the polluted shrine. Nevertheless, God promised, "Yet for a little while I have been a sanctuary for them in the countries where they have gone" (Ezek. 11:16). However, the priestly prophet focused on a future time when God, in covenantal fidelity, would give his believers obedient, undivided, and receptive hearts: "They will be my people, and I will be their God" (11:19–20). In that time, the prophet saw the return of the glory to "the place of my throne and the place for the soles of my feet" (43:7). God himself, more than any monumental building, provokes the desire of his people for worshipful living.

Desire to Be "Like the Nations"

The issue of Israel's priority for royal monuments was akin to a second difference between the construction of God's tabernacle and the temple—the nation's developing ambition to be prestigious among the nations. The tabernacle had been constructed by offerings and Spirit-endowed giftedness among the people (Ex. 35:30–36:1). The temple was underwritten partly by offerings as well (1 Chron. 29:6–9), but David apparently underwrote most of the costs for this palatial structure from his royal treasury (29:1–5). Had an emphasis on personal service at Sinai shifted to a more impersonal bureaucracy at Jerusalem?

The impression is supported by Solomon's large-scale use of conscripted labor for his project (2 Chron. 2), reminiscent of an earlier time in the nation's history, when the elders of Israel asked Samuel for a king "such as all the other nations have" (1 Sam. 8:5). Samuel warned them that human kingship would involve tyrannical oppression. But the people rejected his advice and insisted that they wanted to be like other nations (8:20). The desire to be like everyone else carries a sense of false security and comfort that amounts to little more than an attitude of, "If we go down, at least everyone will go down with us." We can detect a similar declension in Solomon's reign. The king quickly consolidated his power with crucial alliances, with a significantly enhanced military establishment, and with maximum utilization of Israel's strategic position on the major north-south trade routes between Egypt and Syria. He became enormously wealthy for a time as reflected in his lavish temple. In spite of a booming economy, he spent more than he could afford. The outward display camouflaged a decline in worship, a chronic financial shortfall, and an endemic labor shortage with devastating consequences. Buechner described Solomon as "the first of the big-time spenders . . . unfortunately, the price for all this was pretty high, and it was his subjects who had to pick up the tab."[15] Solomon's cession of towns to the king of Tyre evidenced his financial straits (1 Kings 9:10–14). A king does not yield strategic territory apart from necessity, nor can he satisfy his debts with inferior cities that are rejected as unacceptable payment!

Solomon's policies pointed in a similar direction. First, he replaced the tribal arrangement, a familial social order that was based on the descendants of Jacob/Israel, with twelve administrative districts to enhance tax revenues (1 Kings 4:7–19). This change consolidated power in the royal bureaucracy, but it undermined the presence of God in Jerusalem's holiest place as the unifying center of the nation. The tribes had been grounded in the law and in traditional values that focused on the need to faithfully remember God's deliverance in the exodus and guidance through the wilderness. The center of the nation had shifted from a focus on divine presence to the financial maintenance of an extended empire.

Second, Solomon resorted to enforced labor for Israelites and slave labor for Canaanites (1 Kings 9:20–22). The family-oriented tribes were transformed into a new, centralized authority in which gaps between privileged rich and oppressed poor

---

15. Frederick Buechner, *Peculiar Treasures: A Biblical Who's Who* (San Francisco: Harper and Row, 1979), 159–60.

began to widen. Consequent injustices were a primary concern of the prophets: "You oppress the righteous and take bribes," Amos lamented characteristically, "and you deprive the poor of justice in the courts" (Amos 5:12). Transporting the ark to Jerusalem enabled the new order to annex the Mosaic tradition and, ultimately, led to a faith in the security of the state based on the divine claims of the royal dynasty and religious institutions.[16] However, the transition meant that the effective basis of social obligation was the state rather than the Lord's covenant, so that the law was increasingly ignored in daily affairs.

Third, the royal policies resulted in compromised worship, because Solomon had married outside the faith to cement alliances. First Kings 10:23 and 11:1–2 underscore the point:

> King Solomon was greater in riches and wisdom than all the other kings of the earth. . . . King Solomon, however, loved many foreign women besides Pharaoh's daughter—Moabites, Ammonites, Edomites, Sidonians, and Hittites. They were from nations about which the LORD had told the Israelites, "You must not intermarry with them, because they will surely turn your hearts after their gods." (cf. Ex. 34:16)

God's blessing was perverted into the burden of idolatry (1 Kings 11:3–13). Moses had known that God's presence was the nonnegotiable distinction between the Lord's people and all the other peoples (Ex. 33:16). The distinction was lost in the pressures of state. Without a vital sense of the presence, Israel divided. Jeroboam, a leading administrator in Solomon's labor force, was prompted by Ahijah the prophet to rebel against Solomon and his successor Rehoboam (1 Kings 11–12; 2 Chron. 10). From that rebellion Israel and Judah diverged to pursue their different destinies.

16. Edmond Jacob notes, "As early as the time of Isaiah, the temple had become for many Israelites a sort of talisman which kept them in illusory security." *Theology of the Old Testament*, trans. A. W. Heathcote and P. J. Allcock (New York, Evanston: Harper and Row, 1958), 260.

We have seen a progression from a comparatively simple tent in the midst of the pilgrims to an elaborate complex that dominated its world. The Chronicler emphasized the continuity of the successive sanctuaries, thus highlighting God's loyal love for his people from Moses through David. From the tent to the temple, Israelites were "joyful and glad in heart for the good things the LORD had done for . . . his people Israel" (2 Chron. 7:10; 1 Kings 8:66). The supreme good, however, was the presence of God himself. Moses had cautioned them: "When you have eaten and are satisfied. . . . then your heart will become proud and you will forget the LORD your God, who brought you out of Egypt, out of the land of slavery" (Deut. 8:10, 14). In New Testament terms, "they became lovers of pleasure" rather than worshipers of God (2 Tim. 3:4). In contemporary terms, they would probably have said that they were too busy with the weighty matters of empire to take time to rest and remember on God's Sabbath. Godly believers in the nation, on the other hand, looked forward to when "I will be their God, and they will be my people. Then the nations will know that I the LORD make Israel holy, when my sanctuary is among them forever" (Ezek. 37:27–28).

In summary, the pattern of Israel's worship transitioned to God's mobile presence in her midst on the way to the chosen city. The training of encampment yielded to the wilderness pilgrimage with the Lord. The principles of unified worship and corporate obedience did not change. However, the nation changed. Instead of a focus on God's presence, the people desired to be like the nations, and their kings prioritized monumental structures in the city. The shift from security in the Lord to worldly display shredded the nation's Davidic unity with compromised worship, financial burdens, and impersonal bureaucracy. As we look to the chapter on the prophets, we can hear the words of Abijah on Mount Zemaraim, "You [Israel] have forsaken him [the LORD]. God is with us [Judah]; he is our leader" (2 Chron. 13:11–12). Thus, with unity lost, a remnant of believers was left to carry the promises of the presence forward.

The Presence in Our Worship

This chapter addresses our pilgrimage with fellow believers in our churches. Yancey pointed to the problem at the beginning of the chapter, when he identified contemporary misdirections in the church's purpose and widespread fuzziness about the meaning of worship. These issues are difficult, because they bring to the fore differences of background, preferences in spirituality, and desires for family worship that span generations. Can we ever embrace the wide spectrum of options that are characterized as "traditional" and "contemporary" forms of worship? Wouldn't we all like to ignore the problems and hope that they will somehow dissipate? But we can't. The introduction to the chapter presented a caveat that so-called "sacred" and "secular" distinctions, so familiar to us, cannot be found in the Bible. Worship, from its Old English roots, literally means "worth-ship," meaning our acknowledgment of God's supreme worth in our lives. The underlying theme of holiness, as we noted in Leviticus, underscores the fact that worship in all of our routines is a serious matter in the eyes of the Lord. Now we will attempt to apply principles from Mosaic worship to contemporary churches that struggle with "worship wars."

Contemporary Struggles

During the last decade I have been asked to chair several boards. They all struggled with a common set of problems that typically characterize organizations in times of change. Here I will limit myself to my own church as a representative example. Several years ago I was asked to chair the board of elders at a time of conflict that threatened the existence of the church. Four of us were elected to replace the former board of nearly thirty people. I remember our prayers for a "resurrection," since we suspected on several occasions that the church had died. When we began to serve, we inherited a body of people who had experienced numerous confrontations with a consequent loss of members. How many? I am not sure, but over the course of several weeks

112

the congregation had shrunk to about two hundred participants in an auditorium that seated twelve hundred! The church's identity is irrelevant, because it exemplifies countless other churches that have shared the same problems, in whole or in part. Now, years later, the church has regained its vitality and seems to be very healthy in the Lord.

As we unpack the church's problems and look for solutions, we must begin with the problematic relationship of church and culture in the United States, which resembles the Israelite tendencies in Solomon's reign. Relevance in culture is an abiding concern in every church. However, no church was ever called by God to exemplify culture, namely, to be the incarnation of worldly values to the extent that a church loses its biblical moorings.

The starting point of cultural compromise, in our church's case, was the pervasive institutionalization and professionalization of organizations in America. These trends are desirable and necessary parts of an efficient organization. In time, however, organizations take on an existence of their own, so that the preservation of the church becomes the purpose of its activities at the expense of vital worship and the pastoral care of its congregation and community. This, we recall, was an issue in David's kingdom. Leadership, in the case of churches, becomes more concerned about the size of membership and budget than the vitality of the members' walk with God. Energy is measured by growth, since the Spirit's work in the life of the church cannot be statistically quantified.

I remember the banal comment being tossed around, "If it ain't broke, don't fix it," meaning that the bills are paid, so don't worry. We have all heard this as we settle into comfortable routines. The problem is that churches often break for spiritual reasons rather than budgetary shortfalls. Once they break, it is too late. A sense of "family" is replaced by grief-stricken "divorce." The "children" withdraw and wonder what their role was in the tragedy. In the case of our church, there were divisions on the board and staff, and a bewildered congregation understood little except that a serious storm raged above them. We all realize, of

113

course, that many churches are large because they prioritize godly worship and ministry. However, divisions come, in Solomon's day and now, when these priorities are replaced by self-centered ambitions.

Professionalism, in a negative sense, is characterized by emphasis on job descriptions in the organizational chart to the neglect of personal caring that moves beyond duty to helping in the church "as unto the Lord." Without an atmosphere of godly cooperation, a church is prone to competition that undermines its unity. We are reminded of Jeroboam's rebellion against Solomon and Rehoboam and the consequent division of the nation. People become more concerned with organizational perks than they are with the privilege of godly service. One can attend a professionalized church with anonymity, not having to care or be cared for. Most people today experience a variety of painful circumstances, but fear exposure even as they seek help. They do not trust people around them, because they do not know them well enough to share sensitive information. Loving God and his people requires trusting relationships and is very time-consuming. In short, when a church loses its sense of God's presence and a personal touch, it becomes a charitable agency that neglects its members' needs for worship and service in the Spirit.

With frequent meetings and gatherings for prayer, our church regained its heart. The oft-repeated phrases were "pursuing Christ with passionate love" and "every member a minister." Will I ever forget them? I doubt it. The major areas of need were analyzed, and initiatives addressed them: expanding the outreach of the church in the neediest areas of our city and around the world, involving gifted members in pastoral care and conflict resolution, launching small-group ministries to encourage close relationships, rotating leadership to provide fresh perspectives, and bathing every activity in prayer.

We must realize as well that a church's culture affects not only its organization but also the content of its services. A comparison of past and present programs and practices in churches will demonstrate that entertainment is a large part of worship today. With technological advances, various forms of theater have made contemporary services increasingly visual with a distinctive new language for expressing spiritual needs.

We see similar changes and struggles in the Old Testament. With the aesthetic precision of God's pattern, the cloud of divine presence guided Israel on the pilgrimage to the land. We probably wish that we had a cloud to give us clarity on our journeys. We wonder what the experience of a theophany and a charismatic leader such as Moses would have been like. However, we remember that the Israelites sinned in the presence of God's theophany! We also know that the people behaved only after God's disciplinary visitation in Exodus 32. Moreover, within a few years, jealousy infected Moses' own siblings (Num. 12), as in the case of Korah and his followers. The menu was not tasty enough, and their thirst could not be quenched. Sweetened by nostalgia, Egypt had never looked so good, and Moses was blamed for leading the people to a desert that had no milk and honey. Hebrews 3 and 4, quoting Psalm 95:7–11, remembered the wilderness generation as "hardened by sin's deceitfulness," rebellious, and "not able to enter" God's rest (Heb. 3:12, 19). The author of the Epistle to the Hebrews exhorts his readers and us to have faithful hearts that endure in the Lord's presence. Our desire for the visibility of God should not be a detour from the endurance of an obedient heart that walks in his Word.

All of these changes must be filtered by wisdom. I used to have lunch with Tim, a student of mine for several years. One day, after years of fellowship, I sensed that Tim was at a low point in his educational experience. He was mired in a cycle that is typical among many Christians and ministries. We all seem to pass through these phases in our own ways. I asked Tim about his problem. He responded that he had made wonderful grades and could successfully engineer every kind of program that he had been taught. But he had lost the zeal for his seminary training and felt far from God compared with his beginnings in graduate study. He described himself with the cliché "burned out." I was not surprised because his decline had been noticeable to his good friends. He explained that, after two years or so, he had begun to question the relevance of what he had learned. The "what" had been replaced by "so what?" We discussed this gradual transition, and he seemed to be rejuvenated by the importance of biblical knowledge. In the last year or so, he had seen a growing gap between ancient texts and his industrialized, technologically advanced world. His "so what," which he had begun to digest, now transitioned to "how do I live out and communicate what I know?" In accord with our day, his questions seemed to indicate a desire for techniques that would not require a great deal of effort. Often what happens at this stage of development, for individuals and churches, is that we return to "what we know" and redefine it in terms of our contemporary world.

Tim had completed the circle: What? So what? How to? and then a reformatted What? I wish that I could say that he finished his degree, but he didn't. I wish that I could say that all wounded churches recover their vision. Sometimes they don't. The pressures of wage earning, home, study, and the world in general sent Tim back into the business that he had left years before. But I think that his training enriched him and gave him an appreciation for serving God in the world.

Foundational Principles

Perhaps no word has been redefined more than *worship*. In a media-driven, self-absorbed environment, its meaning has narrowed from broad-based, God-honoring service, to a Sunday morning service, and now to the music in the service. A Christian author recently observed that "worship is something we do for twenty minutes on Sunday," which seems strange to most people in the world who sacrificially give all of their time and resources for the success of their business ventures. The dictionary, by the same token, is not specific in its definitions: appropriately honoring worth, reverence, devotion, veneration, and so forth. So, the question becomes: How do we redefine worship for today's needs using principles from Israel's tabernacle/temple as guidelines?

Acknowledging that divisions, splits, and conflicts in the church usually have many causes in a complex world, we would do well to recall that the Old Testament calls us back to basic practices for imperfect people. First and foremost, all members in their churches must conduct services and carry out programs and projects with a sense of God's presence. The Holy of Holies was precisely designed to be the center of Israel. Now, with a similar emphasis, each of us is "a temple of the Holy Spirit" (1 Cor. 6:19). Leadership must be vigilant to maintain a conscious awareness that the Lord is the head of the church, and all of our efforts should be for his glory. Church members must realize that ministry is a team effort under God, and that everyone's role is vital (1 Cor. 12). This humility is a significant part of personal holiness and was a primary emphasis in Old Testament ethics. Pride was Israel's problem, both in jealousy over another's position and in complaining about God's insufficiency.

No one exemplified the sufficiency of God's presence more winsomely than Brother Lawrence. In the last chapter, we discussed his view of conversational prayer, talking with God as we walk through life. Now we need to show how prayer, for him, engendered a worshipful sense of God's presence. He assumed, we noted, that the living God loves us and desires to be loved in return. He also believed that we should live in light of the fact that the Holy Spirit indwells us, and should seek his presence in the spirit of Deuteronomy 4:29: "You will find him if you look for him with all your heart and with all your soul." Brother Lawrence lived with a disarming confidence in God's love. We should not pray for favors, he believed, but for the strength to love God in all circumstances. Suffering is a "sure sign of the way God is taking care of you," since we need to be weaned from self-centeredness that is the greatest barrier to "living in his presence": "Our only concern in this life is to please God, and everything else is folly and vanity."[17] The effect is a peace and joy beyond understand-

17. Brother Lawrence of the Resurrection, *The Practice of the Presence of God*, critical edition, ed. Conrad De Meester, trans. Salvatore Sciurba (Washington: ICS Publications, 1994), 67.

ing that validates the Spirit's presence. Since these evidences are the fruit of the Spirit, we should not compare or analyze them as if God could be manipulated into greater grace. In Brother Lawrence's words, such divine favor should be joyfully celebrated without noise (that is, without even a hint of boastfulness): "We don't have to make a lot of noise because He's closer than we can realize."[18]

In this framework, Brother Lawrence viewed worship as prayerfully loving God in all of life. Love, prayer, and worship are almost synonymous in his writings. In the "Fourth Conversation," worship in his kitchen is described:

> He found no better way to approach God than by the ordinary works required in his case by obedience, purifying them as much as he could from all human respect, and doing them for the pure love of God. [He said] that it is a big mistake to think that a period of mental prayer should be different from any other. We must be as closely united with God during our activities as we are during our times of prayer.[19]

In brief, he would have understood the threat of the world to the well-being of the church. But he would have affirmed that we must take worship into the world, so that we can keep the world from bringing quarrels and fights into the church (James 4:2).

Second, service that is consciously performed with a sense of God's presence must be nurtured by God's Word. One cannot come to the Bible with holy priorities without seeing the Lord in the midst of his people. I know a large number of people who dislike the Scriptures (and God) because of the narratives that this chapter has covered. Frankly, I rarely hear tabernacle/temple texts in lists of favorite passages; we don't prefer them because we recognize that Israel's problems are ours as well, from discontent with our circumstances to our preoccupation with "empires" that

---

18. Robert Elmer, *Practicing God's Presence: Brother Lawrence for Today's Reader* (Colorado Springs: NavPress, 2005), 49.
19. Brother Lawrence, *Practicing the Presence*, critical edition, 78.

require all of our finances and labor. Beware of "Diotrephes," the apostle John warned, "who loves to be first" (3 John 9). This means that every member of our churches should master central teachings of the Bible such as: "Be completely humble and gentle; be patient, bearing with one another in love. Make every effort to keep the unity of the Spirit through the bond of peace" (Eph. 4:2–3).

Third, worship must be defined broadly and taken beyond the walls of our sanctuaries. Earlier in the chapter, we noted that the Bible described worship without sacred-secular distinctions. All of life was viewed as sacred under the Creator, who formed his people from the crucibles of empires. If worship is understood as celebrating God's worth on a daily basis, then we could contribute to our churches in surprisingly creative ways. Paul expressed such celebration explicitly in his exhortation to "employees" in Colosse: "Whatever you do, work at it with all your heart, as working for the Lord, not for men" (Col. 3:23). Peter spoke of godly labor as being particularly effective under ungodly "bosses," in a sermon that proclaims Christ's example with irrefutable clarity and power (1 Peter 2:13–25). Worship, with this meaning, would make all believers ministers in their churches' mission. And each church should be aligned with God's mission for the world. Israel, God said, was called to be "a light for the Gentiles, that you may bring my salvation to the ends of the earth" (Isa. 49:6). That is our call as well. When Israel began to look inward at her administrative districts, then the nation divided at the expense of the families of God. When churches exist for their own glory, then they too divide and the sense of a family under God is lost. There were hundreds of years between a generation that said, "We will do everything the LORD has said" (Ex. 19:8) and the generation that will "refuse to listen to my words, who will follow the stubbornness of their hearts and will go after other gods to serve and worship them" (cf. Jer. 13:10). Thus, the Bible has taught us that every generation needs to reconsecrate itself in the presence of the Lord to worship in the mission.

Guide me, O Thou great Jehouvah.
Pilgrim through this barren land;
I am weak, but Thou art mighty;
Hold me with Thy powerful hand;
Bread of heaven, Bread of heaven,
Feed me till I want no more,
Feed me till I want no more.

Open now the crystal fountain,
Whence the healing stream doth flow;
Let the fire and cloudy pillar,
Lead me all my journey through;
Strong Deliverer, strong Deliverer,
Be Thou still my strength and shield,
Be Thou still my strength and shield.

—John Hughes

The Presence
and the Prophets

It is part of our very existence to be faithful to the future, to keep alive the beginning by nursing the vision of the end. Hope is the creative articulation of faith. We misunderstand events past unless we are certain of events to come. . . . Pagans have idols, Israel has a promise. We have no image, all we have is hope.—Abraham Joshua Heschel[1]

A person can live forty days without food, three days without water, twelve minutes without air, and one second without hope.—Author unknown

PEOPLE HAVE an abiding desire to experience the presence of God as indicated by the progress of the book to this point. Their desire reflects God's engraved image from creation, a relational path that had been illumined by his Word. But the desire is double-edged from a human viewpoint. We have seen how presence is no panacea, as it is often hedged by fears of being too close

1. Abraham Joshua Heschel, *Israel: An Echo of Eternity* (New York: Farrar, Straus, and Giroux, 1969), 94, 101.

for comfort or by pain that comes from loss of relationships. Some people, for example, do not desire accountability. They prefer a shell of anonymity to the closeness of intimate friendships. They attend churches or gatherings to meet a perceived spiritual need without exposing themselves to others whom they fear would judge them if they really knew their weaknesses or mistakes. It was true of the patriarchs, who became deceitful when their paths were obscured by threatening circumstances. I suspect that the fear was true of Aaron, when Moses encountered him at Sinai with the question, "What did these people do to you, that you led them into such great sin?" (Ex. 32:21). Many people think that too much presence, divine or otherwise, can erode good relationships. We all know that familiarity can breed contempt. Knowing someone intimately can cause us to compare and compete as in sibling rivalries, thus undermining healthy relationships. Perhaps this was the case when Moses' family and associates became disgruntled in the wilderness (e.g., Num. 12). Others want to protect their privacy in today's digital revolution, when everything about everyone is being exposed. Or, we can take presence for granted until we no longer have it. I had wonderful times of fellowship with my father. Since his death thirty years ago, I have longed to share just one good conversation with him. I have things that I need to say to him, but I can't. A number of people join cults that claim to facilitate communication with departed loved ones. We cannot accept the error, but we need to realize that people need the comfort and assurance that an abiding presence brings.

All of these reservations about presence can be found in the Israelites' relationships with God and each other. The first chapter concerned Jesus Christ as the Word, who became flesh and "tabernacled" in our midst as God's incarnate presence (John 1:14). If we want to see God, we must abide in the Word of life (1 John 1:1–3). He is the Truth and the supreme expression of divine grace, whom John compared to Moses, Israel's lawgiver who received the blueprint for worship in Israel's tabernacle and temple. But how can a carpenter's son be "God with us"? The second and third chapters discussed the importance of God's presence in his people's pilgrimages through concepts such as obedience and prayer. These chapters centered on Moses' face-to-face encounters with the name and glory of the Lord as he led the Israelites from Egypt toward the land. But how can God be present, when the good old days in Egyptian slavery seemed better than wandering faith in the wilderness? The fourth chapter focused on the tabernacle and temple as God's dwelling and the center of corporate worship. The law revealed a pattern that centered the holiness of God for the Israelites in their camp and on the march. As the people approached life in Jerusalem, they desired to be more like the nations, an inclination that led to a lethal mixture of political compromise and idolatrous practices. Israel had adopted the pagan idols around her in spite of the distinguishing promises of the presence. How could God's presence be special, when the grass was greener on the nations' side? Why, we wonder, was God's presence not enough to keep the Israelites from seeking other gods?

God's presence in the prophets is a daunting topic that covers a substantial portion of the Old Testament. My approach will use Jeremiah as a representative of the seventeen books that covered approximately four hundred years. His is the longest biblical book, and we know more about him than any other prophet. The length of Jeremiah, however, forces us to further limit our discussion to three crucial parts of his "collection": his temple sermon (chapter 7), his letter to the exiles (chapter 29), and the book of consolation (chapters 30–33). This chapter will treat these three parts of Jeremiah:

- The Presence in Spite of Ungodly Leadership (Jeremiah 7)
- The Presence in Messianic Hope (Jeremiah 29–33)
- The Presence in Godly Families (Jeremiah 7:18; 29:3)

This chapter picks up Israel's narrative at the final question above—why was God's presence not enough for the Israelites? They illustrate the restless wandering of Cain-like characters who leave the ways of God to stride in the steps of the flesh. The prophets constantly reminded the Israelites of the Mosaic covenant after the exodus from Egypt and, when confronted with another exile, they pointed forward to the messianic future of the nation and world. One of the foremost scholars on the Old Testament prophets in the last generation, Heschel, reminds us of the importance of hope in Israel's history. These special servants ministered in times of corrupt kings and false competitors who preached popular messages that sanctioned the easygoing idolatry around them. Hope seemed to be hopelessly frayed as imperial marauders taunted the divided and doomed Israelites with paltry propaganda and obscene charades for worship. But light is often most evident in times of darkness. When we seem to have little hope, we can know that God intervenes for his family of believers. The exiled Israelites desperately needed hope, and God responded with his plans for their future. His ultimate plan was to incarnate himself as the Messiah to accomplish the fulfillment of all things. The relentlessness of his gracious interventions in the world validated his plan. The interventions also serve as a bridge between Jeremiah's wisdom and our struggles with similar issues. Jeremiah's courageous, uncompromising stand for the Lord reminds us, as God told Paul: "My power is made perfect in weakness" (2 Cor. 12:9).

The Presence in Spite of Ungodly Leadership

Jeremiah built his understanding of the presence of God on the foundation of the divine presence and the sanctuary. His temple sermon in chapter 7, in conjunction with his call (chapter 1), is a suitable window for viewing the broader themes of the subject. The sermon is a stern warning that is structured around three contrasts between God's revealed truths and the false practices of the nation—contrasts in worship, the prophetic office, and God's presence.

True Versus False Worship

Jeremiah delivered his prophetic sermon "at the gate of the LORD's house" (7:1; cf. 26:2). The sanctuary was suitable for his messages because of the large number of pilgrims "who come through these gates to worship the LORD" (7:2). But what were the people like who were coming to worship? Their character is a central issue in Jeremiah, because their pilgrimages revolved around their rebellious attitudes.

The prophet's sermon called for a change in Israel's life-style, so that they could "live in this place, in the land I gave your forefathers for ever and ever" (7:7; cf. 7:3). However, the prophet foretold discipline for God's people and destruction for his "house" for several interrelated reasons. First, the Israelites were enmeshed in idolatrous habits: "to your own harm . . . [you] follow other gods you have not known" (7:6, 9; chapter 2). Their pagan offerings were listed, which indicated the depth of their unbelief as they mimicked the Canaanite society around them (7:9, 17–18; cf. Ezek. 22).

Jeremiah 10:1–16 spells out the classic prophetic argument against idolatry. The Lord Almighty is "the Maker of all things, including Israel, the tribe of his inheritance." He is "the living God, the eternal King," the incomparable Ruler of the nations (10:16, 10, 12–13). Worship is his due (10:7)! The idols were the creations of human creatures, fraudulent and worthless (10:3, 14–15; 51:17–19). They were carved from wood, plated with precious metals, clothed with royal colors, and hammered to a base to keep them from tottering (10:3–4, 8–9; cf. Isa. 40:18–20). "Like a scarecrow in a melon patch," they were impotent, immobile, and incapable of answering prayers (10:5; cf. Hab. 2:18–20). Their only message was the senselessness of their makers. Thus, the house of Israel was not to learn "the ways of the nations" (10:2).

Second, the corollary of false worship was a plethora of injustices among the people: oppression of aliens, stealing, murder, adultery, perjury, and the shedding of "innocent blood" (7:5–6, 9; 19:4–5; 22:17; cf. Hos. 4:2). The latter sin probably refers to

125

child sacrifice (Jer. 7:31; cf. Lev. 20:1–5) and to the persecution of righteous people, notably prophets, who resisted royal policies as in the reign of Manasseh (2 Kings 21:16; Jer. 26:23). In 26:15 Jeremiah had to defend himself before the leaders and people as follows: "Be assured, however, that if you put me to death, you will bring the guilt of innocent blood on yourselves and on this city and on those who live in it, for in truth the LORD has sent me to you to speak all these words in your hearing."

The prophets were unambiguous on the connection between idolatry and injustice.[2] In his case against Israel, Micah memorably declared, "And what does the LORD require of you? To act justly and to love mercy and to walk humbly with your God" (Mic. 6:8). The contrast had been sketched earlier: "All the nations may walk in the name of their gods; we will walk in the name of the LORD our God for ever and ever" (Mic.4:5). God reviewed the exodus and his provision of leadership in 6:3–4. Then Micah argued that one who loves the Lord will love his people as well. How can we claim to walk with God, if we dishonor and oppress his people (Jer. 22:15–17)? How could a people claim to worship God, when their temple had become a perverted place of commerce, where people became rich by taking advantage of the poor (Amos 2:8)? Micah's answer summarized prophetic themes that illumine a righteous walk before the Lord: Amos 5:24 ("act justly"), Hosea 6:6 ("love mercy"), and Isaiah 29:19 with Jeremiah 9:23–24 ("walk humbly with your God").

Third, Israel would be disciplined because their persistent disobedience had hardened the "stubbornness of their hearts" (Jer. 9:14). Jeremiah's distinctive "again and again" underscores God's persistence in calling for Israel's repentance. But they had confused dead stones with their living God. The effect was a rationalizing of their behavior to the point that Jeremiah's words were shocking. The Israelites were living in a delusion that their

2. R. K. Harrison, *Jeremiah and Lamentations*, Tyndale Old Testament Commentaries (Downers Grove, IL: InterVarsity Press, 1973), 85. "As they experience spiritual renewal they will become aware of the gross inequalities existing in contemporary society, and out of loving concern for the helpless they will set about remedying existing abuses."

abundant sacrifices in the temple of the Lord guaranteed their safety, and they "stand before me in this house, which bears my Name, and say 'We are safe'—safe to do all these detestable things" (7:10; cf. 5:12). "Friend deceives friend, and no one speaks the truth," God lamented; "the heart is deceitful above all things and beyond cure. Who can understand it?" (9:5–6; 17:9–10). Their threefold repetition of "the temple of the LORD" amounted to pagan babbling that indicated their trust in "the place I gave to you and your fathers" (7:4, 14; cf. Matt. 6:7). In fact, they had transformed "this house, which bears my Name," into "a den of robbers," the center of their corrupt practices (7:11; cf. Isa. 56:7 with Matt. 21:13; 23:23 and parallels). In words that recall Israel's idolatry at Sinai (Ex. 32:7–10), the Lord declared, "But I have been watching!" (7:11; cf. Hos. 7:2).

The proof that security is in the Lord personally, rather than his "dwelling," was the precedent at Shiloh, "where I first made a dwelling for my Name, and see what I did to it because of the wickedness of my people Israel" (7:12; cf. 26:6). The psalmist recalled that, on that occasion, God abandoned the center of worship and allowed his ark to be captured by the Philistines (Ps. 78:60–61). Thus, the priests, prophets, and people were alarmed that Jeremiah predicted the desolation of the sanctuary and city "like Shiloh" (Jer. 26:9), because they had dismissed the necessary connection of sanctuary and holiness. The words struck at the heart of their confidence in the status quo.

The image of Jeremiah, standing alone at the temple's gate before a hostile crowd, is the sort of scene more likely found in our nightmares than our dreams. Idolatry seems to be a dusty, old sin that modern people would prefer to leave in their haunted attics. However, we cannot afford to dismiss the uncomfortable subject so cavalierly. We all agree that the world is unfair, but the myriad of injustices indicates that other gods are alive and well. When people do not love God, they cannot love their neighbors. In the absence of the standard, the law of the jungle prevails, even though flattering language usually masks carnivorous behavior. Biblical teaching about idols helps us to see that the problem has always been a human infatuation with gods that cater to selfish drives and desires. Habakkuk 1:11 indicts the Babylonians as "guilty men, whose own strength is their god." And Colossians 3:5 with Ephesians 5:5 identifies idolatry as greed or covetousness. Paul in Romans 1:21–23 identifies idolatry as the worship of creatures or created things rather than the Creator (cf. Acts 17:16–34 for his application of the principle to an Athenian audience). Putting all of this together, we can say that we worship what we covet to make us strong and self-sufficient apart from God. We trust in our own abilities or accomplishments, or perhaps our own networks and organizations that keep us from glorifying our Lord. Of course, we should not expect unbelievers to be true worshipers any more than Jeremiah expected the Canaanites to be like Israel.

So how should we respond to easily besetting sins that people around us commit today? I would suggest that we list several values or practices that dominate the time and spending habits of our society. Recently I have observed addictions, lying, cheating, winning at any cost, and related problems. The media are a good measure of cultural values. Or we may be able to reflect on contemporary idols from our own experiences. Then we should ask ourselves, as believers in the Word, whether we are controlled by those priorities, "like the nations around us." The answer to this question will bring life to the messages of Jeremiah and his fellow prophets. Jeremiah tells us that these kinds of likenesses are serious and should be dealt with. He says that walking in the good ways of the Lord is the best form of repentance (Jer. 6:16; cf.18:15).

True Versus False Prophets

Behind the idolatrous practices of the people were the teachings of false prophets, the second of the contrasts that structure Jeremiah's sermon at the temple. The rulers and populace had chosen to believe "deceptive words that are worthless," that reinforced their privileged positions in the nation (Jer 7:8, 4; cf. 23:25–26; Isa. 30:10–11). Jeremiah, an exemplar of true prophecy, said whatever the Lord commanded him (Jer. 1:7; 7:1), while the false prophets sought popularity by validating the leaders and institutions of the land: "From the least to the greatest, all are greedy for gain; prophets and priests alike, all practice deceit. They dress the wound of my people as though it were not serious" (8:10–11). Jeremiah proclaimed the truth about bad news, while his opponents told lies to curry favor. Willem VanGemeren summarizes the problem well, when he notes that the Israelites "sought to eternalize the present and to institutionalize the Spirit in space and time."[3] In other words, they sought to "eternalize" their privileged status under the auspices of approving institutions. They worshiped according to pagan principles and embezzled from their fellow citizens for their own aggrandizement. The effect was to entrench the people in their spiritual blindness, so that they could not see the blessings of the living God. They lost all understanding of the way in which God was present at the time, so they failed to prepare for the judgments that were around the corner. In a word, the false prophets were self-appointed heralds of false information.

Perhaps we might think that the old prophets were too harsh with people's sincere desire to succeed on their own terms. The truth, however, is that the personal quality of the covenant relationship was at stake. The prophets passionately resisted anything that detracted from personal accountability before God in the daily affairs of the Israelites. According to Walther Eichrodt, "God becomes an impersonal source of magical power, which can be manipulated with no feeling of reverence whatsoever simply by means of a meticulous routine; for, so far as his will, the core of his personality, is concerned, man by such an attitude declines to recognize the claims of his divine Lord."[4] In a word, the people of Israel went about their intensely religious routines as if God did not exist. They paid for their sins with their lives, and their

3. Willem VanGemeren, *Interpreting the Prophetic Word* (Grand Rapids: Zondervan, 1990), 64.
4. Walther Eichrodt, *Theology of the Old Testament*, 2 vols., The Old Testament Library, trans. J. A. Baker (Philadelphia: Westminster, 1961), 1.365.

exposed corpses (7:32–33) indicated that their sanctuary had become their cemetery.

The contrast is particularly clear in Jeremiah's confrontation with the false prophet Hananiah (chapter 28). Jeremiah, like other prophets, dramatized his messages with symbolic gestures. In this episode, he wore a wooden yoke to represent Israel's submission to Babylon for seventy years (25:11; 27:11; 29:10). Hananiah, ever the optimist, contradicted Jeremiah by prophesying that the yoke would be broken and "all the articles of the LORD's house" would be returned within two years (28:1–4). Jeremiah wished that Hananiah could be right, but the true prophets had predicted "war, disaster, and plague" (28:8). Hananiah took the yoke from Jeremiah's neck and broke it as he repeated his prediction. Then the Word of the Lord instructed Jeremiah to confront Hananiah with correction and condemnation:

> You have broken a wooden yoke, but in its place you will get a yoke of iron. . . . Listen, Hananiah! The LORD has not sent you, yet you have persuaded this nation to trust in lies. (28:13, 15)

The false prophets sponsored magical incantations and a frenzy of activity at the temple to mask their misleading messages and the wickedness of the nation. Sacrifices are valid, we are told repeatedly in the prophets, only when they are accompanied by heartfelt repentance and joyful obedience (cf. Isa. 1:10–20).

The prophetic Word as the presence of God involved the prophets' participation in their message, which scholars have called *pathos*. Examples are Jeremiah's yoke as a portrayal of judgment and Hosea's marriage as a vivid enactment of the covenantal love of God. Prophetic messages, blended with visual reinforcement, were living sermons that made "God's presence perceptible."[5] What the people heard and saw in the prophet was a mirror of God's assessment of their condition before him.[6]

---

5. Edmond Jacob, *Theology of the Old Testament*, trans. A. W. Heathcote and P. J. Allcock (New York, Evanston: Harper and Row, 1958), 243.

6. Abraham Joshua Heschel, *The Prophets*, 2 vols. (New York, Evanston: Harper and

These godly servants formed a tradition of truth "from the time your forefathers left Egypt until now, day after day, again and again I sent you my servants the prophets" (7:25; cf. 7:13; 25:4; 26:5; 29:19; 35:15; 44:4). Their unifying message was expressed in the language of presence (cf. Deut. 26:16–19): "Obey me, and I will be your God and you will be my people. Walk in all the ways I command you, that it may go well with you" (7:23; cf. 17:19–27). But God lamented, "They did not listen or pay attention" (7:24; cf. 7:13), so "my anger and my wrath will be poured out on this place" (7:20).

Jeremiah's call in chapter 1 graphically illustrates God's presence with and through his servants the prophets. VanGemeren lists several criteria for these "spokesmen for God" with the distinct call to be his ambassadors: they all were like Moses, their exemplary servant and prototypical prophet; Israelites, called by the Lord, empowered by the Holy Spirit; God's authoritative messengers of the Word; good shepherds of the people; and validated by signs and the fulfillment of their messages.[7] Primarily, the prophet was a mediating presence of God through the Word. Walther Zimmerli summarizes the power of presence in the Word as follows: "In its own history Israel learned by experience that it was not the policies of its kings and their armies that made history, but the word of Yahweh proclaimed by the pre-exilic prophets."[8]

Chapter 1 begins with specific information about Jeremiah's background. He prophesied from 626 to 586 B.C., from the reign of Josiah, his godly kindred spirit, through the wicked kings Jehoiakim and Zedekiah, the ruler at the fall of Jerusalem in 586. The last of Judah's pre-exilic prophets, Jeremiah was a contemporary of Habakkuk, perhaps Obadiah, and Ezekiel, who wrote in Babylon. He was Hilkiah's son and a priest at Anathoth,

---

Row, 1962), 2.1–11. "The prophet of wrath did not merely proclaim it: he lived it, and was conscious of it" 1.115.

7. VanGemeren, *Interpreting the Prophetic Word*, 32–34, 42–43. The reader should note Jer. 1:12 and Deut. 34:10–11 as well.

8. Walther Zimmerli, *Old Testament Theology in Outline*, trans. David Green (Atlanta: John Knox Press, 1978), 216.

when "the word of the LORD came to him" (1:2). His times were tumultuous. Buffer states such as Judah were pawns in imperial transitions. Assyrian Nineveh fell to the Babylonians in 612, and the Babylonian Nebuchadnezzar defeated the Egyptians at Carchemish in 605.

In such a setting, without preparation or credentials and with no right of refusal, Jeremiah was appointed "as a prophet to the nations" (1:4–5). God's election of the priest/prophet was an expression of his sovereign prerogative that he had exercised previously with Moses (Ex. 7:1–2; 33:12): "Before I formed you in the womb I knew you, before you were born I set you apart . . . to uproot and tear down, to destroy and overthrow, to build and to plant" (Jer. 1:5, 10). He was "the weeping prophet of judgment" (9:1), yet he joined other prophets as the bearer of hope in God's new covenant.

Like Moses, Jeremiah was afraid and objected that he could not speak since he was only a child (Jer. 1:6 with Ex. 4:10). God's response, as in Moses' case, was that his presence was sufficient for his calling (Jer. 1:7–8).[9] The prophet must go anywhere that God would send him and say whatever the Lord would put in his mouth (1:7–9, 17). "I am with you and will rescue you," declared the Lord (1:8, 19). Jeremiah's security under divine sovereignty extended to a message that God would use Judah's enemy as his disciplinary agent. In Jeremiah's terrifying calling, God would make him "a fortified city, an iron pillar, and a bronze wall to stand against the whole land," impregnable, strong, and secure (1:18; cf. 15:20).

The Absence of the Presence

The security of God's presence with the prophet brings us to the third contrast that structured Jeremiah's temple sermon, in addition to contrasts in worship and the prophets. Although

9. In some cases, such as Isaiah (chapter 6) and Ezekiel (chapters 1–2), the prophet's calling involved a personal vision of God's glorious presence. Also, with Moses-like imagery, God comforted Elijah with his presence when the prophet was discouraged by the nation's evil practices (1 Kings 19:9–18).

Jeremiah was secure in his calling, God said that he would thrust the people of Judah from his presence, just as he did to the people of Ephraim (Shiloh) (7:15; 52:3). God's announcement of exile is a counterpoint to his earlier appeal for repentance, expressing his desire for his people to live in the Promised Land and worship at his dwelling (7:3, 7). However, they "did not listen" to his prophets (7:13, 27), so the Lord "will not listen" to their cries (7:16). Accordingly, Jeremiah was instructed not to pray for the Israelites in view of their persistent disobedience over time. In startling words, the Lord told his prophet in 15:1: "Even if Moses and Samuel were to stand before me, my heart would not go out to this people. Send them away from my presence! Let them go!"

This divine resolve to exile the nation is prophetically expressed as a "hiding of his face." This was, as we recall, the alienating effect of sin.[10] Heschel noted that God would not have left his people altogether, but he would be among them "like a stranger in the land, like a traveler . . . like a warrior powerless to save" (Jer. 14:8–9).[11] "I will hide my face from this city," the Lord told Jeremiah in his confinement, "because of all its wickedness" (33:5; cf. 32:31).

Israel's rebellion was not a surprise to God. Moses had predicted their idolatry and the Lord's exilic discipline in Deuteronomy 31:16–18: "On that day I will become angry with them and forsake them; I will hide my face from them, and they will be destroyed." Their likeness to the pagan cults was described as prostitution "to the foreign gods of the land they are entering." Especially shameful was the use of God's "dwelling" for "meaningless offerings" (Isa. 1:13). Thus, "when you spread out your hands in prayer, I will hide my eyes from you; even if you offer many prayers, I will not listen" (Isa. 1:15; cf. 54:8; 59:2; 64:7; Ezek. 7:22; Mic. 3:4).

---

10. The prophets also express this ethical alienation in terms of nearness (*qarob*) and farness (*rahoq*). The principle appears in James, where we read, "Come near to God and he will come near to you" (4:8).

11. Heschel, *The Prophets*, 1.112.

True worship and divine presence converge in Isaiah 8:13–17. Arguing against veneration of the corrupted temple, the Lord Almighty claimed that he alone was the One whom his people should worship (8:13). "He will be a sanctuary," the prophet stated with temple imagery, the "cornerstone" of their faith (28:16). If the temple was not to be his house of prayer, then it would be "a stone that causes men to stumble and a rock that makes them fall" (8:14). The image was associated with darkness, where the people stumble over what they cannot see (cf. John 9:39). The cornerstone "in the light" shaped the design of a beautiful structure, but if one did not understand the design, it was merely an obstacle. Isaiah, setting himself apart from the people in his obedience (Isa. 8:11–12), concluded, "I will wait for the LORD, who is hiding his face from the house of Jacob. I will put my trust in him" (8:17).

The prophet Ezekiel paralleled Isaiah, when he wrote of Judah's exile "into the desert of the nations," where he will execute judgment "face to face" on his people (Ezek. 20:35). He "hid" his "face" from them and, accordingly, had "handed them over to their enemies" (Ezek. 39:23–24). But there would be a messianic day, when "I will no longer hide my face from them, for I will pour out my Spirit on the house of Israel," declared the Lord (Ezek. 39:29).

Why did the Israelites embrace the darkness of false worship under the auspices of ungodly leadership and false prophets in spite of God's presence? Because the "glitter" of the nations deceived them into oppressing their own people for personal security and prestige. Sinners worship what they covet to make them appear strong apart from God. This activity causes them to hide from the presence, lest they be shamed by what they want to do (cf. Gen. 3:10). The living God desires the true worship of living people, not the mechanical obedience of robots. He warned his people through true prophets before he allowed the majorities to self-destruct in their idolatrous practices. The true prophets were God's mediating presences as servants of his Word. Whatever the cost, the prophets proclaimed, "Obey me, and I will be your God and you will be my people. Walk in all the ways I command you, that it may go well with you" (Jer. 7:23). The notion of "face" as encounter with the presence reemerged in this section, as the Lord promised a messianic day, when "I will no longer hide my face from [my people]" (Ezek. 39:29). In the words of the psalmist: "The eyes of the LORD are on those who fear him, on those whose hope is in his unfailing love, to deliver them from death" (Ps. 33:18–19).

The Presence in Messianic Hope

Messiah as Cornerstone of the Living Temple

The prophets were pointing to the Messiah, the supreme presence of God on earth, who as "temple" would initiate the fullness of covenantal relationship between God and his people by his glorification through crucifixion, resurrection, and ascension to the right hand of the Father (John 2:18–22). The New Testament authors use the prophetic temple texts with Psalm 118:22 to demonstrate that the Messiah was crucified because the Israelites rejected the Stone who became the Cornerstone of God's spiritual temple, in a scenario that was similar to the pre-exilic generation. That is, they were more concerned with security among the nations than they were with the safety of God himself.

Matthew 20–21 parallels develop God's reversal of values in which service defines greatness, and leadership means not lording authority over the people (Matt. 20:25–28). "Not so with you," the Savior emphasized (v. 26). His model of leadership exemplified service, even as he came "not to be served, but to serve, and to give his life as a ransom for many" (v. 28). This form of servant leadership was an obstacle to people who failed to understand the power of gracious service in the presence of God. Jesus' testimony was that God's absence was temporary and awaited the fullness of times, when he, the Word incarnate, would bring all things to pass. Jesus triumphantly entered Jerusalem as a king on a colt of a donkey, which emphasized his

135

humility (21:2–5; cf. Zech. 9:9). A large crowd acknowledged him with messianic praise: "Blessed is he who comes in the name of the Lord!" (Matt. 21:9, quoting the first half of Ps. 118:26). The second half of the psalm's verse, "From the house of the LORD we bless you," is omitted in Matthew, because Jesus had to cleanse the temple as a "den of robbers" and performed acts of mercy for "the blind and the lame" before the joyful day of his victory (Matt. 21:12–14 with Jer. 7:11; Isa. 56:7). His advent was a divine commission from the Father (Matt. 21:23–27), because Israel's leadership had continued to persecute God's servants the prophets, as well as God the Son and heir (Matt. 21:33–43). Jesus presented this tragic continuum in terms of the temple imagery in Psalm 118:22–23 (Matt. 21:42–44), and he did it in such a way that "The chief priests and Pharisees . . . knew that he was talking about them" (Matt. 21:45).

The emphasis continues as the New Testament proceeds. In Acts 4:5–14, Peter, having performed an act of kindness at the time of prayer, had to defend himself before the Sanhedrin with the Name of the Cornerstone (Ps. 118:22) in the Holy Spirit. Paul in Romans 9:30–33 affirmed that Israel had "stumbled," because they had rejected the Stone on which God would complete the salvation of everyone who trusted him as their sanctuary (Isa. 8:14 with 28:16). The author to the Hebrews defines salvation in terms of the family of God, a family that is formed by believers who "trust in him" (Heb. 2:13 with Isa. 8:17–18; Rom. 10:11). Briefly, the New Testament writers placed themselves in the tradition of prophetic servants, whose message centered in the living temple and divine presence of the messianic King, who would return to establish the new heaven and new earth. "Worship God!" the angel told John. "For the testimony of Jesus is the spirit of prophecy" (Rev. 19:10).

Peter's use of "presence" texts in 1 Peter 2:1–10 is especially noteworthy. He wrote to believers, whom he identified as "strangers in the world" and "shielded by God's power" (1:1–5). He encouraged them to "crave pure spiritual milk" of the Word (2:2). The "word of the Lord" pointed to the "living Stone," who as Cornerstone has shaped believers as "living stones" into a spiritual temple as a holy priesthood (2:4–5). According to the image, Christians are to be a loving community, a temple (or "dwelling") that reflects the presence of God in the world (cf. Eph. 2:19–22). In support of the temple image for the church, Peter quotes Isaiah 28:16 with the promise that "the one who trusts in him will never be put to shame" (1 Peter 2:6). Though humble, neither Christ nor his body or temple will ever be anything other than a living presence, since the living God has accomplished his will through people that the world usually rejects.

"The world was not worthy of them," Hebrews concludes about people of faith (11:38). God's historical parade includes people such as Jeremiah and the unschooled, ordinary apostles (Acts 4:13), while their powerful adversaries pass away. Unbelievers stumble and fall in their blindness, because they reject a living, covenantal relationship with God as predicted by Psalm 118:22 and Isaiah 8:14. In his sermons in the early chapters of Acts, Peter drew a sharp contrast between the rejection of the Messiah by Jewish leadership and his subsequent exaltation by God. The messages are vivid illustrations of his point in 1 Peter. Believers are described as "a holy nation," who manifest the indwelling presence of God, and "a people belonging to God," whose lives become God's worship center in the world (1 Peter 2:9; cf.1 Cor. 3:16–17). They are further described as inhabitants in God's "wonderful light" (1 Peter 2:9; cf. Isa. 49:6), who shine through their godly deeds. Peter's terminology is derived from descriptions of Israel in Exodus and Deuteronomy.

The exilic discipline of the Lord, the prophets declared, was an act of tough love to provoke repentance and to promote the completion of all things. Isaiah's thrilling emphasis signals the shift:

> Comfort, comfort my people, says your God. Speak tenderly to Jerusalem, and proclaim to her that her hard service has been completed, that her sin has been paid for, that she has received from the LORD's hand double for all her sins. (Isa. 40:1–2)

"In a surge of anger I hid my face from you for a moment, but with everlasting kindness I will have compassion on you," says the Lord your Redeemer. (Isa. 54:8)

O afflicted city [Jerusalem], lashed by storms and not comforted, I will build you with stones of turquoise, your foundations with sapphires. (Isa. 54:11)

My house will be called a house of prayer for all nations. (Isa. 56:7)

This is the one I esteem: he who is humble and contrite in spirit, and trembles at my word. (Isa. 66:2)

How beautiful on the mountains are the feet of those who bring good news, who proclaim peace, who bring good tidings, who proclaim salvation, who say to Zion, "Your God reigns!" (Isa. 52:7 with Rom. 10:15).

Behold, I will create new heavens and a new earth. The former things will not be remembered, nor will they come to mind. But be glad and rejoice forever in what I will create, for I will create Jerusalem to be a delight and its people a joy. I will rejoice over Jerusalem and take delight in my people; the sound of weeping and of crying will be heard in it no more. (Isa. 65:17–19)

This is what the Lord says: "Heaven is my throne, and the earth is my footstool. Where is the house you will build for me? Where will my resting place be?" (Isa. 66:1)

"As the new heavens and the new earth that I make will endure before me [in my presence] . . . so will your name and descendants endure. . . . all mankind will come and bow down before me," says the Lord (Isa. 66:22–23).

This is the prophetic word that points to Revelation 21:

I saw the Holy City, the new Jerusalem, coming down out of heaven from God. . . . And I heard a loud voice from the throne saying, "Now the dwelling of God is with men, and he will live with them. They will be his people, and God himself will be with them and be their God." (vv. 21:2–3)

Messiah as Foundation of the New Covenant

Jeremiah's temple sermon transitions to his letter to the exiles in chapter 29 by way of the Babylonian captivity. Prophetic pleas fell on deaf ears, so that discipline was necessary as in the Egyptian precedent. According to Jer. 52:28–30, 4,600 Israelites were carried to Mesopotamia, including King Jehoiachin and his household. Nebuzaradan, the commander of the imperial guard, on the other hand, left behind "the poorest people of the land to work the vineyards and fields" (Jer. 52:16). However, the covenantal love of God was persistent, so the darkness of judgment yielded to the hope of God's consolation later in the book. The letter in Jeremiah 29:4–23, perhaps dating from 594 B.C., was like an urgent office memo from the prophet in Jerusalem to the exiles in Babylon seven hundred miles away. The year was characterized by rumors of a vassal uprising against the empire, apparently supported by false prophets. He "certified" his letter by entrusting it to Elasah and Gemariah, who were members of a trusted family. The communiqué was a prophetic oracle from God. It contained positive instructions and negative warnings in view of the seventy-year length of the exile.

God's Plans and Israel's Hope. The instructions of Jeremiah's letter would have been shocking in their call for a peaceful sojourn in Babylon. Contrary to false predictions that the exile would be short, the Israelites should settle down and raise families (Jer. 29:5–6). Apparently they were settled in colonies with a measure of freedom to nurture children and develop the land (cf. Ezek. 3:15). They were to be good citizens, seeking "the peace and prosperity of the city" (Jer. 29:7). Finally, they were "to pray to the Lord for [Babylon]," so that they would share its prosperity (Jer.29:7). The attitude reminds us of Jesus' counter-cultural instruction "to pray for those who persecute you" (Matt. 5:44). What was good for the Babylonians would be good for the Israelites. If the exilic generation was not going to return, then peace in the city was the best preparation for the later generation that would come home.[12] The term for "peace" (*shalom*) meant a condition of well-being and wholeness in relationships in contrast with fragmentation and alienation.

On the other hand, the instructions were startling, because circumstances were sometimes very harsh as Jeremiah 29:15–23 indicates. The passage describes judgments on unbelieving Israelites and their false prophets. The unbelievers were described as "poor figs" who refused to listen to the Lord "again and again" (29:17, 19). Thus, they were pursued by "the sword, famine and plague" and became "an object of cursing and horror, of scorn and reproach, among all the nations" (29:18). The prophets were described through the examples of Ahab and Zedekiah, who were not the well-known kings with the same names. Nebuchadnezzar burned the deceivers in the fire for agitating against the empire and committing immorality (cf. Dan. 3:20).[13]

Negatively, God warned the Israelites to ignore the deceptions of false prophets and diviners (Jer. 29:8). These addicts of deception continued their practices in captivity, prophesying lies that may have reflected their fleshly desires. "I have not sent them," declared the Lord (Jer. 29:9).

These instructions and warnings were based on the fact that the exile was God's will instead of an unfortunate accident (29:4, 7). When the seventy–year exile was completed, then God would

---

12. R. E. Clements, *Jeremiah*, Interpretation: A Bible Commentary for Teaching and Preaching (Atlanta: John Knox Press, 1988), 172. "The reference in Jeremiah's letter to a period of 'seventy years' (29:10; cf. 25:12) was obviously intended to signify a full human lifetime (cf. Ps. 90:10). None of those who had been taken to Babylon could hope to return to their homeland. Only their children might hope to do so."

13. Jeremiah's message to Shemaiah (29:24–32), a false prophet, is a separate message that is based on the letter. In reaction to the letter's instructions (v. 28), the false prophet requested that Zephaniah the priest reprimand Jeremiah the "madman" and confine him in "stocks and neck-irons." Instead, the Lord cursed Shemaiah and his descendants, declaring that they would not "see the good things I will do for my people."

initiate the fulfillment of his promise to bring his people back to their land (29:10). It was a long time for homesick captives, who would sit and weep by the rivers of Babylon as they remembered Zion (Ps. 137:1). Their proper hope was in the Lord's plans and promises "to prosper you and not to harm you, plans to give you hope and a future" (29:11).

For the Israelite believer, hope was inseparable from the presence of the Lord in his Word (Ps. 119:43, 49). The verbs for hope generally mean "to wait," and the nouns are rendered "confidence" or "expectation." The vocabulary for hope, accordingly, was connected to the true prophets' counsel to await God's word about the return from captivity. Hope and trust stood in close proximity biblically and blended together in the community of believers, where memories of his goodness were a vital part of their heritage. In fact, hope in the faithful God of our salvation was a defining characteristic of relationship with God, a dwelling "in the shelter of the Most High" and a resting place "in the shadow of the Almighty" (Ps. 91:1). This sense of presence was spatially focused on the city of David, an affirmation of the fact that Israel's election necessarily meant God's presence among his people in "this place" (Jer. 29:10).[14]

Much of the Old Testament deals with prolonged periods of hope over lifetimes or centuries, something unthinkable for modern people who have been poisoned by instant gratification and speed. We must remember that seventy years was difficult for the Israelites as well. It meant that many of the exilic generation would not return, and younger survivors "who had seen the former temple wept aloud" (Ezra 3:12, cf. Jer. 29:1). In times of prolonged difficulty, people ask questions about the goodness and purposes of God. We reach out and declare our commitment to God, if he will only intervene in our behalf. Is it true that "in all things God works for the good of those who love him" (Rom. 8:28)? The answer is yes, but the point of Jeremiah's letter is that

14. VanGemeren, *Interpreting the Prophetic Word*, 31: "The eschatological hope of the Mosaic revelation is the presence of God among his people."

God took his people from their homes to generate a hunger for true worship.

Israel's Prayer for God's Presence. "Then," God declared to people who would be starved for the comforts of home, "you will call upon me and come and pray to me, and I will listen to you" (Jer. 29:12). We often wish that discipline would be unnecessary, but the exchange of perversion for purity made the Mesopotamian sojourn worthwhile. Restoration to the land was bound up with a renewed worship of God. Heartfelt prayer is a sure sign of the change, a change that God honors with his recognition that discipline has done its work.

Sincere prayer meant that God's people must seek him with all their heart (29:13). The Israelites would have to forsake the heretical combination of pious language and idolatrous practices. They would have to remember their Mosaic roots, where their exile for idolatry was predicted with an exhortation to seek the Lord with reverent obedience and loving service (Deut. 4:29). They must embrace a dedication that would help them recognize and reject false prophets, so that, in the Lord's time, their fortunes would be restored with worship in the land. Without addressing the false prophets directly, Jeremiah explained that the Lord will listen when his people are willing to listen to his Word through his "servants the prophets" (Jer. 29:12, 19). The clear implication of this reciprocity is that God is living and personal.

God's Consolation and the New Covenant. To this point in Jeremiah, the dominant theme has been God's judgment on his people. The promise of hope in 29:11 now transitions to his book of consolation in chapters 30–33. Hope for the people in exile could not be represented by an abstract assurance that all would be well for Israel in the future. It could only be seen in terms of God's promise of their land and their Davidic ruler who would rebuild their cities, renew cultivation of their land, and promote enjoyment of the Lord's presence. So, the theme of the chapters is God's promise of Israel's return to the land (chapter

30) and their spiritual renewal as his united people (chapter 31). The promise was his unchanging commitment from Sinai: "I will be their God, and they will be my people" (Jer. 31:33). Judgment was not the end of the nation's existence, but rather the means by which God would graciously draw his people into a lasting covenantal relationship (30:11). Discipline did not mean that God had rejected the Israelites. It meant that God took his covenant with them seriously. He would forgive their sins and internalize his Word in their hearts, an inner prompting to love and serve him through his Spirit (31:31–34). The emphasis of the book of consolation is that in punishment God is just, and in salvation he is extravagant.

The Lord instructed Jeremiah to "write in a book" how divine discipline with justice would end, and how, in his time, he would "restore them to the land . . . . They will serve the LORD their God and David their king, whom I will raise up for them. . . . 'I am with you and will save you,' declares the LORD" (30:1–11). "For the LORD will ransom Jacob and redeem them from the hand of those stronger than they" (31:11). Moreover, the Lord promised to heal their wounds and judge their enemies (30:12–17). Zion would be rebuilt, and "the palace will stand in its proper place. . . . Their leader will be one of their own" to lead them closer to the Lord (30:18–24). Thus, "you will be my people, and I will be your God" (Jer. 30:22; cf. Ex. 6:7; Lev. 26:12; Jer. 31:1; Hos. 2:23).

In chapter 31, God's blessing would have occasioned exuberant celebration. He had saved the Israelites in the past "with everlasting love; I have drawn you with loving-kindness" (Jer. 31:3; cf. Deut. 4:37).[15] So, reflecting Jeremiah's calling in chapter 1, again the Lord "will watch over them to build and to plant" (Jer. 31:28). As mourning was turned into gladness, so the remnant's praise would be heard among the nations (31:6–7).

15. Elmer Martens, *Jeremiah*, Believers Church Bible Commentary (Scottsdale, PA: Herald Press, 1986), 191. "Only here in Jeremiah is there mention of love with God as subject. 'Loving-kindness' is too anemic for the Hebrew term (*hesed*), which occurs 245 times in the Old Testament and means 'covenant love, covenant loyalty' (see Exod. 34:6; Ps. 136). In a direct, personable way the Lord gives of himself to his people, for their well-being is his concern."

The Lord's faithful love in saving his people was an act of sovereign grace that was the basis of the nation's hope-filled future (Jer. 31:17). His provision of the new covenant likewise proceeded from an emphatic divine resolve as Israel's husband in spite of the nation's infidelity. The imagery of the chapter was drawn from patriarch Jacob/Israel's blessing of his sons in Genesis 49. The oft-used name for the Israelites in Jeremiah 31 was "Ephraim," Joseph's younger son in Jacob's blessing. The patriarch Jacob adopted Manasseh and Ephraim as his own and blessed the younger brother, who, like himself, represented the prerogative of God. Now, over twelve hundred years later, Israel as "Ephraim" would receive Father God's blessing in their return from Babylon, even as Joseph's two sons were blessed out of Egypt. In spite of the apparent hopelessness of the exiles, "he who scattered Israel will gather them" again (31:10). Songs of thanksgiving, such as chapter 31, are reminders that prayer often was the prompting for divine deliverance. Later Jeremiah's text would be used in Matthew 2:13–23, where the Christ child was spared in Egypt during Herod's cruel slaughter of Jewish boys (Jer. 31:15 in Matt. 2:18; cf. Hos. 11:1 in Matt. 2:15).

Upon their return from captivity, the people "will once again use these words: 'The LORD bless you, O righteous dwelling, O sacred mountain,'" which is the loving language of the Presence with his people (Jer. 31:23). Consequently, the Israelites would live together with their Lord's refreshment and security.

The sequence of events during the time of captivity was not easy, as exemplified by Jeremiah. In the tenth year of Zedekiah, Jerusalem was under Babylonian siege. The king imprisoned the prophet until the city fell (Jer. 32:1–2). Then the Lord revealed to Jeremiah that he must formally purchase Hanamel's field in Anathoth as a guarantee that God would restore Israel to the land after captivity (32:6–15). Reminiscent of Moses' dialogues with God, the confused prophet, hoping against hope, sought the Lord's counsel in view of his knowledge of the nation's impending judgment for idolatry (32:16–35). The Lord reported that he would bring them back, so that "they will be my people, and I will be their God" (32:8). "As I have brought all this great calamity on this people, so I will give them all the prosperity I have promised them" (32:42). The eight occurrences of God saying "I will" (32:37–41) pointed to the assurances of God's new covenant as a message of certainty in times that occasionally confused even his prophets.

John Bright refers to Jeremiah 31:31–34 as "deservedly famous . . . certainly one of the profoundest and most moving passages in the entire Bible."[16] At a critical juncture in Israel's history, Jeremiah reached back to the Torah and carried God's promised presence forward to the Messiah and to the new heavens and new earth. Its hope extended not only to Israel's restoration but also to the nations' glorification of the Lord in Zion. The only use of the title "new covenant" in the Old Testament occurs in verse 31, but its content is expanded in Ezekiel, Isaiah, and elsewhere. Noteworthy is the fact that the designation became "New Testament," which is attributed to the early church father Origen.

The open-ended projection of the passage into the future is indicated by the indefinite phrase "the time is coming" (Jer. 31:31). Of course, a number of exiles returned from Babylon, and the city was rebuilt on a less-than-grand scale (Ezra, Nehemiah). "Many of the older priests and Levites and family heads, who had seen the former temple, wept aloud when they saw the foundation of this temple being laid" (Ezra 3:12; cf. Hag. 2:3). However, the new covenant extends far beyond those blessings. In the church, it was expanded to Gentiles, according to God's earlier promise to Abraham (Gen. 12:3; cf. Eph. 2:11–22). Ultimately, the new covenant formed the eternal destiny of all of God's chosen people (Rev. 21:3).

God's first declaration was that he would make a new covenant that would not be like the one that he made with "their forefathers when I took them by the hand to lead them out of Egypt" (Jer. 31:32). The difference is initially described in terms of the people's need, "because they broke my covenant, though I

16. John Bright, *Jeremiah*, The Anchor Bible (Garden City, NY: Doubleday, 1965), 287.

was a husband to them" (31:32).[17] Israel had persistently failed to keep "the terms of this [Sinaitic] covenant," which had mandated obedience to the law as the central issue of their existence as God's people (Jer. 11:1–8). They had followed the deceitfulness of their hearts (17:9) until they could no longer assess their condition (8:4–7): "Can the Ethiopian change his skin or the leopard its spots? Neither can you do good who are accustomed to doing evil" (13:23).

"This is the covenant," declared the Lord in announcing three differences that would make his unchanging will effective in their lives. First, God would "put my law in their minds and write it on their hearts" (Jer. 31:33) instead of on tablets of stone (Ex. 31:18; 34:28–29) or a reflected glory that distanced a fearful people (Ex. 34:30). Admittedly, the intent of the law was to fix these words of the Lord in their circumcised hearts (Deut. 10:12–16; 30:6, 14; Ps. 37:31). But the difference was in the effective grace within their hearts and minds rather than the Word that was continually before them, which they could deceitfully spin (Jer. 7:22–26). The transformation would be inside out, with God himself inscribing his Word in his people until the Messiah would fulfill the law to the "smallest letter" and "the least stroke of a pen" (cf. Matt. 5:18).

God's promise of internalization concerned the intimacy of his presence according to Ezekiel 36:22–27. God emphasized his promise to give his people "a new heart" and "a new spirit" for the sake of "the holiness of my great name" (36:26, 23). Again, "I want you to know that I am not doing this for your sake" (36:32, 22–23). When he worked through Israel on the international stage, then the nations would "know that I am the LORD" (36:23). He would effect his transformation through the indwelling Holy Spirit: "I will put my Spirit in you and move you to follow my decrees and be careful to keep my laws" (36:27; 11:19–20). The Spirit would change the people's hearts from hardened stone to teachable flesh, so that they would be moved to love and obey

---

17. The emphatic first person underscores the reprehensibleness of the nation's behavior. The term for husband (*ba'al*) may be a play on words for Israel's idolatry.

him with all their hearts. Then the ancient ideal would become a reality: "You will be my people, and I will be your God" (Ezek. 36:28; 11:20; Jer. 31:33).

The second difference that would make God's will effective in people's lives is that, instead of the mediation of wayward kings and false prophets, the indwelling Spirit would ultimately enable believing Israelites from the least to the greatest to know the Lord. This democratization of presence accomplished the covenantal sense of knowledge, a mutual community of encouragement to walk in obedience to the Lord (cf. Jer. 5:4–5; 22:15–17). The implication of such spiritual knowledge was harmony among the people and a consequent justice in the land. Isaiah captures this in 54:13, "All your sons will be taught by the LORD, and great will be your children's peace."

Third, as the cornerstone of the internalized Word, God "will forgive their wickedness and will remember their sins no more" (Jer. 31:34). The foundational emphasis on forgiveness is unmistakable in Ezekiel as well, where the transforming presence of the Spirit is bracketed by "I will cleanse you from all your impurities" (Ezek. 36:25, 29, 33). The words for wickedness and sin mean "departure from" and "rebellion against" God's revealed standards. Together the terms depict aberration from covenant relationship with the nation's jealous Lord. God declared that he would save his people with a gracious pardon from these offenses. In Micah's words, "You will again have compassion on us; you will tread our sins underfoot and hurl all our iniquities into the depths of the sea" (Mic. 7:19). The causal clause (Jer. 31:34b) means that the forgiveness of sins was the necessary premise for knowing the Lord through the indwelling Spirit.

In summary, the new covenant emphatically promised forgiveness from sins and a relationship with and knowledge of God for believing Israelites regardless of their status in the nation. The Lord Almighty swore that he would never "reject all the descendants of Israel" (Jer. 31:36–37; cf. Rom. 11:1–5), a fact as secure as his creation. Thus, his gift of their transformed hearts made this his everlasting covenant. The darkness of the prophets' days would be dispelled by messianic light. He would establish a living temple and a new city. In God's Word, hope is inseparable from God's presence in the Messiah. Through him, God pledged: "I will be their God and they will be my people."

"The days are coming," declared the Lord, when his city would be rebuilt and endure forever (Jer. 31:38–40). The latter section of Isaiah, his "book of comfort," connects the future of Zion and creation. It is the destination of our trail, which leads to the Light of his eternal presence. E. J. Young states, "In particular Jerusalem, the focal point of the new creation and the kingdom of God, is to be created a rejoicing, and her people (those who truly belong to her) are created a joy."[18] God himself would be the light of the city as the advents of the Messiah brought healing and an abundance of living water (Isa. 58:8, 11), the dawning of hope for creation that would attract a Jewish audience at the Feast of Tabernacles (John 7:37–39) and, ultimately, the nations (Isa. 60:1–3). "The Spirit of the Sovereign LORD" would anoint the Messiah to proclaim both forgiveness and wrath under God (Isa. 61:1–2).[19] The glorious presence of the Lord will "shine out like the dawn," transforming the name of the city from "Deserted" and "Desolate" to "My delight is in her" ("Hephzibah") and "Married" ("Beulah") because "as a bridegroom rejoices over his bride, so will your God rejoice over you" (62:1–5). Therefore, this is what the Sovereign Lord says:

> "Behold, I will create new heavens and a new earth.
> The former things will not be remembered,
>   nor will they come to mind.
> But be glad and rejoice forever in what I will create,
>   for I will create Jerusalem to be a delight
>   and its people a joy.

18. Edward J. Young, *The Book of Isaiah*, 3 vols., New International Commentary on the Old Testament (Grand Rapids: Eerdmans, 1972), 3.514.

19. The Messiah himself quoted Isaiah 61:1–2a to relate his good news to God's hope-filled future.

I will rejoice over Jerusalem and take delight in my people;
the sound of weeping and crying will be heard in it no
more."

(Isa. 65:17–19)

His Presence in Godly Families

This chapter has synthesized a vast amount of material that moves from the darkness of Israel's past to the light of God's hope-filled future. The "jeremiads" against false worship and prophets are not the reading that we would choose for a leisure day at the beach. Sometimes, however, the things that we least like to think about are the things that we most need to ponder. If we are nourished on frothy pleasures, we will starve as the passage of time diminishes our lives. We began by describing the false worship that Jeremiah encountered "at the gate of the LORD's house" (Jer. 7:1). We noted that idolatry seems to be an irrelevant, old sin that is ignored by people who want to win at any cost. Ephesians 5:5 reminded us that idolatry in the apostolic church was greed or covetousness. The bleak picture of pre-exilic Israel transitioned, as the chapter developed, to the hope of the new covenant and the advent of the Messiah as the Cornerstone of a living temple in the Spirit.

We find Jeremiah's juxtaposition of the dangers of idolatry with the deliverance of the saving Messiah in John's magisterial first epistle. The connection adds to our understanding that ancient problems must continually be addressed with answers in Christ. The contrasting walks in darkness or light are evidenced in opposing lifestyles that are characterized by lawlessness versus obedience and hatred versus love, respectively (1 John 1–2). "Children of God" are to look forward to the Son's appearance, when "we shall be like him, for we shall see him as he is" (3:2). In the meantime, brotherly love sets "our hearts at rest in his presence" (3:19). Love of fellow believers finds its opposite in a prohibition against "loving the world" (2:15–17). Love is understood as a priority that changes one's behavior to conform to

149

the object of affection. Thus, one cannot love both God and the world. Believers' "fellowship . . . with the Father and with his Son" is opposed by "antichrists," who deny "the Father and the Son" (1:3; 2:22). "The Spirit of God" is distinguished from spirits of the world by the affirmation or denial of God's supreme presence in the incarnation (4:1–6). Finally, in one of the most abrupt conclusions of any biblical book, John commanded, "Dear children, keep yourselves from idols" (5:21).

Jeremiah and John speak directly to present-day idolatries. I have created a file folder of newspaper clippings and magazine articles on our culture's obsession with celebrities. In summary, numerous authors trace the culture's problems to consumerism, which has commoditized human life. People are things to be manipulated for selfish gain rather than personal beings who are to be valued under God. People are devouring goods with an insatiable appetite, hoping to find a satisfaction that can discard family and friends as unnecessary. Various authors agree that the expenditure of fabulous sums of money is a self-destructive divinization of the self. One quoted a media award winner who accepted her recognition with the words, "A lot of people come up here and thank Jesus for this award, but no one had less to do with this award than Jesus." As if that comment was not enough, she concluded, "This award is my god now." That is the very "spirit of the world" that Jeremiah and the apostles condemned.

A couple of verses in Jeremiah have come to mind repeatedly and have left an indelible impression on my memory. They further illustrate how the prophets can speak to us: the generations of Jeremiah can be paralleled with stages in a family's history. The home life we have experienced is a vital connection between what Jeremiah saw and what we experience in our world.

One instance where the family plays a negative role is in Jeremiah's temple sermon (7:18). The prophet was standing at the temple gate, watching the idolatries of the Judahites as they came to offer worship to the Lord. He did not see a nebulous mass of helpless victims who were being coerced by relentless forces.

Instead, he saw "the children gather wood, the fathers light the fire, and the women knead the dough and make cakes of bread for the Queen of Heaven." The queen was Ishtar, a prominent goddess in the Babylonian pantheon. We notice that Israel's idolatry was a family affair. The practices were so widespread that names were unimportant. Everyone was doing it, and if you wanted social acceptance, you had best join the parade. I suggest that the prophet knew a number of these families and had noted their careful organization and diligent training, so that they could magically change their country into an imperial power like Babylon. Perhaps Sabbath instruction included the ways that pagan rituals could be combined with godly observances. One doesn't learn complicated cultic rituals overnight! No doubt, there were generational secrets about which omens and incantations worked best according to circumstances and seasons. Risky behavior is like leaven, and when the few become like the nations, seemingly without consequences, then the majority stampedes to the options of other gods. We know that families were involved on a national scale and that the wrath of God had reached the boiling point.

An instance where family plays a positive role is mentioned in Jeremiah 29:3: "He entrusted the letter to Elasah son of Shaphan and to Gemariah son of Hilkiah." Shaphan and Hilkiah were part of a priestly circle that was instrumental in the reform by Josiah, the last godly king of the Davidic line before the exile. Hilkiah was an ancestor of Ezra and the high priest who found the Book of the Law in the temple. Shaphan was secretary of the royal court (2 Kings 22:3). These men delivered funds to trusted workers to repair the temple, but the king said: "They need not account for the money entrusted to them, because they are acting faithfully" (2 Kings 22:7). This righteous circle was saturated with integrity! Later, when the king heard the words of the Law, Shaphan and his son Ahikam were part of a commission that consulted with Huldah the prophetess (2 Kings 22:14–20). The prophetess, who may have been Jeremiah's relative, informed them of coming disaster on the people and of blessing on Josiah for his "responsive heart." Ahikam also saved Jeremiah's life during Jehoiakim's persecution (Jer. 26:24). Now, during the exile, the important letter was entrusted to another son of Shaphan, who would be accompanied by a son of Hilkiah.[20]

Life must have been lonely for these godly families. Most believers realize the difficulties of raising a godly family in a godless society. The parents must have worried about the boys in their childhood and adolescence: What was being said or done to them in their schools? Were the boys sufficiently mature to stand in the midst of temptations? On the other hand, the boys must have wondered why their parents were so strict: Why was I born into a godly heritage that made our home unlike other families? Why do our folks always seem to say no to things that our peers think are fun? Do we really have to have character, whatever that is, when it sometimes results in hazing from our friends? The boys and their parents must have wondered why their neighbors, who lived by different rules, prospered.

Hypothetical questions like these point to the timeless challenge of raising God-honoring families across generations. Perhaps its difficulty accounts for the "nameless majority" and the "memorialized minority." As I reflect on godly families, I gravitate toward time as the important formative influence in cross-generational godliness. Too many people, I would suggest, say that they love their children or parents, but their priorities lie elsewhere. In innumerable cases, what we do speaks louder than what we say. How often do we hear, "If you love me, why aren't you around when I need you?" Families need to share life together, in serious business and restful play, living through their deepest desires and prayers for one another. They need to know each other well, so that they can encourage one another's strengths and recognize the danger signals when a loved one's faith is tested to the breaking point. Fellowship in godly values, John suggests, is most effective when we appropriately demonstrate love for one another. This is based on the fact that we

20. Gemariah may have been a common name, so that Shaphan had another son with the same name (Jer. 36:10). From his room, Baruch read Jeremiah's scroll to the people.

have been mutually loved by God (1 John 4:11–12). Time among family and friends is an indispensable ingredient in fostering Shaphan-like integrity.

Israel's commission was to "bring my salvation to the ends of the earth" (Isa. 49:6). Often, this privilege rested on the shoulders of a few people with extraordinary dedication. Shaphan must have wondered about his lifelong commitment to godly ideals in times when wrongs seemed so overwhelmingly right. However, one cannot overemphasize the fact that godly people with ingrained integrity are the ones who can be trusted with important tasks in critical times. This kind of integrity comes from honoring God's Word on a daily basis. One must not forget the power that a family can have over a nation, even when its members stand in an oppressed minority. They are emissaries of hope from God, without whom we cannot live one second, as the aphorism at the beginning of the chapter reminds us. Our hope and prayers should be directed toward the membership of our families in such a distinguished legacy. A primary goal of churches ought to be nurturing families like the Shaphans and Hilkiahs, who honor the Word and send their Ahikams, Elasahs, and Gemariahs to bring God's light to the world in succeeding generations.

> O God, our help in ages past,
> Our hope for years to come,
> Our shelter from the stormy blast,
> And our eternal home!
> —Isaac Watts, 1719

153

6

The New Covenant
in the New Testament

*Nothing in Paul's estimate of the Redeemer is more
illuminating than the way in which he correlates Christ
and the Spirit. He was, indeed, almost bound to take
this step by the very nature of the experience through
which he had passed and of the new life into which he
had entered. . . . The gift which had been the privilege
and prerogative of the few would then be poured "upon
all flesh." This was the great hope which the Church saw
fulfilled at Pentecost.—James S. Stewart[1]*

*And surely I am with you always, to the very end of the
age.—Matthew 28:20*

THIS CHAPTER was forged in a hospital. I was living in over-
drive in the weeks before Christmas, attending to the numerous
chores that converge at that time of the year. A week before
Christmas, my right leg began to swell, so I consumed over-the-
counter remedies to maintain the frenetic pace. Finally, one of

1. James Stewart, *A Man in Christ: The Vital Elements of St. Paul's Religion* (New
York: Harper and Brothers, n.d.), 307–8.

my children noticed the problem and notified a heart specialist. I was admitted on an emergency basis with a DVT (deep veinous thrombosis) in my leg, which meant that I was suffering from a sizable blood clot and that my condition was almost catastrophic. Further tests revealed that pieces of the clot had migrated to my lung, resulting in another serious problem called pulmonary embolism, and this meant that I had suffered a "lung attack."

I stayed in the hospital for about a week as my doctors struggled to raise my anti-clotting ability. I responded enough to come home on Christmas day to be with my family. I cannot recall a finer day than this celebration of God's faithfulness in the birth of his Son and in the collection of children and grand-children who have joined Kathy and me over the years in our pilgrimage with the Lord!

A day later, I tried to get out of bed in the evening. In my weakened condition and without blood clotting ability, I pulled a muscle around my stomach and began to hemorrhage. I returned to the hospital with one of the most painful conditions that I had ever endured. I remember the question, "On a scale of one to ten, how do you rate your pain?" My unvoiced response was, "More than fifteen, so could you stop asking questions and do something about it!" I discovered that I was trapped between the rock of needing to dissolve blood clots and the hard place of needing to avoid the bleeding that accompanies anti-coagulant treatments. An additional week of hospitalization was required before I could continue recovery at home.

My illness will form the backdrop for this chapter, because it illustrates vividly our need for God's presence. The Spirit is present regardless of circumstances. However, extraordinary conditions are lenses that focus the most important truths in life. Here we will discuss the presence of the Spirit in the church in light of pivotal passages such as John 14–17, Hebrews 8–10, and 2 Corinthians 3. Along with indispensable doctrines such as the Trinity, the Word, and salvation, God's presence in his people lies at the heart of the New Testament. We can ill afford to neglect it.

How have we traveled to this point in his presence on our pilgrimage? In the last chapter, the section on "The Presence in Messianic Hope" brings us back to "Incarnation as Presence" in the first chapter, where God dwelt among us in the Son's incarnation. With the coming of the Messiah, the temple imagery in Isaiah 28:16 and related passages was linked to the messianic Cornerstone, who would become God's fulfilling sanctuary for his people in the new covenant. We have discussed how the vision of God's prophets was based on the prototype of Moses, who experienced the presence as Word, face, glory, and Name. The prophets' imagery looked back to the pattern of the tabernacle, which was a copy and shadow of an eternal dwelling to come.

As we return to John's gospel, we will structure our discussion around the promise of the new covenant in Jeremiah 31. Earlier, the covenant was described in terms of its divine author and Israelite recipients: "I will be their God, and they will be my people" (Jer. 31:33). This everlasting relationship would be accomplished by his forgiveness of their sins and the internalization of his presence in their lives (cf. Ezek. 36:27). Here we will examine:

- God: The Provider of the New Covenant
- Forgiveness: The Provision of the New Covenant
- Believers: The People of the New Covenant

First, understanding God as the "divine provider," we will unfold the internalization of the Trinitarian presence in John's gospel. I must emphasize that this is not a treatment of God's single, divine essence in three distinct persons, who are coequal and coeternal.[2] God is Trinity, but here we will describe, in human

---

2. The church's traditional position on the Trinity as stated in the creeds of Nicea and Chalcedon is assumed here as a doctrine in systematic theology. The subject of "presence" belongs in biblical theology and examines the Trinity from the viewpoint of the apostles, who were listening to the Savior in the upper room. What did they hear, and how did they receive what they heard? In this perspective, a small verse such as John 14:18 is filled with meaning: "I will not leave you as orphans; I will come to you." This chapter is a discussion of that meaning.

perspective, how God is with us as Father, Son, and Spirit, successively. John wrote with an emphasis on the theme of "the Father in the Son" (John 1–12), which is followed by "the Father and the Son in the Spirit" (John 14–17), resulting in a distinctive Trinitarian presence in believers. He will not abandon us "as orphans" but will be in us forever through the Holy Spirit. Jesus was leaving the earth to be with his Father in heaven, but the Trinity would continue to be with the disciples through the Spirit. Second, the provision of forgiveness will emphasize the accomplishments of Christ's perfect sacrifice as spelled out in Hebrews 8–10 in light of our preceding study of the Old Testament. Finally, we will discuss believers as recipients of new covenantal blessings with special reference to the olive tree in Romans 9–11. A correlation of these themes and passages leads to the conclusion that believers are the "living stones" of God's temple in the present. The divine intention is that our lives are to be "living epistles" that manifest his presence to all our "readers" (2 Cor. 3:1–3).

God: The Provider of the New Covenant

The Father in the Son

John 1–12. The apostle John presents the Son as the fulfilling revelation and representation of God the Father on earth (cf. Heb. 1:1–2). In our first chapter, this truth was presented as "the Word" who "was with God in the beginning" (John 1:1), who "became flesh and made his dwelling among us" (1:14), and "who is at the Father's side" and "has made him known" (1:18; 17:25–26). The Son declared, "Before Abraham was born, I am!" (8:58), which his audience understood as a blasphemous claim of deity. The enfleshed Son declared, "I and the Father are one" (10:30), a oneness of being and work in which the Son came "in" his "Father's name" (5:43; cf. 6:41–44). In John 3:16–17, the Father "so loved the world that he gave his one and only Son, that whoever believes in him shall not perish but

158

have eternal life" (cf. 8:51–52). The Father sent the Son "from above" to speak the words of God, having "placed everything in his hands" (3:31–36; 6:57; 8:42). This authority applies to judgment as well as the gift of life (5:19–30; 17:2–3). The Father and Son say and do the same things and receive worship equally (3:2; 5:23). The "tandem" between the Father and the Son is an eternally loving relationship with mutual affirmation that is reflected in constant prayer (11:41). In the Upper Room Discourse, Philip requested, "Lord, show us the Father and that will be enough for us" (14:8). In response, Jesus summarized his Trinitarian relationship with his Father in verses 9–11 as follows:

> Anyone who has seen me has seen the Father. How can you say, "Show us the Father?" Don't you believe that I am in the Father, and that the Father is in me? The words I say to you are not just my own. Rather it is the Father, living in me, who is doing his work. Believe me when I say that I am in the Father and the Father is in me; or at least believe on the evidence of the miracles themselves.

Thus, John initiated his distinctive doctrine of the tandem relationship of the Trinity's presence on earth in terms of the Father and the Son.[3]

Jesus' summary was shared in proximity with the completion of his saving work. "My children," he declared, "I will be with you only a little longer" (John 13:33). Then he prayed, "Father, the time has come. Glorify your Son, that your Son may glorify you" (17:1; cf. 13:31–32). "I have brought you glory on earth by completing the work you gave me to do. . . . Glorify me in your presence with the glory I had with you before the world began" (17:4–5).

3. By "tandem," I mean that John presents Trinitarian presence in terms of a succession of presences on earth, one after another. The key to his presentation is the incarnation, in which Christ brought the presence of the Father near. When Christ ascended to the right hand of the Father, he remained incarnate, so he is present now through the Holy Spirit.

Jesus' words have two implications for the issue of Trinitarian presence on earth. First, his tandem identification indicated that the Father was the monotheistic emphasis of the Old Testament. Our Trinitarian God was present with Israel, but the emphasis was on the one and only, living God, unseen except in the various forms of his presence. When the Son of God came as the Son of Man, the emphasis of God's presence on earth changed to the Second Person of the Godhead, "the Lamb of God, who takes away the sin of the world!" (John 1:29). We can say that the Son was the proxy (or representative) presence of the Father, accomplishing God's redemptive work for creation.

John 7:37–39. Within John 1–12, a crucial passage introduces the Holy Spirit as the abiding presence of the Trinity. The Messiah's accomplishment of his saving mission introduced the second implication, which was a possible departure of God's presence from the earth. This was a profound crisis in the lives of Jesus' disciples. If the Son was to be glorified by crucifixion, then how could God continue to be present with his people on earth? Jesus previewed the looming crisis with a new covenantal promise at the Feast of Tabernacles in John 7:37–39. On "the last and greatest day of the Feast," Jesus proclaimed loudly, "If anyone is thirsty, let him come to me and drink. Whoever believes in me, as the Scripture has said, streams of living water will flow from within him."[4] "By this," John explained, "he meant the Spirit, whom those who believed in him were later to receive" (7:39). Surprisingly, he added, "Up to that time the Spirit had not been given, since Jesus had not yet been glorified."

The last of the three Jewish pilgrimages, Tabernacles was a joyous harvest festival around early October. Participants camped in homemade shelters for a week (cf. Lev. 23:33–43; Deut. 16:13–

---

4. Edwin Freed, *Old Testament Quotations in the Gospel of John* (Leiden: E. J. Brill, 1965), 23, states, "This quotation is the most difficult one in Jn. . . . The evidence at present is insufficient to determine the exact O. T. source or sources and text or texts used." Freed's point, made years ago, is still valid.

17; Neh. 8:13–18). At dawn, priests would fill a golden pitcher with water from the pool of Siloam and parade to the temple "with joy . . . from the wells of salvation" (Isa. 12:3). Choirs would sing Hallel psalms (Pss. 113–118) amid cries of "Give thanks to the Lord." The males would shake fronds that signified a completed harvest. Every evening, the pilgrims would celebrate in the light of enormous candelabra in the temple's court of the women. The ceremonies recalled the provision of God when the people lived in booths after the exodus. They also anticipated covenantal fellowship in the future, when "the river of the water of life" will flow from the throne of the Father and the Lamb (Rev. 22:1; Ezek. 47:1–12). A chosen priest would pour offerings to God and lift his hand to signify that he had discharged his duty.

Though not explicitly stated, we can infer that Jesus' proclamation was at the moment of the upraised hand on the seventh day to signify the completion of the ceremony.[5] Characteristically, John places Jesus at the center of memory and hope. Jesus synthesized the occasion by focusing the promises of the new covenant on himself. "If anyone is thirsty, let him come to me and drink," and I paraphrase, "whoever believes will overflow with an abundance of living water" (John 7:37–38). The effect would have been stunning, since the multitude would have understood that their past salvation as a nation, present worship, and future hope were being celebrated in Jesus as Messiah (cf. 7:40–46). "The Christian life is eating and drinking Christ, or it is nothing at all," Keddie affirms.[6] It is the "water" that brings the joy of relationship in the presence of God.

We should not be surprised that John 7 resonates with the opposition of Jewish authorities to Christ. Initially hesitant about going to Judea, Jesus began to teach halfway through the feast, and provoked a heated discussion about his identity. His teaching

5. Raymond Brown, *The Gospel according to John I–XII*, 2 vols., The Anchor Bible (Garden City, NY: Doubleday, 1966), 1.320, 327. Also, George R. Beasley-Murray, *John*, 2d ed., Word Biblical Commentary, vol. 36 (Nashville: Nelson Reference and Electronic, 1999), 113–17.
6. Gordon Keddie, *A Study Commentary on John*, 2 vols., Evangelical Press Study Commentaries (Auburn, MA: Evangelical Press, 2001), 1.303.

angered the crowd, who questioned his credentials. His rejoinder was that his teaching was "from him who sent me" (7:16–18, 28–29, 33).

The Father and the Son in the Spirit

Jesus' proclamation at Tabernacles particularly connected the Scriptures and the Spirit with the "living water." He was summarizing a number of Old Testament passages about Tabernacles and the new covenant. The issue here is the earthly presence of God with his people after the Son's return to the presence of the Father. God's presence, in turn, involves the inauguration of the new covenant in the saving work of the Messiah and in Pentecost (or, the indwelling presence of the Spirit in all believers from the least to the greatest): "John wants it clearly understood that the living water is a metaphorical bridge between the water poured out at the Feast of Tabernacles and the work of the Holy Spirit in the post-Pentecostal church."[7]

John 14–17. Jesus' announcement of his departure initiated anxiety and fear among his disciples (John 14:1, 27). He understood their sense of abandonment and assured them, "I will not leave you as orphans; I will come to you" (14:18). In the upper room he described his continuing presence with them through the Spirit in terms that precisely paralleled his own representing the Father. The connecting link is the title *Paraclete*, the Spirit being "another [*allos*] Paraclete" like Jesus (14:16).[8] Jesus is "the Truth," and the Spirit is "the Spirit of Truth" (14:6, 17). Jesus has been with the disciples, but he will be "in" them through the Spirit (14:17). In the presence of the Spirit, the disciples will realize "that I am in my Father, and you are in me, and I am in you" (14:20; cf. 17:23–26). Andreas Köstenberger views this important verse as an

7. Ibid., 306.

8. Leon Morris, *Commentary on the Gospel of John*, New International Commentary on the New Testament (Grand Rapids: Eerdmans, 1971), 648, n. 42: "*Allon* is said to mean 'another of the same kind,' whereas *heteron* would mean 'another of a different kind'. . . . The Spirit is thus said to be a Comforter like Christ."

outgrowth of the covenantal phrase "I will be their God, and they will be my people" (Jer. 31:33).[9] The Spirit will be sent from the Father and the Son to guide the disciples "into all truth" (16:12–15) and to convict the hostile world around them (15:18–16:11). Brown cautions that the title *Paraclete* should not be translated. Instead, it should be understood as the enabling presence of God in the multifaceted demands of Christian living:

> By way of summary we find that no one translation of *parakletos* captures the complexity of the functions, forensic and otherwise, that this figure has. The Paraclete is a *witness* in defense of Jesus and a *spokesman* for him in the context of his trial by his enemies; the Paraclete is a *consoler* of the disciples for he takes Jesus' place among them; the Paraclete is a teacher and guide of the disciples and thus their *helper*. . . . We would probably be wise also in modern times to settle for "Paraclete," a near-transliteration that preserves the uniqueness of the title and does not emphasize one of the functions to the detriment of the others.[10]

Thus, he correctly concludes, "It is our contention that John presents the Paraclete as the Holy Spirit in a special role, namely, as the personal presence of Jesus in the Christian while Jesus is with the Father."[11] The Spirit will comfort their fears and anxiety: "Peace I leave with you; my peace I give you. I do not give to you as the world gives. Do not let your hearts be troubled and do not be afraid" (14:27).

New Testament Validation. The Trinitarian presence, as presented in the upper room, is evident throughout the New Testament. In Romans 8:9–11 the indwelling Holy Spirit is identified

9. Andreas Köstenberger, *Encountering John: The Gospel in Historical, Literary, and Theological Perspective* (Grand Rapids: Baker, 1999), 155. The author is insightful as well in his use of "substitute presence" in the sense that "the Spirit's presence with the disciples will replace Jesus' presence with them on earth" (157). Also, D. A. Carson, *The Farewell Discourse and Final Prayer of Jesus: An Exposition of John 14–17* (Grand Rapids: Baker, 1980), 53.

10. Brown, *Gospel according to John*, 2.1137.

11. Ibid., 1139.

as "the Spirit of Christ" and "the Spirit of him who raised Jesus from the dead." "When the time had fully come," Paul wrote in Galatians 4:4–6, "God sent his Son . . . to redeem those under the Law, that we might receive the full rights of sons. Because you are sons, God sent the Spirit of his Son into our hearts, the Spirit who calls out 'Abba, Father'" (cf. 1 Cor. 2:12; Phil. 1:19).

The implication of the presence of the Spirit of Truth is that John's comfort is an abiding relationship with God rather than abstract notions of "spirit and truth."[12] With this in mind, Jesus' explanation of worship apart from Samaria and Jerusalem takes on a new emphasis (John 4:21–24). The issue is not a proper place but rather personal worship of the "Truth" in the "Spirit." The Samaritan woman seemed to understand, because she responded, "I know that Messiah is coming." She did not inquire about a new place, but rather a new relationship with God. Jesus then declared, "I who speak to you am he" (4:25–26). Many in her town believed and worshiped the Messiah, whom they recognized as "the Savior of the world" (4:39–42).

This is the correlation of "Christ and the Spirit," which Stewart alluded to in the introductory quotation. This is the "era of the Spirit," when the prerogative of the few was poured out "upon all flesh." The Christ-Spirit tandem should be understood first as an issue of presence before it is explained as revelation of comforting truths. As Jesus promised, "I will come back and take you to be with me that you also may be where I am" (14:3). Admittedly, the Spirit "will guide" us "into all truth" under the Father and the Son (16:13). But that aspect of his abiding work is secondary to more foundational concerns for the apostles and us.

The Spirit in Us

John 14 is a critically important part of God's Word, because it reflects the deepest needs of human existence. Its underlying

12. Morris, *John*, 700, n. 30: "The words do not mean that the church will be led to a full knowledge of the truth on all manner of subjects. What is meant is the specific truth about the Person of Jesus and the significance of what he said and did. Perhaps we could say that the words must be interpreted in the light of 14:6." I agree with Morris's emphasis.

theme is a cluster of concepts whose matrix is fear (or anxiety). From the admission of Adam to the present, we are fearful creatures, often unconsciously so: "I was afraid because I was naked; so I hid" (Gen. 3:10). No one is exempt. People have always been fearful in innumerable ways about what they know as well as what could happen should life take a wrong turn. Anxiety characterizes everyone, because its ultimate cause is death. Sometimes we try to dodge the monster by saying, "I am not as afraid of dying as I am about the process of death—how I might join the departed." This is only a cover, because we are too familiar with violence and pain, and we all want to "fall asleep" without them.

The disciples were filled with anxiety in the upper room. They had experienced social ostracism with their Master. They were shocked by Jesus' revelation of an unknown traitor in their midst and stared at one another, "at a loss to know which of them he meant" (John 13:22). When their Master revealed his imminent departure from the world, Peter blurted out, "I will lay down my life for you" (13:37). Why? Because he and the others did not want to be alone, when life's fragility and the world's hostility were so evident (15:18). The intensity of their feelings was seen later in Peter's vehement denial that he was a follower of the Way, even as his Savior was on trial and the crackling fire offered little warmth.

We may not be apostles, but we live with the same emotions, even if our circumstances are less threatening. Besides death and dying, we fear failure, loss of things that we worked hard to gain, rejection, various catastrophes, unknown dangers, loss of control, and a multitude of daily phobias. Sharon Begley wrote recently about fear as a political motivator: "Half a century of research has shown that fear is one of the most politically powerful emotions a candidate can tap, especially when the fears have a basis in reality."[13] Beyond politics, people are created with basic instincts in which even imaginary fears such as indestructible enemies can cause unparalleled rushes of emotional energy.

13. Sharon Begley, "The Roots of Fear," *Newsweek* (December 24, 2007), 37.

Humanity has responded to its pervasive fears with a passionate pursuit of "the good life." We hear, "You only go around once in life, so grab all the gusto you can." As with fear, there are no exceptions. Everyone pursues countless pleasures, legitimate and otherwise. No one can point fingers—because all of us do it—from Las Vegas casinos to the monasteries. In today's world, these pleasures usually relate to the satisfaction of our physical senses and our ability to enjoy leisure and luxuries. Jesus acknowledged that pursuits of pleasure provide a limited measure of satisfaction: "I do not give to you as the world gives" (John 14:27).

However, I have never read about any connection between hospitals and "the good life." Their food, accommodations, and locations are not promoted with star ratings, and we do not hear that anyone had a wonderful vacation in a five-star hospital. Yet who would deny the necessity of health care centers and their goodness in meeting human needs? We need more than the good life, and, for our purposes, Jesus identified this as "the godly life" in terms of our awareness of God's presence in our anxious moments. "Do not let your hearts be troubled and do not be afraid," he emphasized (14:27; cf. 14:1).

I have discovered through years of ministry that intangibles such as faith, hope, and love are as important as physical pains and pleasures. The godly life may be the good one, but the connections are more subtle than religious marketing would lead us to believe. I am aware that John 14 offers relational answers. Fearful people want the certainty of right questions with instantaneous answers. Let's face it, there are some answers like that, but most of life is saturated by less-than-clear solutions to our concerns.

When admitted to the hospital, I wanted to know "why me, why this, why now?" After another week at home, I was admitted for a third time to the hospital, this time to treat a pervasive clotting condition that extended to my midsection. I spent more than a week in intensive care and had several operations to try to clear my veins. People told me that they had prayed continually for me. How could I look at this serious episode as an answer to the prayers of my family and friends? On the other hand, would precise answers have helped my physical problems? Outwardly, I was thankful for the precision of my doctors. But they could not answer the questions either, even though they could skillfully treat the disease.

What I really needed was peace, which is the biblical answer for the fears that easily beset us. I needed a sense of well-being in spite of my proximity to the face of death.[14] People experience inner turmoil in crisis situations. In the upper room, Jesus offered a release from anxieties when life spins out of control, "when sorrows like sea billows roll." I remember pleading with the Lord for his peace-giving presence out of my suffering. In answer he blessed me with a wellness in my soul in spite of the pain; it was a prize for "practicing the presence of God." "Peace I leave with you; my peace I give you" (John 14:27). What did the peace of the Spirit feel like? How can I arrange to have this peace when I need it? I cannot tell you, because I experienced it as his gracious gift. I thought almost constantly of Paul's stunning promise in Philippians 4:5–7: "The Lord is near. Do not be anxious about anything, but in everything, by prayer and petition, with thanksgiving, present your requests to God. And the peace of God, which transcends all understanding, will guard your hearts and your minds in Christ Jesus." I remembered Horatio Spafford as well, when he penned one of the most beloved affirmations of this promise as he viewed the place where four of his daughters had drowned:

When peace, like a river attendeth my way,
When sorrows like sea billows roll—
Whatever my lot, Thou hast taught me to say,
It is well, it is well with my soul.

14. Catherine Marshall expressed this need when she was diagnosed with tuberculosis (or histoplasmosis). She poured out her heart to the Lord: "I'm desperately weary of the struggle of trying to persuade you to give me what I want. . . . Nevertheless, a strange, deep peace settled into my heart." *The Best of Catherine Marshall*, ed. Leonard LeSourd (Grand Rapids: Baker, 1993), 60–61.

With Spafford I discovered in the worst of times that I was not alone. I could rest in contentment, knowing and experiencing the Paraclete's presence within me. You don't have to be in trying circumstances to experience this blessing, but a little darkness makes the light shine brighter. In the language of a contemporary advertisement, we can say, "Priceless!"

Forgiveness: The Provision of the New Covenant

The New Covenant and the Crucifixion

At the end of John's gospel, the crisis was Jesus' impending crucifixion. The apostles were troubled by the death and departure of their Savior, for they had followed him to gain significance in his kingdom. Their difficulty was in the apparent contradiction between eternal life and sacrificial death, but salvation is only possible through the forgiveness of sins. The new covenant was given in Jeremiah 31 with the Lord's assurance of forgiveness. We can recall the fivefold "I will" in Jeremiah 31:39–41 and "declares the LORD" as in Jeremiah 31:34: "For I will forgive their wickedness and will remember their sins no more." This promise was inextricably connected to the glorification of the Son of God, whose death on the cross accomplished his atonement for sin (cf. Heb. 12:2).

This book has been developing to this climactic point. As we review its contents, Christ appears on every page and in every sentence. We may not have seen these points earlier, but now they show that he is the summary of "presences" in God's Word. He is the Center of Biblical Journeys. He is

- the precise image of God (Gen. 1:26–27; 2 Cor. 4:4; Col. 1:15)
- the offspring of the woman (Gen. 3:15)
- the living Word of God, Creator of the earth (John 1:1)
- the supreme revelation of God (Heb. 1:1–2)
- the perfect example of obedience (Heb. 5:7–8)
- the model pilgrim (Phil. 2:5–11), whose mission was the priority of his presence (John 13:1; 17:1; Matt. 28:19–20)

- the Light on the path of life (John 8:12; 12:35)
- the Mediator between God and man (John 1:18; 1 Tim. 2:5)
- the perfect example of prayer (John 17)
- the I AM (John 8:58)
- the Glory as the One and Only (John 1:14; 2 Pet. 1:16–17)
- the Lamb of God (John 1:29, 35)
- the eternal High Priest (Heb. 8)
- the Holy One of God (John 6:69)
- the fulfillment of the Law (Matt. 5:17–18)
- the living Stone of the living temple (1 Peter 2:4–8)
- the Messiah of God's promises (John 1:45; Luke 24:27; Rev. 19:10)
- the Security of his people (John 10:28)
- God with us (Matt. 1:23), the face and dwelling of God in our midst (John 1:14)
- the way to the Father (John 14:6)

Our present concern is Jesus' role as "the author and perfecter of our faith" (Heb. 12:2), as the mediator of the new covenant (Heb. 12:24). We are at the center of the Center, where all Christian paths intersect. We are at the Easter time of his crucifixion and resurrection.

The Lord's Supper is the familial celebration of thankful believers for their forgiveness through Christ's atonement. The Lord instituted the feast on Passover, the celebration of Israel's salvation from Egypt. It represented joyful worship in the fellowship of the Savior, looking forward with a living hope to the time when the Messiah will "drink it anew with you in my Father's kingdom" (Matt. 26:26–29; Mark 14:22–25; Luke 22:15–20). The scene was the upper room, a special place of presence before Christ's body was broken and "my blood of the covenant [was] poured out for many for the forgiveness of sins."

Paul received an authoritative mandate from the Lord that the Supper was a love feast "in remembrance" of his sacrificial death in our place (1 Cor. 11:17–26). He sternly rebuked the Corinthian indulgences and excesses in light of the fact that the Messiah's broken body and the new covenant in his blood were for us. We share the celebration with ethical awareness of Christlike living in the church until he comes.

The New Covenant in Hebrews 8–10

Hebrews 8–10 develops new covenantal forgiveness in rich heavenly detail. A thesis statement of the sermonic letter is in 8:1–5, in which the author magnified Christianity's unique high priest who sovereignly serves "at the right hand of the throne of the Majesty in heaven." "The point of what we are saying is this . . ."(8:1).[15] The Messiah as high priest was presented as fulfilling the types, patterns, and shadows of the Old Testament. Thus, his humanity was emphasized by names and titles such as "Jesus" (10:19), or "Christ" (9:11, 14), or their combination (10:10), whereas in 1:3 "Son" of God focused on his deity.

The argument of Hebrews presented the Messiah as better than the Old Testament patriarchs and institutions. His sacrifice for sin was complete and perfect as uniquely God and man. It was the decisive pivot between the old and the new arrangements for forgiveness. This perfect sacrifice was expressed as a contrast between earthly and heavenly sanctuaries. Christ serves in "the true tabernacle set up by the Lord, not by man" (8:2). In the Old Testament, as we have seen, Levitical priests "serve at a sanctuary that is a copy and shadow of what is in heaven" (8:5), a fact that is accompanied by a quotation of Exodus 25:40 (in 8:5). The superiority is further expressed as the fulfillment of the "better promises" of the new covenant.

Interestingly, the Old Testament sanctuary in Hebrews is the tabernacle rather than the temple. The author has two reasons for preferring the tent. First, the "pattern" for Christ's heavenly

---

15. George Guthrie, *Hebrews: The NIV Application Commentary* (Grand Rapids: Zondervan, 1998), 278, brackets "the great central section" as 4:14–16 through 10:19–25. "Hebrews 8:1–2 stands at the mid-point of this whole discussion."

service was revealed at Sinai, and Solomon's temple was a mere copy. Even beyond that is the author's view that earthly life is a pilgrimage to the heavenly goal. Christ is the believer's file leader and supreme example in the march to the Holy of Holies that has been prepared by God for his people (12:2). Abraham looked forward to the city "whose architect and builder is God" (11:10), in company with believers who "admitted that they were aliens and strangers on earth. . . . longing for a better country—a heavenly one" (11:13–16). In faith they came "to Mount Zion, to the heavenly Jerusalem, the city of the living God" (12:22–24). And Jesus suffered "outside the city gate" as an example for us, who are "looking for the city that is to come" (13:11–14). Thus, believers are on a pilgrimage in the wilderness on the way to the heavenly city, where we will live forever in the Holy of Holies of God's Trinitarian presence.

The sacrifice of Christ, involving his own blood as the unique Mediator, is developed in Hebrews 8:8–12 in a complete quotation of new covenantal promises from Jeremiah 31, the longest quotation of the Old Testament in the New Testament. It summarizes the fulfillment of "better promises" in Christ as the personal goal toward which the Mosaic sacrifices pointed. The quotation is followed by a summarizing statement that in Christ the tutorial role of the law was completed (cf. Gal. 3:15–25). That is, the law defined God's righteousness, which Christ fulfilled.

The foundation for covenantal relationship is the forgiveness of sins, so Hebrews 9 develops the theme of the Messiah as God's final sacrifice (vv. 1–14). The author reviews "the regulations for worship and also an earthly sanctuary" in 9:1–10, but not "in detail now." The tabernacle was designed to focus beyond the holy place and the curtain to the Most Holy Place of God's presence, a space that contained the golden altar and the ark, which was crowned by the cherubim of the Glory.

The Old Testament regulations for worship specified regular ministries by priests in the holy place (Heb. 9:6–10). Only on the Day of Atonement (cf. Lev. 16) could the high priest enter the Holy of Holies alone—never without blood—to cover his own sins and the people's sins "committed in ignorance" (Heb. 9:7). "The life of a creature is in the blood" (Lev. 17:10–14), so sacrifices portrayed the deadly consequences of sin as life was drained from the victim. "The blood of the covenant" ritually (or, outwardly) cleansed the worshiper in a confessional sense that acknowledged the need for forgiveness to maintain a holy relationship with the Giver of promises for an eternal inheritance (Heb. 9:15–22; 13:12). In Paul's words, "For no matter how many promises God has made, they are 'Yes' in Christ" (2 Cor. 1:20; cf. Gal. 3:16). The Holy Spirit used the illustration of the tabernacle, according to the author of Hebrews, to demonstrate that "the way into the Most Holy Place had not been disclosed" by the "food, and drink and various ceremonial washings" of the old order (Heb. 9:8–10).[16] The demonstration centered in the need of the high priest to offer repeated sacrifices for sin (9:25).

Christ, on the other hand, entered the holiest place by his own blood, "through the eternal Spirit," a perfect sacrifice that "cleanses our consciences from acts that lead to death, so that we may serve the living God" (9:14).[17] Hebrews emphasizes that God has satisfied himself with the reconciliation of his people (cf. 2 Cor. 5:11–21). In other words, God has lovingly freed believers from the guilt and fearful consequences of sin. In his presence we are free to serve him boldly until he returns (Heb. 10:1–4). Christ, accordingly, is better than Moses as "the mediator of a new covenant" (9:15), who brought the old shadows to the reality of "heaven itself. . . . at the end of the ages . . . by the sacrifice of himself" (9:23–27). He was sacrificed "once to take away the sins of many people," and he will return "to bring salvation to those who are waiting for him" (9:28).

16. We can infer that this was the meaning of Jesus as "the Way, the Truth, and the Life" in John 14:6. A part of the sufficiency of the new covenant is the transition from the old institutions to the forgiving presence of God himself (Ezek. 36:26–27), an eternal relationship with Christ beyond mere service for him.

17. The law is "holy, and the commandment is holy, righteous and good" (Rom. 7:12). However, as a clear indicator of sin, it reinforces our guilt, alienation from God, and need for a Savior.

According to Hebrews, the shadows of the good things in Christ were foreseen at the first advent, when Christ quoted Psalm 40:6–8 to the Father as a mission statement:

> Sacrifice and offering you did not desire, but a body you prepared for me; with burnt offerings and sin offerings you were not pleased. Then I said, "Here I am—it is written about me in the scroll—I have come to do your will, O God." (Heb. 10:5–7)

The psalm was David's praise (or, "new song") for God's deliverance from trouble. In turn, David pledged lifelong service to his Deliverer ("my ears you have pierced," in Ps. 40:6, as a sign of dedication by a servant). Perhaps the psalm was part of a celebration at his enthronement, since he desired from his heart to fulfill his covenantal office (Ps. 40:8).

The author of Hebrews applies three aspects of Psalm 40 to Christ. First, he notes the incompleteness of Old Testament sacrifices as practiced apart from the intent of the law. Second, he notes Christ's attitude of obedience to the Father's will, with his God-given body as his offering (cf. Heb. 8:3). His incarnate, final sacrifice perfectly satisfied the forward-pointing shadow of the law to the extent that "there is no longer any sacrifice for sin" (10:18). Third, in accomplishing the will of God, Christ's followers "have been made holy [that is, fully and finally forgiven] through the sacrifice of the body of Jesus Christ once for all" (10:10). Several verses later, Christ's broken body is paralleled with the tearing of the curtain "from top to bottom" (10:20; see Mark 15:38), an act of God that opened his presence to all of his people, "from the least of them to the greatest" (Jer. 31:34).

The Lord's victory over sin was followed by his enthronement at the right hand of God as Priest-King in the order of Melchizedek (Heb. 7:11–22): "After he had provided purification for sins, he sat down at the right hand of the Majesty in heaven" (1:3). The finality of his sacrifice is underscored by his sovereign position in the heavenly sanctuary (8:1). Now he awaits the subjection of all his enemies, notably death as the antithesis of life, when the eternal inheritance that God promised in the new covenant will come to pass (10:12–18).

God's Forgiveness and Us

Therefore, the author concludes in Hebrews 10:19–20, we can confidently "enter the Most Holy Place by the blood of Jesus, by a new and living way" based on his high-priestly office and sacrifice. This is an invitation to believers to mutually enjoy the presence of God "through the curtain" of Christ's "torn flesh."[18] Elizabeth Achtemaier captures the drama of the Savior's accomplishment:

> What is needed is someone to come and open the [prison] door! What is needed is a Savior who will free people from their captivity to sin. And that is what God promises his erring people in this new covenant—freedom from their imprisonment, freedom from their slavery to sin, and power given them to do the right and to live new lives of faithfulness to their Lord.[19]

The accomplishment of Jesus' obedience on the cross (10:5–10) is accompanied by a threefold exhortation in 10:22–25 that corresponds to the cardinal virtues of Christianity; namely, faith, hope, and love. Let us look at these in turn.

First, "let us draw near to [or, approach] God with a sincere heart in full assurance of faith" (Heb. 10:22). We can follow Jesus into God's presence, because we have trusted in his perfect offering for the forgiveness of our sins. The author's clear intent is to emphasize the full and free access that Christians have in contrast with restrictions in the structure and regulations of the tabernacle. Thus, we approach God to receive comfort and strength for our pilgrimage through the world. Harold Attridge distinctively con-

---

18. Donald Hagner, *Encountering the Book of Hebrews: An Exposition* (Grand Rapids: Baker, 2002), 135, interprets the parallel between curtain and flesh as "a deliberate allusion to the tearing of the curtain before the Holy of Holies at the time of the death of Jesus, symbolizing the end of the old regime and the beginning of the new."

19. Elizabeth Achtemeier, *Jeremiah*, Knox Preaching Guides (Atlanta: John Knox, 1987), 92.

nects Christ's obedience in his opening of the way to God with his example for our drawing near to God by faith.[20] How do we draw near? We follow the path of love to the Lord who has loved us, and the presence of God will be reflected in our mutual love as shown in the third exhortation below.

The motif of a guilty conscience stands in contrast with the assurance of believers in spite of trials that they endure in this world. They are sinful, and they tend to "shrink back" from accountability in shame, fear, and often conflict (10:39). An example is James 4:1–10, where "fights and quarrels" had broken out among people whose "friendship with the world" reflected their "hatred toward God." James encouraged them to "wash your hands . . . and purify your hearts." They should "come near to God," who, in turn, "will come near" to them." So, Hebrews counsels us to "draw near to God . . . having our hearts sprinkled to cleanse us from a guilty conscience and having our bodies washed with pure water"(10:22).[21] Like John Bunyan's Christian, we come to the cross by faith, where our burden of guilt is removed from our backs and rolled into the Lord's tomb.

A positive example of approaching God in faith is found in Acts 4:23–31.[22] Peter and John were arrested in Jerusalem for proclaiming Jesus' crucifixion and resurrection in the wake of a miraculous healing. The authorities threatened and then released them because of a groundswell of support for their ministry. The apostles retreated to a gathering of believers to draw near to God in prayer: "Now, Lord, consider their threats and enable your ser-

20. Harold Attridge, *The Epistle to the Hebrews*, Hermeneia Commentaries (Philadelphia: Fortress Press, 1989), 285–87.

21. George Guthrie, *Hebrews*, 348, cautions that "commentators have rushed too quickly to reading baptismal imagery in the references to 'sprinkling' and the washing of our bodies 'with pure water.' The author here gives no indication that he is doing other than continuing to draw on important images found in the old covenant system. Such sprinkling and washing are pictures the author uses to point to the greater and more perfect cleansing from sins found in the sacrifice of Christ."

22. William Lane, *Hebrews 9–13*, Word Biblical Commentary, vol. 47B (Dallas: Word, 1991), 286, makes an important point for our purposes: "The use of this terminology elsewhere in Hebrews (7:25; 11:6; 12:18, 22) indicates that earnest prayer is a significant expression of the relationship between God and his people promised in the new covenant (8:10–12; 10:16; cf. Jer. 31:33; Ezek. 36:26–27)."

vants to speak your word with great boldness" (4:29). After their experience of God's presence in prayer, "they were all filled with the Holy Spirit and spoke the word of God boldly" (4:31). Thus, forgiven believers can have assurance of God's presence, even in grave difficulties. The assurance brings a peace that "we are more than conquerors through him who loved us" (Rom. 8:37).

Second, "let us hold unswervingly to the hope we profess" (Heb. 10:23). The exhortation flows from Jeremiah 29:11, which promised the unchanging plans of God "to give you hope and a future." The language reminds us of the initial part of the central section of Hebrews, where we are to "hold on to our courage and the hope of which we boast" (3:6). In 3:14 we are to "hold firmly till the end the confidence we had at first." In 4:14 we are to "hold firmly to the faith we profess." In 6:18–19 we are "to take hold of the hope offered to us" that we "may be greatly encouraged. We have this hope as an anchor for the soul, firm and secure." In Hebrews, faith and hope are conjoined, because they rest in the character and accomplishments of God. Thus, the reason for hope's encouragement is that "he who promised is faithful" (10:23).

Again, the presence of God through the Son is an issue. The indwelling of the Spirit is a pledge of our Christ-centered presence in the future. I think of the assurance of John in 1 John 3:2–3: "we know that when he appears, we shall be like him, for we shall see him as he is. Everyone who has this hope in him purifies himself, just as he is pure."

Third, "let us not give up meeting together, as some are in the habit of doing, but let us encourage one another" (Heb. 10:25). "These three remain: faith, hope, and love," Paul wrote. "But the greatest of these is love" (1 Cor. 13:13). Christian beliefs can be skeletons, if they are not enfleshed in the supportive fellowship of believers who share a common faith and hope in Christ. John has a similar emphasis in the familial language of his oft-repeated "my little children," a concept that was based on the mutual indwelling of the Trinity's presence in the Spirit.

We tend to think of peer group pressure as a negative drag on our youth. However, we should appreciate its power, when used positively, to "spur one another on toward love and good deeds" (Heb. 10:24). The term for "spur" means that we should notice the contributions of our fellow believers and "provoke" (or motivate) them concerning their value to the church. We hunger for appreciation of our contributions to the congregation. When we are criticized for what we try to do well, we remember almost every negative comment about our work. On the other hand, a word of appreciation brings refreshment and a determination to do more for the Lord and his people.

Encouragement is so important that we are told to "rivet our attention" on it. ("Consider" [*katanoeo*] fails to express the emphasis of the exhortation.) Hebrews 3:13 tells us that this should be practiced daily. In 10:32–33 we are informed that, in the past, these believers had suffered well and supported their brothers and sisters in persecution. For lack of encouragement, they had fallen away from their ministry to one another. Forgiven believers should not dwell on the shortcomings of their fellow pilgrims. Nor, even when circumstances are less than ideal, should we miss out on the fellowship that we desperately need.

The power of Christian fellowship was illustrated for me during a trip to California with my family. We visited the giant redwood forests, and I wondered what kept the huge trees from toppling over, especially when storms swept through the forest. I directed the question to a park ranger: What keeps the trees stable, so that they can grow for hundreds of years? Her answer was that the trees surprisingly have relatively shallow root systems, but they interlock their roots for strength and stability. The forest stands together, even though the trees have endured a constant barrage of severe weather. The author of the Epistle to the Hebrews tells us that we should mesh our faith, hope, and love together in Christ to withstand the storms of life.

Believers: The People of the New Covenant

A final aspect of the new covenant is the covenantal people, the recipients of God's grace who will receive his blessings. In Jeremiah 31 the covenant was promised to "the houses" of Israel and Judah as a reunited nation (also Ezek. 37:15–28). The indwelt people would all know the Lord "from the least of them to the greatest" (Jer. 31:34).

The People in the Spirit and Word

Jesus comforted the apostles in the upper room with the fact that they would not be left as "orphans" (John 14:18), for they would experience the indwelling presence of the Spirit as promised in Jeremiah and Ezekiel 36:26–27 (cf. John 7:37–39). The effect in believers would be "hearts of flesh" that would express love for God by obediently abiding in his Word. Jesus declared, "Whoever has my commands and obeys them, he is the one who loves me" (John 14:21). The matrix of believers' obedience can be summarized in their mutual love for one another as a reflection of the love of God in their lives (John 13:34–35; 15:9–12; 1 John 3:11–24; 4:7–21).

The way of biblical love is one of mutual indwelling in Trinitarian presence. The Lord said that after his resurrection, "You will realize that I am in my Father, and you are in me, and I am in you" (John 14:20). The Father and the Son will live in every believer, and "will come to him, and make [their] home with him" (14:23). Jesus' intercessory prayer in John 17 emphasizes that Trinitarian presence should be evidenced in the unity of the church:

> I pray also for those who will believe in me through their message, that all of them may be one, Father, just as you are in me and I am in you. May they also be in us so that the world may believe that you have sent me. (John 17:20–21; cf. 17:11, 22–23, 26)

178

This unity may await a future fulfillment, though the new covenant was inaugurated by the crucifixion of Christ. A crucial problem in salvation history surfaced with the recipients of the covenant's blessings in light of the fact that the Word "came to that which was his own, but his own did not receive him" (John 1:11).

The People as an Olive Tree

Paul addressed the problem of the relationship of Jews and Gentiles in the new covenant in Romans 9–11.[23] These chapters have been called Paul's theodicy; that is, his vindication of God's justice in light of his promises to Abraham's lineage. He developed three themes based on Israel's distinctive past, provocative present, and promised future.

The Distinctiveness of Israel. Paul initially reviews Israel's blessings as evidenced by her divinely bestowed privileges and promises. Paul's sentiment about his people Israel was rooted in their unique calling. He emphatically expressed his passion for the salvation of "my brothers, those of my own race" (9:1–3; cf. 10:1; 11:1). In Romans 1:16 he underscored his zeal for the gospel, "the power of God for the salvation of everyone who believes: first for the Jew, then for the Gentile," a priority that resonates throughout the letter. The Jews, especially their leaders, had largely rejected their privileged opportunities and condemned Paul for his conversion from Pharisaism.

Paul further describes Israel's distinctiveness in terms of a divinely bestowed ancestry, worship, and revelation. To the nation belongs "adoption as sons," chosen for a unique relationship with the only living God (Rom. 9:4; note Ex. 4:22). Significantly for us, Israel was chosen as the dwelling of the divine glory (cf. Ex. 33:14). The Israelites received covenants of promise that would bless the

---

23. An expanded version of this discussion can be found in Lanier Burns, "Israel and the Church of a Progressive Dispensationalist," in *Three Central Issues in Contemporary Dispensationalism: A Comparison of Traditional and Progressive Views*, ed. Herbert W. Bateman IV (Grand Rapids: Kregel, 1999), 263–303.

earth through their mediation. They received the revelation of the law to make them wise about righteousness (cf. Rom. 2:17–29). Divinely prescribed temple worship was the awe-inspiring center of national life. To them alone belonged the promises of God and the patriarchs. The Jewish Messiah was the hope of the world (Rom. 9:4–5). This crescendo of blessings begs for faith to break through the persistent hardness of Israel, the apple of God's eye.

Israel's collective memory, however, had been marred by the majority's unbelief, a wilderness pilgrimage of unlearned lessons, a seemingly endless rupture of the national fabric, and harsh discipline from the Lord at the hand of pagan empires. If the law was a privilege, then zeal for its laws should be virtuous, but this approach to divine favor had led to an endemic legalism that obscured the righteousness of faith. Wasserberg's observation is perceptive: "The key issue for Paul, as I see it, is not whether or how the Gentiles have access to God's promises but, rather, why Israel has by and large thus far rejected Jesus as its Messiah."[24] Even messianic promises were elusive, since Jesus of Nazareth experienced a criminal's death instead of a heroic initiative against Rome. Nevertheless, Paul, a "Hebrew of Hebrews" (Phil. 3:5), was miraculously called to bring the message of justification by faith to the Jews first as well as to Gentiles.

In the eyes of his fellow Jews, even more disturbing than Paul's conversion was the lingering suspicion that God had reneged on his promises and compromised his Word: "It is not as though God's word had failed" (9:6). His explanation is that "not all who are descended from Israel are Israel. . . . It is not the natural children who are God's children" (9:6, 8). Confusing the chosen part of Israel with the nation as a whole has sometimes

---

24. Gunther Wasserberg, "Romans 9–11 and Jewish-Christian Dialogue: Prospects and Provisos," in *Society of Biblical Literature 1998 Seminar Papers* (Atlanta: Scholars Press, 1998), 7. An excellent summary of first-century polemics between Christians and Jews can be found in Craig Evans, "Introduction, Faith and Polemic: The New Testament and First-century Judaism," in *Anti-Semitism and Early Christianity: Issues of Faith and Polemic*, ed. Craig Evans and Donald Hagner (Minneapolis: Fortress, 1993), 1–17. For the Jewish perspective, see Claudia Setzer, *Jewish Responses to Early Christians: History and Polemics, 30–150 C.E.* (Minneapolis: Fortress, 1994).

obscured the biblical emphasis on Jewish remnants of faith, which demonstrated continuity between the ages. The remnants are identified as the chosen offspring of Isaac and Jacob (9:7–13).

The truth of sovereign election raised a further question about God's justice (9:14–29). Had God been unfair to promise blessing for some but not all of Abraham's offspring and, by extension, for some but not all of humanity? Paul responded with his oft-repeated "Not at all!" in 9:14–10:21. With a chain of Old Testament support, he argues that the mercy of God the "Potter" is sovereign and not subject to objections by the "clay" (Rom. 9:19–24; cf. Jer.18:1–10). Moses is quoted for the principle that God will have mercy on whom he wants (Rom. 9:14–18; cf. Ex. 33:19). Hosea is cited for God's delight in grafting Gentiles into covenantal relationship by faith (9:25–26; cf. Hos. 1:10; 2:23). Isaiah 1:9 and 10:22–23 remind us that "though the number of the Israelites be like the sand by the sea, only the remnant will be saved" (Rom. 9:27). We can conclude that the Gentiles obtained righteousness by faith in Christ, while Israel's majority had "stumbled" in spite of their zeal instead of "walking" according to the example of father Abraham (Rom. 4:9–17). Salvation by faith alone in the finished work of Christ emerges in 9:30 with messianic validation (9:30–10:8; cf. Isa. 8:14; 28:16). "If you confess with your mouth, 'Jesus is Lord,' and believe in your heart that God raised him from the dead," Paul emphasized, "you will be saved" (Rom. 10:9–18). From Deuteronomy 32:21 we are reminded that God would provoke Israel to faith by making them "envious" of believing Gentiles, who did not inherit their privileges (10:19–21; cf. 9:1–5). The next stage of Paul's argument elaborates this strategic envy in terms of an olive tree metaphor.

The Distinctiveness of the Church. Romans 11 describes the relationship of Jews and Gentiles as God's people from the vantage point of the present age. Paul uses his prior arguments for Israel's distinctiveness and justification by faith as preludes to his explanation of how the church relates to God's promises. The chapter is keynoted by two rhetorical questions about the possibility of God's rejection of his people (11:1) and about whether Israel's unbelief renders their "recovery" impossible (11:11). Both questions pertain to the validity of God's Word (9:6), and Paul answered both with his emphatic, "By no means!"

The first question was an issue of divine rejection, and Paul included himself as part of a remnant that indicated that God had not rejected his "people whom he foreknew" (11:2). The connection of the remnant to the "people" bridged the believing minority to a larger ethnic fullness in verse 26. That is, had God rejected Israel, then Paul would not have been chosen for salvation and apostleship to the Gentiles (11:13).[25] He used the precedent of Elijah (11:2–4) to illustrate God's faithfulness at a time when national unbelief had seemed to short-circuit his promises for Israel, a situation that Paul paralleled with his own. As God had graciously carried his people in former times, so now Jewish believers could see themselves as a pledge of his commitment to the fulfillment of his covenants. By combining Deuteronomy 29:4 and Isaiah 29:10 (in Rom. 11:8–10), Paul established a continuum for the remnant theme as a basis for future fullness in Romans 11:27, as Isaiah had predicted.

The second question (11:11) focused on the possibility of human disqualification for salvation, introducing the constructive tension between Jews and Gentiles as the divine strategy of provocation (cf. 10:19). The church validates God's faithfulness to his Word and people and serves, by means of "envy," as the vehicle of bountiful blessing for the world (11:12).

In the remainder of Romans 11, the firstfruits and olive tree metaphors expand on God's use of Gentiles to provoke Paul's Israelite kinsmen to faith. Consonant with the remnant theme, the offered part of the firstfruit dough (cf. Num. 15:17–21) and the root of the tree consecrated the full harvest and the branches, respectively. As the Numbers passage addressed mutually edifying

25. Karl Barth, *Church Dogmatics, vol. II.2: The Doctrine of God*, trans. G. W. Bromiley et al. (Edinburgh: T & T Clark, 1902), 268: "To admit that God has rejected his people would mean the annulment, not only of Paul himself, but above all (and this alone is absolutely 'impossible') of his office, his commission, and its whole content."

worship by Israelites and Gentiles in the land, so Paul apparently was calling for a similar amicability among the Romans. His parallels (Rom. 11:16) prepare his readers for a fullness of faith, a process that he hoped would lead to the salvation of a kinsman remnant in his own ministry (11:13–14).

The olive tree figure combines the themes of sovereignty, faith, and provocation in a description of how Gentiles and Jews are engrafted, pruned, and regrafted into the tree until God's covenantal promises reach their fulfillment. The tree is singular. Thus, the passage clearly supports continuity in God's plan of salvation—there is one people of God. The root is given greater space, indicating that relationships in faith are nourished by irrevocable, patriarchal promises (11:17, 32). Beneath the present expressions of divine mercy ("now," 11:31), we can discern the root that "supports" (11:18), even as divine election proceeds to its perfect conclusion in spite of pervasive unbelief throughout history. Thus, the best way to reconcile patriarchal promises and the irrevocability of divine gifts and calling is to identify the root as God's loyal commitment to his covenantal stipulations (notably faith, 11:20) and promises.

The tree, accordingly, would refer to salvation by faith that is based on Israel's new covenant in particular, since it incorporated Gentiles in the Messiah's provision of forgiveness (11:27). The point is the center of the Messiah's provision rather than notions of ethnic supremacy that were undermining unity in the Roman church.

Paul used the grafting process to issue an emphatic warning about pride as the disqualifier from the "nourishing sap" of God's presence (11:17–21): "Consider therefore the kindness and sternness of God: sternness to those who fell, but kindness to you, provided that you continue in his kindness" (11:22). The "regrafting" of the Israelites by faith is a crucial point in Paul's argument that God has not rejected his people. The remnant of Hebrew Christians, in turn, becomes a pledge of the fulfillment of divine promises. The tree remains natural, awaiting the faith of its own branches as wild branches (believing Gentiles) provoke envy by thriving on its nourishment.

Paul's intent was to inform the Romans about "this mystery, brothers, so that you may not be conceited" (Rom. 11:25). His use of "all Israel" and the Old Testament allusions in 11:26–27 lead to larger integrative questions about disobedience, divine mercy, and the gospel. He combined Isaiah 59:20–21 and 27:9 and Jeremiah 31:33–34 to remind his readers that the goal of God's promises encompasses events that are associated with the second coming of Christ. His use of Isaiah affirms that God's dealings with the olive tree "will turn godlessness away from Jacob." The new covenant will be fulfilled when God forgives and delivers his people. So, Israelites are unbelievers (or, "enemies on your account"), but in terms of election "they are loved on account of the patriarchs, for God's gifts and his call are irrevocable" (11:28–29). God's mercy is extended to the obedience of faith, whether Jew or Gentile (11:30–32). The ultimate goal is doxological: "Oh, the depth of the riches of the wisdom and knowledge of God!" (11:33). God's wisdom, judgments, and ways must be praised, because his strategic plan marches through every enemy, objection, and obstacle without compromise or failure (11:33–36).

Two other metaphors enrich our understanding of the distinctiveness of the church. The first one is the "body," which is traceable to the account of the temple's cleansing in John 2:12–22. Finding that the temple had become a place of commerce at Passover, Jesus scattered the merchants and money changers in a demonstration of zeal for proper worship (cf. Ps. 69:9 in John 2:17). The Jews demanded a "miraculous sign" to prove his "authority to do all this" (John 2:18). The episode deeply impressed the crowds and surfaced later as a charge against Jesus and believers such as Stephen (cf. Matt. 26:61; Acts 6:14). Jesus responded, "Destroy this temple, and I will raise it again in three days" (John 2:19). The sign prompted a wordplay between "temple" and "body." The Jews interpreted the response as a reference to the physical temple, which seemed to be an absurd claim. But "the temple he had spoken of was his body" (John 2:20–21). After his crucifixion

184

and resurrection, proper worship would be reconstituted and focus on himself and the Holy Spirit (cf. 4:23–24). His disciples also recalled his response, when "they believed the Scripture and the words that Jesus had spoken" (2:22).

In accord with our earlier discussions, the New Testament uses the "body" of our glorified Savior with the indwelling of the Spirit to combine the "body" of the church with the living "temple of God": "Don't you know that you yourselves are God's temple and that God's Spirit lives in you? . . . God's temple is sacred, and you are that temple" (1 Cor. 3:16–17). Later, Paul wrote about Christ's "body": "We were all baptized by one Spirit into one body—whether Jews or Greeks, slave or free—and we were all given the one Spirit to drink" (1 Cor. 12:13). To the Ephesians (Eph. 2:11–22) he elaborated a new, equal status in the church. Contrary to Israel's special calling in Romans 9:4, Gentiles were "uncircumcised . . . separate from Christ, excluded from citizenship in Israel . . . without hope and without God in the world" (Eph. 2:11–12). However, because of the normative principle of salvation by faith, they could have been saved by messianic faith through a proselytizing relationship with Israel (cf. Jonah). But now in Christ, who is their "peace," believing Gentiles have been made one with Jews, "one new man" with equal access to the Father through the Spirit (Eph. 2:14–18). Finally, Jews and Gentiles as "fellow citizens with God's people and members of God's household" are being "joined together . . . to become a holy temple in the Lord" (2:19–22). The foundation of the temple is "the apostles and prophets, with Christ Jesus himself as the chief cornerstone."

All this means that a new covenantal ministry is in force in which indwelt believers are Christ's continuing body on earth. They are the temple in which God dwells to accomplish his Word in the world. With presence language, Paul affirms that "in him" believing Gentiles too "are being built together to become a dwelling in which God lives by his Spirit" (Eph. 2:22).

At the end of our pilgrimage through the Scriptures from Christ through tabernacle, what does it mean for us, who are not God, to reflect his presence in the church and world? In

2 Corinthians 3, we will try to understand how we, with faltering steps, can march in the Spirit.

God's Presence in Christ's "Body"

Paul describes the new covenantal presence in believers in a chapter that defends the power of the Spirit in his ministry as amplified by his sufferings (2 Cor. 11). According to Scott Hafemann, "A close reading of the text also makes clear that the central theological theme of 2 Corinthians is the relationship between suffering and the power of the Spirit in Paul's apostolic experience."[26] The apostle introduced his explanation with praise to "the God of all comfort, who comforts us in all our troubles . . . with the comfort we ourselves have received from God" (1:3–4). His ministry has been characterized by sincerity as one sent from God (2:17).

Does he need commendation to or from the Corinthians (2 Cor. 3:1–3)? The question draws comparisons between the Mosaic and new covenants as in Hebrews 8–10. First, in contrast with letters of recommendation, Paul states, "You yourselves are our letter, written on our hearts, known and read by everybody" (3:2).[27] The Corinthian church, as "a letter from Christ," is "written not with ink but with the Spirit of the living God, not on tablets of stone but on tablets of human hearts" (3:3). For Paul, commendation through Christ before God instilled a confidence that "our competence comes from God . . . as ministers of a new covenant" that evidences the life-giving Spirit (3:4–5).[28] A constant refrain is the comparison between external tablets that condemn lawbreakers and the transforming presence of the

26. Scott Hafemann, *2 Corinthians: The NIV Application Commentary* (Grand Rapids: Zondervan, 2000), 34.

27. Richard Hays, *Echoes of Scripture in the Letters of Paul* (New Haven: Yale University Press, 1989), 127: "The argument is a potent one: the very existence of the church in Corinth is manifest evidence of the efficacy of Paul's apostleship. They cannot question the legitimacy of his ministry without simultaneously questioning the legitimacy of their own origins as a community." This is a reminder that, in Christianity, arguments about life have precedence over arguments from letters, if hypocrisy is to be curtailed.

28. Peter Naylor, *A Study Commentary on 2 Corinthians*, 2 vols. (Auburn, MA: Evangelical Press, 2002), 1.169–82, has a very helpful discussion of new covenantal ministry through 4:6, which we have not included because of our limited scope.

Spirit within. Thus, Paul's God-centeredness relates believers to the gracious Author of the covenant who was discussed earlier in this chapter. Contrary to his opponents, his defense has no place for self-glorifying boasts.

Second, in contrast with the fading glory of Moses' radiant face at Sinai (cf. Ex. 34) is the abundant glory of ministry that brings righteousness through the Spirit (3:7–11).[29] Paul does not minimize the Mosaic radiance, but he underscores the surpassing, enduring glory of the Spirit.

Therefore, Paul concludes, God's abiding presence should lead to a boldness in believers' "unveiled" lives (2 Cor. 3:12–18). The old veil "covers their [the Israelites'] hearts," when the Old Testament is read, and dulls their response to the presence of God in their midst. The problem in the past (continuing into the present) was the inability of the people to look steadily at the Glory in view of their habitual unbelief (3:7). The same condition of "veiledness" has continued "even to this day" in the Israelites' rejection of the Messiah, to whom their law pointed. Only in the Messiah can it be removed, so that "whenever anyone turns to the Lord, the veil is taken away" (3:14, 16). Moses veiled himself to mediate the renewed covenant in contrast with Paul, who in Christ could boldly minister unveiled (3:13). The Spirit is the presence of the Lord and relates new covenantal ministry to Moses' experience at Sinai.

In the freedom of the Spirit, we believers, "who with unveiled faces all reflect the Lord's glory, are being transformed into his likeness with ever-increasing glory" (2 Cor. 3:18). The allusion to the image and likeness of God (3:18; cf. Gen. 1:26–28), which has been perfectly revealed in Christ (2 Cor. 4:4), points forward to Paul's identification of the new covenant with our new creation, and ultimately the Holy City to come. Hafemann summarizes the apostle's point:

29. Ralph Martin bridges "glory" and Paul's authority as follows: "There is also the small point that the issue, centrally placed in this letter, of Paul's 'authority' is aptly explored by a sermon on *doxa*, usually rendered 'glory' but which also can be construed as a possession conferring authority on God's representatives whether Moses or Paul," *2 Corinthians*, Word Biblical Commentary, vol. 40 (Waco: Word, 1986), 59.

To say that we are being transformed into his likeness *"unto glory"* means that the final result of becoming more and more like him in anticipation of the final consummation of this age is that we will one day participate in his glory in all its fullness. Our life with God begins and ends by entering into his glorious presence—now in the Spirit, then face to face.[30]

Our display of the Lord's glory is a transformative process that is based on abiding in God's presence. The "Trinitarian presence" of the Spirit obviously is an essential part of the process. However, we are prone to discount the presence of believers as "living epistles" as being essential. The transformation causes believers to conform to the likeness of Christ "from glory to glory." Glory does not mean that believers become divine, but it does mean that we reflect God's presence and character ("from glory") until we "see him as he is," face to face (1 John 3:2).

What does this mean? What is the freedom of the Spirit that changes us into mirrors of Christlike glory? How can people read "living epistles"? Obviously, Paul is teaching personal transformation from the inside out in a comprehensive sense. But within that larger picture he is speaking of "the fruit of the Spirit" (chiefly, love) as the new covenantal trait (see Gal. 5:13–26). In brief, where God is present in the Spirit, there is God-honoring love.

We can now conclude the saga of the hospital. God himself was there as Paraclete, bringing comfort to me in painful circumstances. But there is a more tangible presence for those of us who like truth with "flesh" on it. An unbroken stream of family and friends came to my bedside in spite of holiday traffic and frigid weather. Friendly visits were welcome breaks from the bare walls and sterile routines. These were times of sharing our mutual love of the Lord and one another. One doesn't have these celebrations apart from the common Spirit. These were tablets of the heart where God's blessing in our lives was unveiled for

---

30. Hafemann, *2 Corinthians*, 162. Cf. Philip E. Hughes, *Commentary on the Second Epistle to the Corinthians*, The New International Commentary on the New Testament (Grand Rapids: Eerdmans, 1962), 117–21.

all to see. My elders came by to pray over me, and I told them how they had blessed me with their authentic commitment to me and to God's Word (cf. James 5:14). "Do you want to limit or stop your visitors?" I was asked. I am aware that many people would have said yes for good reasons. But I was writing this chapter, and the family of God helped me to read "living epistles" and experience God's presence in an unforgettable way. "Let us not give up meeting together"—in church, home, hospital, and wherever else, Hebrews echoed in my heart—"but let us encourage one another—and all the more as you see the Day approaching" (Heb. 10:25). Thus, as we draw near to God in his holiest place, he gives us a special closeness in his Spirit.

> Pardon for sin and a peace that endureth,
> Thine own dear presence to cheer and to guide;
> Strength for today and bright hope for tomorrow,
> Blessings all mine, with ten thousand beside!
>
> Great is Thy faithfulness!
> Great is Thy faithfulness!
> Morning by morning new mercies I see;
> All I have needed Thy hand hath provided—
> Great is Thy faithfulness, Lord unto me!
> —Thomas Chisolm, 1923

The Presence
in the New Jerusalem

People want to experience God's presence. The Future Church's battle cry is a return to biblical spirituality, one that is rooted in guiding others to experience God's presence.[1]—Jim Wilson

[Knowledge of the last things] is the hope of believing people that the incompleteness of their present experience of God will be resolved, their present thirst for God fulfilled, their present need for release and salvation realized. . . . It is the logical conclusion of the biblical doctrine of creation, in the attempt to foresee the fulfillment of creation's purpose.[2]—Brian Dailey

Behold, I will create new heavens and a new earth. The former things will not be remembered, nor will they come to mind. But be glad and rejoice forever in what I will create, for I will create Jerusalem to be a delight and its people a joy. I will rejoice over Jerusalem and take delight in my people; the sound of weeping and crying will be heard in it no more.—Isaiah 65:17–19

1. Jim Wilson, *Future Church, Ministry in a Post-Seeker Age* (Nashville: Broadman and Holman, 2004), 38.
2. Brian Dailey, *The Hope of the Early Church: A Handbook of Patristic Theology* (Cambridge: Cambridge University Press, 1991), 1–2.

The Wizard of Oz has been acclaimed as the cultural property of almost every American. Frank Baum wrote the book in 1900, and it was made into a movie in 1939. The story is about Dorothy and her dog, Toto, who live on a farm in Kansas with Auntie Em and Uncle Henry. The narrative begins with the girl and her pet fleeing from Miss Gulch, who has been bitten by Toto. They encounter Professor Marvel, an itinerant charlatan who counsels Dorothy to go home where she belongs. After falling asleep and dreaming during a tornado, Dorothy wakes up in Munchkin City in Oz, where she finds herself trapped between good and bad witches. Glinda, Good Witch of the North, gives her ruby slippers that formerly belonged to the Wicked Witch of the East. Dorothy befriends Scarecrow, Tin Man, and Cowardly Lion, who wish for a brain, heart, and courage, respectively. They share struggles and adventures on the Yellow Brick Road as they make their way to the Wizard in his Emerald City. But they discover, to their chagrin, that the Wizard is a fraud, whose majestic image is based on pulling switches and pushing levers. Glinda instructs Dorothy that she can return home, if she says "there's no place like home" three times and magically clicks her ruby slippers. The story closes with Dorothy and Toto in Kansas once again, having learned that home is not so bad after all.

Interpreters of *The Wizard of Oz* have generally agreed that it is a story about nostalgia for home. Nostalgia has been defined as a "yearning for the world as it had been," as an "expression of hope for what it might become."[3] Usually the desire is couched in a sense of loss of something that was good and a hope to recover optimism about the future. Linda Hansen has argued that *The Wizard of Oz* is about a religious quest to find "home" at a time of unsettling change, technological revolution, and secularization in twentieth-century America.[4] By growing up, Dorothy is empow-

3. Robert McElvain, *The Great Depression: America, 1929–1941* (New York: Times Books, 1984), 220–21.

4. Linda Hansen, "Experiencing the World as Home: Reflections on Dorothy's Quest in *The Wizard of Oz*," *Soundings* 67 (1984), 91–102. Bryan Wilson defined "secularization" as the process of transferring meaning from institutions with a supernaturalist frame of reference to institutions that operate with empirical, pragmatic criteria, in

ered to embrace being at home in the world. She exemplifies an education about the past that transforms the present and offers hope for the future.

Everyone hopes for a better future, and sometimes people imagine an ideal outcome. In secular forms, an ideal society is utopian; it is a beneficent end to the chaos of history through the incremental progress of humanity. Sometimes utopians have abandoned their idealism, because their dreams of Oz have been shattered by a fraudulent Wizard. In traditionally Christian forms, the ideal future is God's kingdom, which is understood as a creational and personal passage from Eden through the chaos of history to the fulfillment of God's promises in the New Jerusalem. God's people will find their "home" in his presence in accord with his promises.

These themes are the subject of this chapter. The ideals and thoughts of heaven have prompted innumerable writings and sermons about the destiny of Christians after death. In most cases, they are projections of this life onto an immense stage, where God gives us whatever we have always wanted. This is understandable, since we can only project as far as the limits of our experiences on earth.

We can, however, interpret what God has told us about eternal life in his Word. What does the Bible say about the future of the earth and his people? To answer this question, we will discuss the New Jerusalem in Revelation 21 and 22. We should notice first that God's kingdom will culminate in a new city that is set in contrast with "the great city" of "Mystery Babylon." So, we will develop the chapter along four lines:

- Differences between Two Cities
- Descent of the Holy City (Rev. 21:1–8)
- Description of the Holy City (Rev. 21:9–21)
- Divine Presence as Temple and Throne (Rev. 21:22–22:6)

"Secularization: The Inherited Model," in *The Sacred in a Secular Age: Toward Revision in the Study of Religion*, ed. Philip Hammond (Berkeley: University of California Press, 1985), 11–12.

A section on the deliberate contrast between the old and new creations and their respective cities will keynote the chapter. A second section will describe the heavenly city's descent to the new earth with an assurance of its certainty by God himself. The third section will picture the city in terms of the radiance of its perfections and God's eternal presence with his people. Finally, we will focus on the city's divine presence as temple and throne.

Several interpretive challenges have caused me to adopt a different approach in this chapter's composition compared with the previous ones. First, while the other chapters have attempted to make ancient texts meaningful to our present context, this one must make a perfect future meaningful for our very imperfect daily lives. I have struggled through every word written here, and, in the end, I confess that I have tried to faithfully translate John's own attempts to tell us about the Holy City. The city is heavenly in origin, and even John with angelic guidance did not have an earthly language that could fully describe what he saw and heard. This has led, in turn, to my flexibility with past and future tenses. Generally, I have used tenses according to stylistic convenience; the past refers to John's experience, and the future is the realization of our hope in his vision. In the end, they have the same meaning because of God's trustworthy guarantee of his revelation.

Second, we will not offer a straightforward exposition of Revelation 21–22. Clearly, John wrote the Revelation in the Spirit to encourage his churches in chapters 2 and 3. The future was meant to encourage embattled saints to overcome in their struggles in Asia Minor toward the end of the first century. The Revelation was meant to encourage us as well. Dailey's introductory quotation connects our hope with the resolution of present issues. Thus, each section deals with timeless human desires and needs, ten in all, which generate hope as we await God's future city. These desires are grounded in John's description of the Holy City. Our fascination with our future stems in part from its insights about our desires in the present.

Finally, readers will recognize that the Holy City is a composite of the themes of presence and pilgrimage that we have been discussing from Genesis to the Revelation. All along our hope for the Glory of the Lamb of God has been the unifying foundation. This chapter is the culmination of the book's journey, the bloom of God's tree that has grown from its roots in Eden. With a view to the dwelling of God with us forever and the wiping away of every tear from our eyes, we turn toward our eternal home with him.

Differences between Two Cities

G. R. Beasley-Murray skillfully introduces John's vision of the New Jerusalem: "The introductory sentence of verse 9 [Rev. 21:9] not merely echoes but uses identical language to that in John's introductory statement to the vision of the harlot, the antichristian city (17:1). The Revelation as a whole may be characterized as *A Tale of Two Cities*, with the sub-title, *The Harlot and the Bride*."[5] He is alerting us to the fact that the end of John's vision is about two cities. In fact, the city is a corporate metaphor that is entrenched in the Bible from its earliest narratives.

The Great City

The first city in the Bible was named Enoch after Cain's son (Gen. 4:17). Cain had been condemned by God for murdering Abel and was cursed with a life of restless wandering on a sterile earth (4:8–14). He understood the deadly implications of the punishment: "My punishment is more than I can bear. . . . I will be hidden from your presence; I will be a restless wanderer on the earth, and whoever finds me will kill me" (4:13–14). Thus, the city Enoch was a gathering of Cain's descendants to find security apart from the Lord. The rebellion in the city was evident in its representative

---

5. G. R. Beasley-Murray, *The Book of Revelation*, New Century Bible (Greenwood, SC: The Attic Press, 1974), 315. G. K. Beale, *The Book of Revelation: A Commentary on the Greek Text*, The New International Greek Testament Commentary (Grand Rapids: Eerdmans, 1999), 1063–65, 1118–19, discusses contrasts between the cities in detail.

inhabitant Lamech, who boasted about his bigamy and murders (4:23–24). The boast was a rebellious challenge directed toward two of the basic values in Eden, marriage and life.

After the flood, the great city is traced to Nimrod, "a mighty warrior," whose Mesopotamian kingdom encompassed Babylon, Erech, Akkad, and Nineveh among others (Gen. 10:8–12). The "mighty hunter" in his "great city" suggests imperial conquests (10:9, 12). The spirit of the culture is clearly presented in Genesis 11:1–4: "The whole world had one language" and settled in Shinar and resolved to "build ourselves a city, with a tower that reaches to the heavens, so that we may make a name for ourselves and not be scattered over the face of the whole earth." Their city was a presumptuous enterprise to gain security and significance. They were united in a godless effort to dominate the world. From that time "Babel" became the prototype of the pride that characterized godless societies in biblical perspective (cf. Isa. 14; see Ezek. 28 for a similar oracle against Tyre).

In the patriarchal era, Sodom and Gomorrah acquired a proverbial reputation for corruption. Egypt, though not a city, was an imperial society that oppressed God's people (Ex. 1:14). Similarly, Babylon became the oppressor during Israel's exile. All of these cities and societies could anticipate God's wrath. Isaiah 13:19 accordingly declared: "Babylon, the jewel of kingdoms, the glory of the Babylonians' pride, will be overthrown by God like Sodom and Gomorrah." Similarly, Jeremiah 50 and 51 state:

> "As God overthrew Sodom and Gomorrah along with their neighboring towns," declares the LORD, "so no one will live there; no man will dwell in it". . . . Babylon was a gold cup in the LORD's hand; she made the whole earth drunk. The nations drank her wine; therefore they have now gone mad. . . . You who live by many waters and are rich in treasures, your end has come, the time for you to be cut off. (50:40; 51:7, 13)

Thus, in Revelation 11:7–10 the two witnesses lie in "the great city, which is figuratively called Sodom and Egypt, where

196

also their Lord was crucified."[6] This great city is later identified as "MYSTERY BABYLON THE GREAT, THE MOTHER OF PROSTITUTES AND OF THE ABOMINATIONS OF THE EARTH" (Rev. 17:5; cf. 17:18; 18:10, 16, 18–19). A clue to the identity of the city can be found in 2 Thessalonians 2:4, where Antichrist will set "himself up in God's temple, proclaiming himself to be God." Thus, at the end of the old order, John seems to be contrasting the old Jerusalem in unbelief with the New Jerusalem that will experience the fullness of God's presence.

The Godly City

Parallel to this line of ungodly societies is God's deflective choice of Jerusalem. The city initially appeared as Salem under its priest-king Melchizedek (Gen. 14:18–20). Its significance must be understood in relationship with God's promise of land to Abraham (Gen. 12:1; 15:18; 17:8) and his promise of kingship to David (Deut. 17:14–15). "David's city," which was centered in its fortress Zion, became the dwelling of the Lord in the Holy of Holies of the temple. It was praised as "the city of our God, his holy mountain":

> It is beautiful in its loftiness,
> the joy of the whole earth.
> Like the utmost heights of Zaphon is Mount Zion,
> the city of the Great King. . . .
> As we have heard,
> so have we seen
> in the city of the LORD Almighty,
> in the city of our God:
> God makes her secure forever. (Ps. 48:2, 8)

Jerusalem's security, however, was compromised by the Israelites' desire to be like the nations. Idolatrous worship exposed

---

6. G. B. Caird, *The Revelation of Saint John*, Black's New Testament Commentary (Peabody, MA: Hendrickson, 1966), 185–86, can be consulted for insightful commentary on the verse.

her flank to the caprice and avarice of surrounding invaders. The Israelites lost sight of the fact that their security was in the Lord rather than rituals and ramparts. The Messiah's tearful lament is even more poignant in this perspective:

> O Jerusalem, Jerusalem, you who kill the prophets and stone those sent to you, how often I have longed to gather your children together, as a hen gathers her chicks under her wings, but you were not willing. Look, your house is left to you desolate. For I tell you, you will not see me again until you say, "Blessed is he who comes in the name of the Lord." (Matt. 23:37–39)

Israel and Jerusalem will see their Lord again, because the Prophets are saturated with promises of the city's inviolability. For example, consider Isaiah 49–66 as represented by Isaiah 65:17, 19:

> Behold, I will create new heavens and a new earth. The former things will not be remembered, nor will they come to mind. . . . I will rejoice over Jerusalem and take delight in my people; the sound of weeping and crying will be heard in it no more.

In Jeremiah's new covenantal promise (31:38, 40), we read:

> "The days are coming," declares the LORD, "when this city will be rebuilt. . . . The city will never again be uprooted or demolished."

And Ezekiel related the return of "the glory of the LORD" to the temple "through the gate facing east" (Ezek. 43:4) to a divine proclamation that

> This is the place of my throne and the place for the soles of my feet. This is where I will live among the Israelites forever. . . . Now let them put away from me their prostitution and the lifeless idols of their kings, and I will live among them forever. (Ezek. 43:7, 9)

Thus, after the judgment of the harlot city, John saw "the new Jerusalem, coming down out of heaven from God" (Rev. 21:2).[7]

Descent of the Holy City

Presentation of the City

After the first heaven and earth "had passed away," John "saw" the new creation (Rev. 21:1). His account emphasizes visionary sight and hearing, because finite reason, language, and experience cannot fully comprehend or describe the magnificence of what he saw. The term for "new" is qualitative, meaning new in kind. However, each aspect of the chapter reflects intimations of immortality in our present experience, so that there is both continuity and discontinuity between our current lives and our eternity with God and one another. The Bible describes time and space in terms of creation from the beginning (Gen. 1:1) to its goal (Rev. 21:1). "The first" and "the new" concern heaven and earth, so God declares, "I am making everything new!" (Rev. 21:5). Jerusalem is still the "dwelling" of God's presence, but it is not an earthly metropolis in the new order. The New Jerusalem has a permanence and splendor that could only come down out of heaven, having been prepared by God. Creation and God's chosen people have been made new, for they have been freed from sin and glorified for their unending service in God's presence. The analogy between the first and the last makes the Holy City discussable, because "the new" is the perfect "pattern" that God showed Moses on the mountain (Ex. 25:8, 40).

---

7. The "tale of two cities" continued in Christian tradition through works such as Augustine's *City of God*. After identifying pride as "the start of all sin," he distinguished two branches of mankind as follows: "The two cities then were created by two kinds of love: the earthly city by a love of self carried even to the point of contempt for God, the heavenly city by a love of God carried even to the point of contempt for self. Consequently, the earthly city glories in itself while the other glories in the Lord." Finally, "I speak of these branches also allegorically as two cities, that is, two societies of human beings, of which one is predestined to reign eternally with God and the other to undergo eternal punishment with the devil." *City of God against the Pagans*, trans. Philip Levine, Loeb Classical Library (Cambridge: Harvard University Press, 1966), IV.25, 405, 413 [XII.vi, XIV.xxviii, XV.i].

The newness of creation may be seen in the words "there was no longer any sea" (Rev. 21:1). This may be literal, since the absence of sea is a counterpoint to the "spring of the water of life" (21:6) and the "river of the water of life" (22:1). John seems to have noticed the stunning perfection of the Holy City, and how it contrasted with the old, sinful order with its "sea" and beast, which symbolized the chaos of that order. Appearing at a point of transition in the chapter, sea seems to be an all-inclusive term for evils that have permeated the world with grief. The "beast from the sea" will captivate the world with his blasphemous claims, idolatrous practices, and tyrannical authority (13:1–10). The harlot city sponsors the same vices and rests on chaotic waters, which are "peoples, multitudes, nations and languages" (17:15). The prophets had looked forward to the end of such wickedness and the advent of peace. Isaiah, for example, comforted righteous people in Isaiah 57:19–21:

> "Peace, peace, to those far and near,"
>   says the LORD. "And I will heal them."
> But the wicked are like the tossing sea,
>   which cannot rest,
>   whose waves cast up mire and mud.
> "There is no peace," says my God, "for the wicked."

With the passing of the chaotic old order and in the glorious presence of God, "there will be no more death or mourning or crying or pain" (Rev. 21:4). The fact that God "will wipe every tear from their eyes" (21:4) is a gracious gesture to celebrate the end of death and pain. In his eternal dwelling God can eliminate weeping, because he has judged and banished "death and Hades . . . into the lake of fire. . . . the second death" (20:14).

How would the Holy City have encouraged believers to overcome adversity under Roman rule? What does it indicate about our needs and desires now? In the rest of this chapter we will examine ten of these needs and desires. First, everyone lives with ideals of perfection, even though the entire world around us is flawed in varying degrees. Life has always been this way! We always try to perform, dress, speak, or behave perfectly, because we have been taught that life is graded according to categories such as failure, bad, or poor; average, good, better, and best. The spoils of the world belong to "the best," which is usually equated with a number one on the list of the top ten. America has had a long love affair with the superlatives that describe exceptional— most, best, -est, or simply perfect.

The truth is that nothing is perfect, because people in this diverse, conflict-filled world cannot agree about what perfection is. We never will agree in this life, because everything we touch leaves a smudge. We hear a beautiful concert and then read the critics. A magisterial piece of art or literature can be adored by some people, yet panned by others. Champions in sports have high mountains along with their low valleys. Valedictorians often are not accepted at their preferred schools, because the admissions committees decide that the students would be an imperfect fit at their institutions. Perfection in competitions may mean undefeated, but records, once perfect, are made to be broken, and competitors have always sought to win at any cost. Circles of leadership define standards in any endeavor, and one individual's potion may be another's poison. Christians have held that the only perfect life was lived by Jesus Christ. But, most people will ask, can perfection be defined by the manger, his sacrificial life, and his death on the cross? I would answer in the affirmative, but I would have to jettison every notion of "flawless" that I have been taught.

John was awed by the absolute perfection of the New Jerusalem. Its perfection will be the result of its preparation by God. What is the eternal "dwelling" of God like? John, in the Spirit, told us that we could not appreciate it fully in this life. His description points to a likeness that is not the reality. We might even feel fearful, because we cannot escape the suspicion that our shortcomings and weaknesses may be judged. But the city is God's perfection, and we attain glory not by performance but only by God's grace. Believers can know that their ideals will be a reality in his perfect presence.

Second, everyone wants to live. Ideally, in the words of Jesus, we want to "have life, and have it to the full" (John 10:10). His strongest claims revolved around preservation through salvation: "I am the resurrection and the life. He who believes in me will live, even though he dies; and whoever lives and believes in me will never die" (11:25). Our hearts break beneath the burdens of pain, suffering, loss, and death. Tears are our constant companions on earth. We weep not only for ourselves but also for untold numbers of people who die tragically—or even "naturally"—and for other countless numbers who grieve in times of loss. Most people do not want the mire, mud, doom, and ruin of harlot cities.

We must note, however, that vast multitudes die in "MYSTERY BABYLON THE GREAT." Unbelief generates a fascination with the risks of violence, immorality, magical arts, idolatry, and untold rebellions that flourish in quests for political power (Rev. 17) and economic prowess (Rev. 18; cf. 21:8). Revelation 18:7 teaches that glory and luxury generate a feeling of invulnerability in the great city of Babylon's citizens: "Give her as much torture and grief as the glory and luxury she gave herself. In her heart she boasts, 'I sit as a queen; I am not a widow, and I will never mourn.'" Those in rebellion seem to forget that "there is a way that seems right to a man, but in the end it leads to death (Prov. 14:12; 16:25). Everyone must choose, because no one can be citizens of both cities. In their end, devotees of the old order "will throw dust on their heads, and with weeping and mourning cry out: 'Woe! Woe, O great city . . .'" (Rev. 18:19). After all, for them the presence and perfection of God would be eternal torment.

John tells us that the Holy City, on the other hand, will be a place of life and godly prosperity. God's "dwelling" with his people will be free from all suffering, tears, and death. What will this be like? Believers must wait to find out, because we think of life in terms of time, which will vanish when we are in a place of love where there is no night. Thus, "the Life" defines eternal life as knowing the living God (John 17:3). Meanwhile, we cannot escape the chaotic consequences of sin until our pilgrimage takes us home!

The celebration of the end of death is presented in the context of the greatest blessing that we can anticipate according to Scripture—unending life, face-to-face with the presence of God. John saw "the Holy City, the new Jerusalem, coming down out of heaven from God" (Rev. 21:2). In the city, God's servants will serve him as they "see his face, and his name will be on their foreheads" (22:4). In other words, believers will find their ultimate identity in the presence of their Creator and Redeemer. This is the fullness of the biblical hope of faith. We recall that Moses could not see the face of God and live (Ex. 33:20). In Matthew 17:2–3, Peter, James, and John were allowed to preview the future because of their foundational role in the church: "His [Jesus'] face shone like the sun, and his clothes became as white as the light. Just then there appeared before them Moses and Elijah, talking with Jesus." Followers of the Lord will live in the feature presentation forever. They will live before his face without shame. Their new identity will be God's name and will be grounded in fidelity to God through the trials and vicissitudes of life: "I will write on him the name of my God, and the name of the city of my God, the new Jerusalem, which is coming down out of heaven from my God" (Rev. 3:12). The inscription of the name of God is opposed to "the mark of the beast," which will be branded forcibly on the unbelieving inhabitants of the earth (especially 13:16–17; 19:20). In summary, citizens of the Holy City will see and serve God without sin or temptation in a purity of worship that we can scarcely comprehend, for "now we see but a poor reflection as in a mirror; then we shall see face to face" (1 Cor. 13:12).

The New Jerusalem will be divinely "prepared as a bride beautifully dressed for her husband" (Rev. 21:2). Revelation 20:9 identifies God's people as "the city he loves," an equation that is validated in 21:9, "I will show you the bride, the wife of the Lamb." Thus, life in the city will focus on the loving relationship between God and his "wife," who is collectively presented as his people and city. Marital language is frequently used in the Bible to describe God's covenantal bond with his chosen people. When he gave the law, God commanded, "Do not worship any other

203

god, for the LORD, whose name is Jealous, is a jealous God" (Ex. 34:14; cf. 20:5). Jealousy alludes to the covenantal relationship in terms of marriage. In Jeremiah 31:32, the new covenant passage, the Lord declared, "They broke my covenant, though I was a husband to them." And in 3:14, the Lord proclaimed through Jeremiah, "Return, faithless people . . . for I am your husband." The references to Israel and Judah (and Jerusalem) as unfaithful, adulterous sisters support this understanding (cf. Jer. 3:6–10; Ezek. 16, 23; Hos. 2:16–17).[8]

The eternal presence of God brings two themes of the book to fruition. In the first theme, "a loud voice from the throne" triumphantly proclaimed, "The dwelling of God is with men, and he will live with them" (Rev. 21:3). We are familiar with the concept of "dwelling" from our discussions of the incarnation, the sanctuary in the wilderness (tabernacle) and in Jerusalem (temple), and the church as the Spirit's "indwelt temple." God's dwelling with us is the goal of our salvation. In the introductory words of Dailey, this is the fulfillment of our hunger and thirst for God and the realization of our need for release and the completion of our salvation. We must be careful to specify once again that God's infinite attributes prohibit even his heavenly dwelling from "containing" him. "Dwelling" is a term of presence throughout the Old and New Testaments, so that the metaphor means a place and a throne where believers will experience his presence.

In the second theme pertaining to God's presence, the notion of eternal dwelling necessarily means covenantal fulfillment: God "will live with them. They will be his people, and God himself will be with them and be their God" (Rev. 21:3). Eternal dwelling is the full realization of God's oft-stated covenantal axiom (Gen. 17:7; Ex. 6:7; 29:45; Lev. 26:12; Deut. 29:13; Jer. 7:23; 11:4; 24:7; 30:22; Zech. 8:8). Packer underscores the importance of the verse for this book: "The goal of the covenant love of God is that He

8. The metaphor is best understood in terms of God's grace in granting covenantal relationship (husband) as well as Israel's faith in accepting his initiative (wife). Thus, adultery is idolatry, the unfaithfulness of the Israelites in worshiping other gods. The wordplay on *ba'al* (husband and Canaanite deity) supports this interpretation.

should have a people on earth as long as history lasts, and after that should have all his faithful ones of every age with him in glory. Covenant love is the heart of God's plan for His world."[9]

Again, how would the Holy City encourage believers to overcome imperial pressures in John's setting? We have already discussed what we have labeled the first and second of our deep-seated desires, the ideal of perfection and the desire to live. We will now add three human needs that are central to biblical motivation. These are faith, hope, and love, which Paul highlights in 1 Corinthians 13:13.

Third, in terms of our basic needs and desires, everyone wants to be vindicated for his or her faith on earth. Of course, we are speaking of faith as personal trust rather than religious affiliation, which is a popular use of the concept; namely, I am a "person of faith" because I belong to such and such a church. People want to trust in the right things or belong to the right groups to gain what they believe they want. There is "good faith" in true and trustworthy people who can help us with our needs on earth. We trust political officials for a secure, stable society. We trust our employers for fair, meaningful work. We trust in professionals with integrity who can provide for us in catastrophic circumstances. However, we sometimes trust the wrong people and experience "bad" faith. We may trust our mates for family and love only to experience abandonment and abuse. We trust our fellow travelers but suffer grievous loss, if they are reckless or drunk. We negotiate contracts that may be voided or altered according to differences in interpretation. Faith is a pervasive aspect of everyday life, and we yearn for the vindication of our good faith.

Fourth, everyone hopes for a good tomorrow. No word is more inextricably connected to human desires than *hope*. We hope for perfect choices and results, for a full life, for trustworthy companions, for loving friendships, and for everything else that is precious to us. Like faith, hope can be good or bad. Bad hope leads to despair, a brokenness that can be humanly devastat-

9. James I. Packer, *Knowing God* (Downers Grove, IL: InterVarsity Press, 1973), 155.

ing. Biblical hope is summarized in the axiomatic expectation of dwelling—not in the Emerald City of Oz but in the eternal city of God, "We will be his people, and God himself will be with them." At that time we will realize that faith, hope, and love in God, however feeble and imperfect in the present, will have been the perfect thing for us to have cultivated in our days on earth.

Believers spend much of their time in trusting God as well. In Hebrews 11, the biblical chapter on faith, the "righteous men made perfect" looked for "the city with foundations, whose architect and builder is God, the heavenly Jerusalem, the city of the living God" (Heb. 11:10, 13–16; 12:22–24). "Therefore God is not ashamed to be called their God, for he has prepared a city for them" (11:16). In Revelation 21 God proves the goodness of faith in his promises with the permanent reality of the New Jerusalem on the new earth.

We briefly pause, because faith and hope are too important to relegate to the transitory whims of a generation. I am well aware that heaven is not "in hand," and that my culture is seeking its own name and fame (that is, significance and immortality) in a frantic pursuit of attention and applause. Life has become a driven present that discards history and ignores the future. But if this life is all there is, then what is the point of awards that gather dust in attics, inheritances that are squandered as quickly as spending allows, plaques that corrode with time, and memorialized buildings that are demolished after a few years as outdated? The world is passing away. Perhaps the majority of undiagnosed illnesses today are profound disappointments (from bad faith) and broken dreams (from bad hope). We are mere specks in a vast universe of people and space that becomes more complex with the passage of time. In this light my confidence in God's city seems to increase in stability and certainty. I share the sight of the city of the living God with millions of believers over millennia of history. This is not a whim; it is an expectation of the heavenly Jerusalem, an expectation with strong foundations in the history of salvation. Hebrews assures us that "a great cloud of witnesses" has been commended for the certainty of things hoped for (11:1; 12:1). It is an affirmation that the Lamb of God did not die in vain or emerge in resurrection life without purpose:

> In my Father's house are many rooms; if it were not so, I would have told you. I am going there to prepare a place for you. And if I go and prepare a place for you, I will come back and take you to be with me that you also may be where I am. (John 14:2–3)

I say these things about a spectacular future beyond imagination without condemning those who do not yet share my hope, because if I had not grown in my knowledge of God, his Word, and his people, I too would be seeking immortality on my terms.

Fifth, people seek unconditional love, which in biblical terms is self-giving, agapic love. Agapic is an adjective from an important Greek word for God's love—*agape*. In thirty years of teaching, I would conclude that love is one of the most powerful human needs. Godly love is so rare that people frequently confess with tears that they thought that they were loved until they realized that they were only being manipulated. John was unmistakably clear on the importance of godly love. Now we know that "we love because he first loved us" (1 John 4:19). We know that "whoever lives in love lives in God, and God in him" (4:16). We know that "whoever loves God must also love his brother" (4:21). But sometimes we don't feel loving or loved. Accordingly, biblical love is tethered to obedience (John 15:9–12). We must always realize, strengthened by hope, that unconditional love is an ideal that was real at Calvary and will be real when we will be "beautifully dressed" for our ever-loving Husband.

Proclamation of the Lord

Emphatic statements by the Creator himself follow in Revelation 21:5. The pastoral urgency of the divine statements for suffering churches is evident in that God speaks for the first time since Revelation 1. First, he says, "I am making everything new!" Second, "Write this down," God continues, "for these words are trustworthy and true." The new creation may have seemed too good to be true for John's readers in view of their trials in the world. One cannot watch contemporary shows and programs without realizing that their mantra is "trust me," thus indicating a prevailing doubt and distrust in society at large. Similarly, John's audience would have craved assurance that God's promises would come to pass. God knows the human desire for certainty, so he guarantees the truth of the new heaven and earth in writing, because he is completely trustworthy. Third, God then proclaims to John, "It is done," in vision as it will be done in the future. At the end of creation, God pronounced his work "very good" and rested. The purpose of God's salvation is as certain as the creation that we experience now, and he invites us to rest in his personal guarantee for our future. Fourth, certainty resides in God as "the Alpha and the Omega, the Beginning and the End" (21:6). As the first and last letters encompass the Greek alphabet, so he embraces all of existence in himself. As the eternal, living Author of all reality, he promises to make all things new in the Holy City, which will never pass away.

The recipients of blessing are then compared with people who are excluded: The one "who overcomes will inherit all this, and I will be his God and he will be my son" (Rev. 21:7). Recalling promises to "overcomers" in letters to the churches in Revelation 2–3, God's commendation is directed particularly toward believers who faithfully persevere in the face of persecution. Sonship often has a sense of heir in the Bible and relates particularly to inheritance in the Holy City (cf. Rom. 8:17). By inference this introduces an important exclusionary principle, which assures us that only those whose names are in the Lamb's Book of Life will inhabit the city. In Revelation 21:8, "the cowardly, the unbelieving, the vile, the murderers, the sexually immoral, those who practice magic arts, the idolaters and all liars" are excluded from the New Jerusalem, and "their place will be in the fiery lake of burning sulfur . . . the second death" (cf. 20:6, 14–15). "Cowardly" heads the list of vices that characterize the harlot city. However, as the paragon of evil, its inhabitants will exemplify the plight of unbelievers in general.

Description of the Holy City

John's observation of the descent of the Holy City is continued in 21:9 with its description. One of the angels who administered the bowl judgments transported him to a closer look at the "wife of the Lamb": "He carried me away in the Spirit to a mountain great and high, and showed me the Holy City, Jerusalem" (Rev. 21:10). The summons is similar to 17:3, where John viewed the prostitute in a desert on a scarlet beast with blasphemous names. The similarity of language reinforces the contrast between the harlot and the Holy City. "In the Spirit" (cf. 4:2) he was taken to a high mountain, which was associated with God's dwelling in the Old Testament. Similarly, Ezekiel was taken to the holy land and was placed on a very high mountain on which was the city (Ezek. 40:1–2). Psalm 48 equates the city of God with his holy mountain (Ps. 48:1). The emphasis of Revelation 21:10, therefore, is that God will bring his Holy City down to dwell with his people, and it will be "beautiful in its loftiness, the joy of the whole earth" (Ps. 48:2). As such, the New Jerusalem will complete the highest ideals of the Old Testament pattern.

The Radiance of the Glory

The dominant characteristic of the city is a luminescence that radiates the glory of God's presence, at once substantive yet beyond description. Its "brilliance was like that of a very precious jewel, like a jasper, clear as crystal" (Rev. 21:11). In verse 18, jasper describes the fabric of the wall and in 4:3 the appearance of God. Zechariah similarly identifies the wall and the presence: "'And I myself will be a wall of fire around it,' declares the LORD, 'and I will be its glory within'" (Zech. 2:5). Perhaps we can conclude that the city will be diamond-like, clear and sparkling to the extent that it is identified with the glorious presence. The city, as the Holy of Holies, will shine with a shimmering radiance, a cosmic iridescence that will fill the new heavens and earth. We can think of the glow that large cities make in the distance at night. In the New Jerusalem, the glory of God will shine everywhere, because there will be no night. We think of the joy that a few carats bring to a prospective bride, and then we think of the infinite sparkle that will be ours as the bride of the Lamb. What will eternity be like? We will be in God's presence and will be awed by the sheer clarity of his glorious light. That is all that we can say now, when analogies fall far short of the power of divine Perfection.

The city is the wife of the Lamb. We tend to associate the image of the Lamb with sacrificial weakness, and in a scene of unparalleled power, we would expect the majestic Lion of the tribe of Judah or its royal equivalent. However, the Lamb is the means by which the city will be populated by the redeemed bride in resurrection. In the words of Isaiah, "Then you will know that I, the LORD, am your Savior, your Redeemer, the Mighty One of Jacob" (Isa. 60:16). The Lamb is the memorial that God's new-covenant promise of forgiveness will be fulfilled in the indestructible city (Jer. 31:34, 40). The Lamb, in fact, is "the Lion of the tribe of Judah, the Root of David," who will inherit creation, which he made (Rev. 5:5–6; cf. John 1:1–5). Accordingly, he will be praised forever with the "new song" of salvation (Rev. 5:9–12).

Three features of the city are noted for emphasis: its wall, gates, and foundations. The wall will share the gem-like transparency of the city, and seems to give the New Jerusalem its radiant, crystalline appearance (Rev. 21:11–12). Its functions, besides being a traditional feature of ancient cities, are to emphasize the city's security in the Lord and to delineate the shape of the Holy of Holies. The wall contains twelve gates, each with an angel, apparently serving as a worshipful guardian. The gates will never be shut (21:25), so the angels would suggest security as well. Three gates are on each directional side, and the names of the twelve tribes of Israel are inscribed on the gates (Ezek. 48:30–34). Perhaps we can infer that they memorialize the patriarchs as the covenantal entry to the presence, now open for all believers to worship, from the least to the greatest (cf. Jer. 31:34). They will be radiantly white, each made of a single pearl. The wall also rests on twelve foundation stones, which are inscribed "with the names of the twelve apostles of the Lamb" (Rev. 21:14). The Lamb, of course, is the Cornerstone and Capstone of the temple and will reside on the throne (cf. Ps. 118:22; Matt. 21:42). The foundations will be jewel-like with a variety of stones and hues, radiating a color-ful spectrum of divinely illumined beauty. The recurrence of the number twelve with tribes and apostles indicates the complete-ness and union of all believers in the city. The "great street" of the New Jerusalem will be "of pure gold," a highway which, like other features, is clear "like transparent glass" (Rev. 21:21).

The Symmetry of the Sanctuary

The angelic escort carries a golden measuring rod to mea-sure the enclosing walls of the city. Interestingly, the rod is "by man's measurement," which seems to indicate an intent to relate the spectacular sight in as comprehensible terms as possible (Rev. 21:17). Measurement indicates the size and symmetry of the eternal dwelling place. In the end, the city is squared in its length, width, and height. In other words, the Holy of Holies is a cube, featuring the presence of the Lord according to the Mosaic pattern.[10] Ezekiel closes with the "name of the city" as "THE LORD IS THERE" (Ezek. 48:35). That is the emphasis of Revelation as well.

Again, we ask how the Holy City would have encouraged John's churches in their trials. How can it inform us about our needs and desires? Thus far, we have identified five of these: the

---

10. Most scholars do not think that we can convincingly demonstrate the identity or arrangement of the jewels. Many of the terms occur only in Revelation in the New Testament. Here we will be content with their rarity, varied colors, and combined beauty. Robert Mounce, *The Book of Revelation*. The New International Commentary on the New Testament (Grand Rapids: Eerdmans, 1977), 380, notes: "This particular shape would immediately remind the Jewish reader of the inner sanctuary of the temple (a perfect cube, each dimension being twenty cubits; 1 Kings 6:20), the place of divine presence. A city foursquare would be the place where God has taken up residence with his people."

211

ideal of perfection, the desire to live, the vindication of faith, the hope of eternal fellowship with God, and the fullness of unconditional love. These five dreams lead to three additional needs: security, peace, and beauty.

Sixth, everyone seeks security in a fearful world. The passage indicates that there will be no tears (Rev. 21:4) or fear in the New Jerusalem. In our present world, we insure and deposit our valuables. We install multiple locks and alarm systems in our houses. We place "walls" around our computers and fear pandemics because of elusive viruses. A large number of people arm themselves against unwanted intrusions, though they know that they may not have the time or ability to defend themselves. People do these things for good reasons. Individuals, families, and nations have suffered ambushes, attacks, and full-scale wars. In our lifetime, the threat of an Armageddon has become real with the development of nuclear and biochemical weapons. The violence in the harlot city's destruction has a ring of plausibility. Will we ever be safe and secure from the dangers that encircle us, real or imagined? The best answer is no in this old order of the world. John's churches were in peril and were tempted to seek the shelter of compromise. We are challenged and tempted as well, even though we sometimes feel invulnerable behind the anonymity of our technological walls. On the other hand, we have the assurance that in the "walls" of God's presence we can rest in his omnipotent love. In the words of Augustine,

> They [the Platonists] make no mention of the tears of confession or of the sacrifice that you [God] will never disdain, a broken spirit, a heart that is humbled and contrite, nor do they speak of the salvation of your people, the city adorned like a bride, the foretaste of your Spirit, or the chalice of our redemption. In them no one sings. No rest has my soul but in God's hands; to him I look for deliverance. I have no other stronghold, no other deliverer but him; safe in his protection, I fear no deadly fall.[11]

11. Augustine, *Confessions*, trans. R. S. Pine-Coffin (Harmondsworth, NY: Penguin Books, 1961), 156 [VII.xxi].

Seventh, a significant part of our future security resides in the peacefulness of our eternal society. We must remember that our desires and needs are both personal and social. For this reason, our future in God's presence is called a "city." Peace is a state of social well-being that results from equitable relationships (or justice). There will be no conflict, because there will be contentment and joy in common standards, service, and goals. The Old Testament's couplet "justice and righteousness" suggests that a right relationship with God will result in just behavior toward other people. That is, a proper love of God will result in the love of our neighbors as ourselves (cf. Matt. 22:34–40). "Babel" stemmed from a prideful lust to pursue god-like power for oneself. Biblical love is the equation of self-interest with the interest of the Other and others (cf. Phil. 2:3). In the New Jerusalem the presence of God will establish a unity of believers in which kings and nations will pass through open gates to give all to God Almighty. The ancient, elusive ideal of the absence of war will be realized in the joy of mutual service and the untarnished rightness of the city's justice and peace. This will be an exhilarating blessing in the new social order.

Eighth, the New Jerusalem also will be a place of ideal beauty. This is another desire that people have had, though they have disagreed about what is beautiful throughout history. Most people have understood beauty as a magnetic awareness of an ideal, and have longed to follow the grail to the inspiration's source. What causes us to be drawn to beautiful scenes and accomplishments? Without belaboring this extensive subject, we can conclude that John obviously wants to communicate the heavenly beauty of what he saw. The fullness of our needs and desires are beautiful in themselves. But the shimmering light, colors, and perfect symmetry of the city with the stunningly adorned bride have an obvious authorial intent—namely, believers will be surrounded by exquisite beauty forever. Beyond that, words cannot capture the surpassing magnificence of God himself and the perfect accomplishments of the Lamb for his bride. Somehow we will enjoy appropriate worship in that day!

Divine Presence as Temple and Throne

The Presence as Temple

The transparency of the city functions as a frame and magnifier of the radiant Glory of God in a breathtakingly colorful way. I have tried to capture this scene by teaching that our entry into the city will result in an "eternal gasp" of joy. "I did not see a temple in the city," John continues, "because the Lord God Almighty and the Lamb are its temple" (Rev. 21:22). The identification of "God Almighty and the Lamb" as the temple supports the notion that the city and the Holy of Holies are to be equated as well. The Holy of Holies as a city, as the dwelling of the presence of God, and as a focus on the Lamb pervades the entire passage.[12] Furthermore, the full deity of the Lamb as coequal and coeternal in the Trinity is affirmed.

This Trinitarian emphasis continues with "the glory of God gives it light, and the Lamb is its lamp" (Rev. 21:23; cf. 18:23 for the harlot's antithetical judgment). In other words, the city does not need the life-promoting illumination of the sun and moon. We see this expectation in Isaiah, when the prophet looked to a future time when "the sun will no more be your light by day, nor will the brightness of the moon shine on you, for the LORD will be your everlasting light, and your God will be your glory" (Isa. 60:19). Certainly, in the absence of sin the perfection of divine glory will bring brilliant light, which transcends our present comprehension.

The Presence as Throne

In the city of Light, "the nations will walk by its light, and the kings of the earth will bring their splendor into it" (Rev. 21:24). The scene lends itself to imprecise earthly interpretations because of its heavenly features. An incorrect view would see nations and

---

12. In these identifications John differs from Ezekiel, whose prophetic imagery parallels Revelation in many ways. Ezekiel spends seven chapters on the temple and its ordinances. John defines the temple as the Presence of God.

kings in a present sense—namely, unredeemed rulers and societies who live outside the city but are attracted to its splendor and bring their riches to trade. This interpretation acknowledges that activities will flourish outside the city, but it ignores the exclusionary principle in 21:8. The unsaved will be condemned to the second death in the fiery lake.

Instead, the text probably refers to the order of the redeemed society in contrast with the chaos of the first earth. The imagery is both prophetic and social. Isaiah 60:3, 11 predict: "Nations will come to your light, and kings to the brightness of your dawn. . . . Your gates will always stand open, they will never be shut, day or night, so that men may bring you the wealth of the nations. . . ." The image is of a godly society "from every tribe and language and people and nation (Rev. 5:9; 7:9) that will offer its splendor to God, because the gains in their eternal occupations are given out of a love for him with all their heart, and soul, and mind (Matt. 22:37). George Ladd relates the presence of God to this social godliness: "So the presence of God will banish all darkness and night. In the Bible, darkness is a standard metaphor for existence apart from the presence of God (Matt. 6:23; 8:12; 22:13; 25:30); all darkness will be abolished in the presence of the radiance of God and the Lamb."[13] We can speculate that the godliness of our present lives will be reflected in our future lives as rewards (cf. 1 Cor. 3:12–15). New Testament authors also refer to crowns, which believers will receive for godly service (1 Cor. 9:25; 1 Thess. 2:19; 2 Tim. 2:5; 4:8; James 1:12; 1 Peter 5:4; Rev. 2:10; 3:11; cf. Isa. 62:11–12). Perhaps these rewards are reflected in the social orders of the redeemed city (cf. Rev. 22:5). We dare not speculate further because of the persistent, pervasive, and materialistic self-interest that clouds our present labors. For example, there will be no concern for prestige, because all Glory is divine; there will be no ambition for power, because there will be a single throne with sovereign Power; and there will be no wealth, because everything

13. George E. Ladd, *A Commentary on the Revelation of John* (Grand Rapids: Eerdmans, 1972), 285. Readers should note John 3:19–21 as well.

will be offered to God. This is underscored in the closing verses of Revelation 21:

> On no day will its gates ever be shut, for there will be no night there. The glory and honor of the nations will be brought into it. Nothing impure will ever enter it, nor will anyone who does what is shameful or deceitful, but only those whose names are written in the Lamb's book of life (Rev. 21:25–26; cf. Isa. 60:11).

John adds the imagery of Eden to the city in Revelation 22:1. Thus, he integrates new features into the Holy City with a focus on the throne of God. The angel shows him "the river of the water of life, as clear as crystal, flowing from the throne of God and the Lamb down the middle of the great street of the city." The theme of "living waters" had been introduced as an inheritance for the "overcomers" in 21:6: "To him who is thirsty I will give to drink without cost from the spring of the water of life." This is the fullness of Jesus' invitation to the Samaritan woman and the pilgrims at Tabernacles in John 4 and 7. This is the water of life that will flow from the throne in 22:1. The Holy City will be the society of the redeemed that completes the creational pilgrimage in the abundance of God's provision. As such, the "living water" stands in contrast with the "maddening wine" in the golden cup of the harlot city's adulteries (18:3, 5; 17:4), which will be brought to ruin by the wrath of God (16:19).

The image of the river harks back to Eden (Gen. 2:10), which remained a part of prophetic predictions (cf. Ezek. 47:10–12; Zech. 14:8). Ezekiel highlighted the primary idea of life: "where the river flows everything will live" (Ezek. 47:9). As we saw earlier when we discussed the human desire to live, the water from the throne means that God is the source of all life on the basis of the Lamb (cf. John 17:3). So, Christ used the figure to personally invite his audiences to find a thirst-quenching relationship with God through faith in himself (John 7:37–39).

The single tree of life was at the center of the garden and God's relationship with Adam and Eve. It visualized the importance of obedience and their dependence on the Lord. The couple was forbidden to eat from the tree after their fall, lest they be immortally sinful: "He must not be allowed to reach out his hand and take also from the tree of life and eat, and live forever" (Gen. 3:22). Like Israel's temple with its Holy of Holies, the tree, the river, and the throne focus the provision of life on the sovereign grace of God, so that in the end of death "God may be all in all" (1 Cor. 15:26–28).

Furthermore, "on each side of the river stood the tree of life bearing . . . fruit every month. And the leaves of the tree are for the healing of the nations" (Rev. 22:2; cf. Ezek. 47:12). The ceaseless nourishment of the fruit and the healing of the leaves is a perpetual memorial that "no longer will there be any curse" on creation (Rev. 22:3; cf. Rom. 8:19–22). Health apparently will not be an issue in the eternal city; instead, the evergreen vitality speaks of abundance and the absence of death, mourning, crying, and pain.

"The throne of God and of the Lamb will be in the city, and his servants will serve him. . . . And they will reign for ever and ever" (Rev. 22:3–4). Serving and ruling under God is not an inconsistency in the Bible. A servant of God is a ruler in the world, because the Lord honors humble ambassadors of his power. This is illustrated in Acts 4, where King David is called "your servant" (Acts 4:25). His messianic lineage leads to "the most exalted of the kings of the earth" (Ps. 89:20–27). Jesus was God's "holy servant," whose humble obedience involved death on the cross (Acts 4:27, 30). He was consequently exalted with "the name that is above every name" (Phil. 2:9–11). Believers are his "servants," who should now humbly speak God's "word with great boldness" (Acts 4:29). Servants of God will reign forever and ever, because he has decreed that we will be fellow heirs with the Lamb.

Finally, how should the New Jerusalem encourage John's audiences, ancient and modern? We have identified eight human needs and desires that will only be perfectly realized in God's presence: our desire for perfection and life; the vindication of our faith in God's promises and our need for hope and love; our need for security and peace, and our desire for beauty. We conclude with two more: our desire for significance and the satisfaction of our appetites.

Ninth, we must remember that God created us in his image and likeness to rule the earth (Gen. 1:26–28). In other words, we were created to live significantly for God's glory. Sin, as we saw in the character of Babylon, has caused us to seek fame obsessively apart from dependence on the Lord of life. So, people have lived self-destructively across history's time line. We want so badly to be self-made captains of our destiny that we look like ancient kings as we use democratic ideals for our own aggrandizement. God's gift of regency is so natural that we hardly realize that our Lord sought the will of his Father to gain "the name that is above every name, that at the name of Jesus every knee will bow" (Phil. 2:10). God promised on the heels of Babel that he would make the name of his special servants "great" (Gen. 12:2; 2 Sam. 7:9).

When followers of Christ arrive on the eternal scene, they will discover that they were right all along to serve the family of God under the Sovereign of creation. The servants of God will reign with him forever! More subtle is the awareness that they reign now. Any student of the New Testament and the history of Christianity can see "a cloud" of servant-kings, whose witness endures to this day, while seemingly powerful empires and enterprises have passed into oblivion (cf. Heb. 12:1–3). We serve a God whose memory is perfect, so we suggest that the sacrificial lives of God's saints will gain a significance in God's city beyond our imagination. God's law of significance honors those who know how to offer their splendor to him.

Tenth, everyone wants to be satisfied in his or her hunger and thirst for personal fulfillment. As we open our eyes, we can see that sin has led to insatiable appetites that we obsessively pursue. Recently, a weekly magazine featured science's quest for "an addiction vaccine." Earlier, a similar publication headlined our society's "driving ambition." Usually the public identifies addictions selectively according to their threat to social order. Drugs, alcohol, and sex usually make the list. We are less prone to identify our drive for significance as "workaholism." We are uncomfortable with speaking of addictions as escapes from reality, because that would hit too close to home.

The obsession with our needs and desires apart from God is precisely the point of the harlot city, and, in antithesis, the fullness of living waters and trees in divine presence. God has created us to find contentment and satisfaction in a prioritized relationship with him: "You will seek me and find me when you seek me with all your heart" (Jer. 29:13; Deut. 4:29). This is mirrored in Christ's claim about his centrality to the relationship: "I am the bread of life. He who comes to me will never go hungry, and he who believes in me will never be thirsty" (John 6:35).

Our pilgrimage through this life is a combination of joys and sorrows, highs and lows, successes and struggles, and stages with changes and transitions that challenge us to the core. Our journey through the Bible has been filled with lessons of challenge and hope. We go on from this book with a conviction that the presence of God is a foundational principle in the Word and in life. The trail is a pilgrimage with a destination. Christ is the compass who guides and guards our daily steps in the Spirit; thus the end of biblical wisdom will be our face-to-face encounter with our Savior.

Face to face with Christ my Savior,
Face to face—what will it be—
When with rapture I behold Him,
Jesus Christ who died for me?

What rejoicing in His presence,
When are banished grief and pain;
When the crooked ways are straightened,
And the dark things shall be plain.

Face to face I shall behold Him,
Far beyond the starry sky;
Face to face in all His glory,
I shall see Him by and by!
—Carrie Breck, 1899

219

Conclusion

AT THE END of our pilgrimage through the book, we can conclude with certainty that "God's presence" is a foundational truth of his Word. Perhaps some of us are not familiar with this truth, because it frames a number of other teachings in its field of meaning. We think about related doctrines such as God's immanence in his creation, his will for our lives, his providential governance of history, and his covenantal relationship with his people. Presence is an umbrella for these and other biblical themes. But it is this hard-hitting, biblical term that forces us to think about "our walk" and "his face."

In writing this book, I have found myself gravitating toward the academic calendar with its deadlines and suspense dates, trying to complete programs and projects that quantify my performance and abilities. In this process I can easily forget about my relationship with God. As long as I am successful with my assigned duties and tasks, then no one, even God himself, seems to care. But my ultimate accountability is to God, and I remember this shameful neglect from time to time, as when I remember that I may not have been with close friends for weeks or years. The other day I was notified of the death of my prayer partner in military service. We had been close friends for several years. Then a hiatus of decades separated us, when responsibilities with family and work blurred the passing days and months. I wish that I could have maintained the friendship. More importantly, I should also be faithful to God, for if I am not, then that "friendship" can fade as well. If I prioritize my gratitude for his love and grace to me, he will draw near to me. I have discovered, however, that close relationships cannot be coerced or neglected. God is the one to whom I must report beyond my human associates on earth. At the same time, I have discovered that when I honor the Spirit's presence in my daily walk, I can serve in a positive way because the divine priority embraces "secular" chores in his "sacred" will. Heaven will have its eternity. But now God's pleasure is for his presence to shine through the earthly journey that he has given us.

The presence of our personal God has surfaced the truth that he does not change. He is incomprehensibly great in all of his attributes that he forms us with our diverse personalities in different ages and cultures into his communities that radiate his presence in the world. He is not some anonymous force out there, but a personal Being with whom we relate as we form relationships around us. From creation God has graciously made his presence a necessary condition for a wise, successful pilgrimage through life. He "clothed" Adam and Eve in their desperately sinful condition. His promises to Abraham have affected history. The patriarchs remind us that the presence of the Word is so powerful that imperfect wandering in strange lands can be immortalized by a simple trust in the promises and provisions of the Creator. The Name, the incomparable I AM, allowed Moses to plead "face-to-face" for Israel and his guidance through the wilderness. Moses of old, like Brother Lawrence in closer proximity, reminds us of the power of a pilgrimage in prayer. God gave us his pattern for reverential worship and a challenge to walk in and beyond the walls of the sanctuary. He led his people with cloud and fire. He spoke through Jeremiah and other prophets to encourage the faithful remnants of the nation. The chapter on the prophets discussed the power of the family and nation to form godly or idolatrous people. The Lord spoke of his covenantal relationship with Israel in terms of marriage, supernatural forgiveness, and an enabling relationship with the Holy Spirit. He could speak of hiding his face from sin without abandoning his people.

Climactically, he came as the Son to live in our midst and to lead us to our eternal home with himself. In the chapters on

222

the New Testament we paused to show how Christ is the center of biblical journeys and that he should be the vine of believers' branches, for "apart from me you can do nothing" (John 15:5). Stated positively, "I can do everything through him who gives me strength" (Phil. 4:13). When Christ encounters us with his love and grace, he gives us a joyful sense of his presence that we would never have known apart from his intervention in our lives. As "living epistles" in the Spirit, we can be bold like the apostles as they proclaimed the good news from Jerusalem to Judea, Samaria and beyond. Finally, the Lamb shows us how his eternal city will meet our needs and satisfy our ideals.

The book points to the fact that the modern problem is not that we have not seen or heard God. The Israelites lived in the midst of miracle and presence in the Exodus, yet insisted on their self-interested creation of a calf that they could control. The problem is that many people refuse to accept Jesus as co-equal and co-eternal with the Father and the Spirit, who must be accepted and worshiped with love and obedience on his terms. Partnership with God on the pathway of life is unequal, and our sovereign Lord has not delegated his authority.

We may not have realized that our culture has reversed the proverbial cart and the horse. We may have come to think that our presence is necessary for his pilgrimage and that life is a self-actualizing journey. We moderns have made ourselves at home in a wilderness of wandering, feeling that our vote is the determining factor of God's will and character. We imagine that if we can garner enough votes, we can change this tragically flawed world into our "brave new world." With this kind of thinking, we are a mere step away from determining who can live and which elite consensus can help us to engineer our utopia.

David Brooks, *New York Times* columnist, recently completed a study of Americans' identity, which he published as *On Paradise Drive: How We Live Now (And Always Have) in the Future Tense.* His data come from research firms and his own travels across the land in the work and recreational spaces that define most of our citizens. He found an incredible diversity that has been blended into a shared mentality, a recent mutation of centuries-old aspirations and impulses. According to Brooks, our surprisingly homogenous population is in feverish pursuit of their image of the "American Dream." He found a materialism that is saturated with enchantment in which affluence has produced mobility, self-reliance, and a quest for the Pilgrims' old "errand into the wilderness" with an addictive twist. We are living with a horizon mentality in which the new Eden is just beyond the next home, the next strategy, the next social hero, the next purchase, the next true love, or the next fantasy with a thousand faces. However, the dream consumes itself, and Brooks concludes:

> This is a brutal form of narcissism. The weight of the universe is placed on the shoulders of the individual. Accordingly, in modern American culture, the self becomes semidivinized. People feel free to pick and choose their own religious beliefs, because whatever serves the self-journey toward happiness must be godly and true. . . . It means that the central question of life is not "What does God command and love?" but rather "What is my destiny and fulfillment?"[1]

He has also labeled the twenty-first century as "The Bad Memory Century," in which we will suffer from an attempt to forget our sins and weaknesses. This will be "especially painful when narcissists suffer memory loss because they are losing parts of the person they love most."[2]

Examples like Brooks's can be multiplied, but he illustrates how thoughtful people address common concerns and arrive at similar conclusions. Our journeys are both individual and communal. We are responsible for our "steps in the Spirit," but our families, friends, churches, affiliations in schools and workplaces, and our nation have formed our distinctive identities. God ordained this balance between individual and community,

---

1. David Brooks, *On Paradise Drive: How We Live Now (And Always Have) in the Future Tense* (New York: Simon and Schuster, 2004), 276.
2. David Brooks, "The Bad Memory Century," *Dallas Morning News* (April 26, 2008), 19A.

so that his light can bring salvation to the diverse ends of the earth (cf. Isa. 49:6).

The balance has two implications for our journeys. First, the diversity of believers means that there is no formula to guide everyone's progress to a common destination. Thus, the balance is unity with diversity. We have the same foundation stones such as a saving encounter with God, the standard of his Word, and a shared community for worship. In this sense "narrow" is "the road" (cf. Matt. 7:13–14). However, the way is as broad as believers around the world that form the body of Christ, the temple of living stones. We tend to be very critical of Christians who differ from our tastes and traditions, but we should avoid the arrogance of taking God's place by defining our ways as the gospel truth. By the same token, many intellectuals may prefer a God who can be controlled by critical analysis, but most people in churches need and desire a personal God, who lavishly responds to faith with grace, forgiveness, and strength in times of need. If we don't have a "Paraclete," some people reason, then we may just as well join the vast multitude—those who are too intoxicated to foresee their doom—in "the great city."

The presence of God is analogous to human relationships, meaning that, while human relationships may not be precisely the same, they help us to understand the blessing and difficulties of relating to the other. The thought of being Christlike in our character helps very different people to build unity as we walk to our common destination. Most of us experience difficulty relating to God as Spirit. And most of us feel that relationships with people are just as difficult in terms of long-lasting, close friendships. The presence of God is a biblical emphasis that encourages authentic relationships between believers in his love.

Second, the common destination of diverse believers has been promised for thousands of years. One of the difficulties of biblical living is persistent faithfulness over a lifetime. Achievers like me struggle if they do "not receive the things promised" as they travel to the heavenly city (cf. Heb. 11:13–16). "The great city" that surrounds us is impressive and seductive. "Come, Lord

Jesus," we cry with legs that are weary from hiking around one obstacle after another on the trail of life (Rev. 20). He encourages us to stay on the well-worn path as we "fix our eyes on Jesus," who has assured us with trustworthy truth that "a mountain great and high" is just ahead (Heb. 12:2; Rev. 21:9–10). In the meantime the Spirit says in the Word, "The grace of the Lord Jesus be with God's people. Amen" (Rev. 22:21).

Questions for Study and Reflection

Chapter 1—Incarnation as Presence

1. What do we learn about God from the fact that the Son of God became flesh to dwell in our midst (1:14)?

2. How is *"Logos"* ("Word") used in John 1:1–2, 14?

3. What does Jesus demonstrate about the importance of "presence" as a biblical truth?

4. Does the use of "flesh" for the incarnation matter (John 1:14)? Why?

5. Why would "incarnation as presence" be offensive to some people?

6. What did John and his contemporaries "see" when they saw the glory of the Lord?

7. What is the point of John's comparison of Jesus and Moses?

8. How can we experience the presence of God in our modern day through an ancient book (the written Word of God) and person (the living Word of God)?

9. Recall one occasion when you had to walk on "the path of pilgrims."

227

Chapter 2—The Presence with the Patriarchs

1. How was God present in creation and Eden? How is he present in our lives today?

2. In what ways does "face" help us to relate to our encounters with God and people?

3. Relate "walk" as a metaphor for God's presence with the patriarchs to our "walking in the truth" (2 John 4).

4. Enoch and Noah walked with God in a totally corrupt generation. What would their lives have been like?

5. What effect did evil have on God's presence in his creation?

6. Why is Genesis 15 such an outstanding "presence" text for us?

7. How does Psalm 119 help us to relate Old Testament spirituality to our walk with the Lord today?

8. What were Jacob's lifelong reminders of his encounters with God?

9. How would you compare Jonathan Edwards's description of the "Christian Pilgrim" with your life?

Chapter 3—The Presence with Moses

1. How does the chapter address Steinsaltz's point (in the quotation that begins the chapter) that people would believe, if they could see something that proves that God exists?

2. Why was God's revelation of his name, "I AM," so important for Moses, and for us?

3. Are Moses' four objections applicable to believers today?

4. What do you think of Moses' incredibly bold and honest relationship with God? Was he irreverent? Why or why not?

5. What does God's "change of mind" in response to Moses' prayer mean, for Israel and for us?

6. God gave Moses so much, yet no more, in his request to have his presence and to see his Glory. Why did God show Moses as much as he did, and as little as he did?

7. Why did the Israelites veil themselves in the presence of Moses' radiance?

8. Why is prayer an appropriate indicator of the presence of God in our lives? How do you deal with the issue of unanswered prayer?

Chapter 4—The Presence and the Sanctuary

1. How would you define worship? Would you agree that it can take place outside church buildings?

2. "Patterned" construction, detailed regulations, and severe penalties indicate the seriousness that God attached to worship in Israel. Are we reverential toward God in our worship?

3. How can we make holiness a more meaningful part of our lives in the midst of our secular culture?

4. The Old Testament mandated a tabernacle and a temple that focused on the presence of the Lord. How can we focus on God's presence today in light of the fact that we do not have a cloud and fire or a Holy of Holies?

5. How would you relate the compromises of Solomon's time to similar pressures that we face? To what extent do we desire to be like the world?

6. What principle in Brother Lawrence's walk with the Lord impresses you the most?

Chapter 5—The Presence and the Prophets

1. How do you feel about relationships in general? Do you fear or want others' presence? Our view of relationships with other people often will affect our desire (or lack of it) for relationship with God.

2. Why did God's presence not keep the Israelites from seeking other gods?

3. How would you have felt if you watched your "friends" practice idolatry "in the name of the Lord" as they oppressed their fellow citizens on a daily basis?

4. How can we recognize idols and false prophets around us? How can we distinguish true and false worship?

5. Review in your mind how each chapter returns to Jesus as the center of biblical journeys. As you do this, consider Jesus' own exposition of the subject in Luke 24:25–27 on the road to Emmaus.

6. How was Israel's prayer related to God's gift of the new covenant? Does the new covenant stimulate your hope for meaningful presences in your life?

7. How can this chapter encourage godly families?

Chapter 6—The New Covenant in the New Testament

1. John 1–12 presents Jesus as the presence of the Father on earth. How can we "see" the Father as we "see" the Son (John 14:9)?

2. What did John mean in John 7:39 when he said, "Up to that time the Spirit had not been given, since Jesus had not yet been glorified"?

3. What would have prompted the Samaritans to conclude that "this man really is the Savior of the world" (John 4:42)?

4. How is the Holy Spirit presented in John 14:16–18? In what ways do you experience the "Paraclete" as God's presence in your life?

5. How can God's presence help us with our anxieties?

6. What are the connections between the new covenant, the Messiah's crucifixion, and the Spirit's advent at Pentecost?

7. How are Israel and the church distinct as we anticipate the fullness of God's chosen people in the future? How are they related in the olive tree? What does this indicate about our personal identities in the diverse body of Christ?

8. The church is identified as the "body of Christ" and the "temple of God" in the New Testament. What do these metaphors mean in terms of believers' unity in Christ, who is our "Head" and "Cornerstone?"

9. What did Paul mean when he spoke of the Corinthians as his "living epistles"?

Chapter 7—The Presence in the New Jerusalem

1. Do you know many people who would think of heaven like Oz?

2. Are you helped by thinking of "the great city" as an adulteress, and God's city as a bride? Think about Ephesians 5:22–33 in these terms. What does it mean for husbands and wives to love and respect one another as do Christ and his church?

3. How can Moses' "pattern" help us to understand God's presence with his people in any period of history as well as in the future? Why is the Holy of Holies central in the new heaven and earth?

4. Can you imagine a world without temptation, suffering, tears, and death?

231

5. The chapter presents ten desires and needs that are fully met only in the Holy City. Which ones impress you the most?

6. Why did God guarantee that his Holy City will be a future reality?

7. How are elements of Eden integrated into the larger vision of the Holy City?

8. Why are serving and ruling not inconsistent in the Bible?

9. Why is the Lamb the most prominent depiction of Christ in Revelation?

Select Resources on God's Presence

Baker, David. *Two Testaments, One Bible: A Study of the Theological Relationship between the Old and New Testaments*. Revised ed. Downers Grove, IL: InterVarsity Press, 1991.

Baylis, Albert. *On the Way to Jesus: A Journey through the Bible*. Portland: Multnomah Press, 1986.

Beale, G. K. *The Temple and the Church's Mission*. New Studies in Biblical Theology, vol. 17. Downers Grove: InterVarsity Press, 2004.

Bernard of Clairvaux. *The Love of God*. Reprint edition. Portland: Multnomah Press, 1983.

Brother Lawrence. *The Practice of the Presence of God*. Revised by Harold Chadwick. Gainesville, FL: Bridge-Logos Publishers, 1999.

Bunyan, John. *The Pilgrim's Progress*. Reprint edition. Grand Rapids: Zondervan, 1966.

Carson, Donald A. *From Triumphalism to Maturity: An Exposition of 2 Corinthians 10–13*. Grand Rapids: Baker, 1984.

Chisholm, Robert, Jr. *Handbook on the Prophets*. Grand Rapids: Baker, 2002.

Fee, Gordon. *God's Empowering Presence: The Holy Spirit in the Letters of Paul*. Peabody, MA: Hendrikson Publishers, 1994.

———. *Paul, the Spirit, and the People of God*. Peabody: Hendrickson Publishers, 1996.

Foster, Richard. *Celebration of Discipline: The Path of Spiritual Growth*. San Francisco: Harper and Row, 1978.

———. *Prayer: Finding the Heart's True Home*. San Francisco: HarperSanFrancisco, 1998.

Gunton, Colin. *The One, the Three, and the Many: God, Creation and the Culture of Modernity, The Bampton Lectures 1992*. Cambridge: Cambridge University Press, 1993.

Gruenler, Royce Gordon. *The Trinity in the Gospel of John: A Thematic Commentary on the Fourth Gospel*. Grand Rapids: Baker, 1986.

Guthrie, Donald. *New Testament Theology*. Leicester, England: Inter-Varsity Press, 1981.

Hinckley, Karen. *The Story of Stories: The Bible in Narrative Form*. Colorado Springs: NavPress, 1991.

Kaiser, Walter, Jr. *Toward an Old Testament Theology*. Grand Rapids: Zondervan, 1978.

Kinlaw, Dennis. *Let's Start with Jesus: A New Way of Doing Theology*. Grand Rapids: Zondervan, 2005.

Ladd, George E. *A Theology of the New Testament*. Grand Rapids: Eerdmans, 1974.

Martens, Elmer. *God's Design: A Focus on Old Testament Theology*. Grand Rapids: Baker, 1981.

McGrath, Alister. *Christian Spirituality*. Oxford: Blackwell Publishers, 1999.

Nouwen, Henri. *Life of the Beloved: Spiritual Living in a Secular World*. New York: Crossroad, 1992.

Packer, J. I. *I Want to Be a Christian*. Wheaton: Tyndale House Publishers, 1977.

———. *Knowing God*. Downers Grove: InterVarsity Press, 1973.

Peterson, Eugene. *Answering God: The Psalms as Tools for Prayer*. San Francisco: HarperCollins Publishers, 1989.

———. *A Long Obedience in the Same Direction: Discipleship in an Instant Society*. Downers Grove, IL: InterVarsity Press, 1980.

Piper, John. *Desiring God: Meditations of a Christian Hedonist*. Portland: Multnomah Press, 1986.

———. *A Hunger for God: Desiring God through Fasting and Prayer*. Wheaton: Crossway, 1997.

Robertson, O. Palmer. *The Christ of the Covenants*. Phillipsburg, NJ: Presbyterian and Reformed, 1980.

Schaeffer, Francis. *How Should We Then Live? The Rise and Decline of Western Thought and Culture*. Old Tappan, NJ: Fleming H. Revell, 1976.

———. *True Spirituality*. Wheaton: Tyndale House Publishers, 1971.

Toon, Peter. *Yesterday, Today, and Forever: Jesus Christ and the Holy Trinity in the Teaching of the Seven Ecumenical Councils*. Swedesboro, NJ: Preservation Press, 1996.

Tozer, A. W. *Man: The Dwelling Place of God*. Harrisburg, PA: Christian Publications, 1966.

———. *The Knowledge of the Holy*. New York: Harper and Row, 1961.

VanGemeren, Willem. *The Progress of Redemption: The Story of Creation to the New Jerusalem*. Grand Rapids: Zondervan, 1988. Paperback edition, Grand Rapids: Baker, 1995.

Yancey, Philip. *The Jesus I Never Knew*. Grand Rapids: Zondervan, 1995.

———. *Reaching for the Invisible God: What Can We Expect to Find?* Grand Rapids: Zondervan, 2000.

Index of Scripture

242

Index of Subjects and Names